THE BATTLE FOR RELIGIOUS LIBERTY

THE BATTLE FOR
RELIGIOUS
LIBERTY

Lynn R. Buzzard
Samuel Ericsson

David C. Cook Publishing Co.

ELGIN, ILLINOIS—WESTON, ONTARIO

ABOUT THE AUTHORS

Lynn R. Buzzard is executive director of the Christian Legal Society, a national organization of Christian lawyers. He also serves as coeditor of the *Religious Freedom Reporter,* a professional legal journal that reports on religious liberty cases, and is on the board of the Committee on Religion and Law, the Church-State Institute at DePaul University, and the Prison Reform Task Force of Prison Fellowship. He is coauthor of *Tell It to the Church* and *Freedom and Faith: the Impact of Law on Religious Liberty.*

Lynn received his undergraduate and graduate degrees in history and theology at Duke University, did his doctoral work in law and theology at San Francisco Theological Seminary, and has studied at Notre Dame College of Law and DePaul College of Law.

Samuel Ericsson is national coordinator for the Center for Law and Religious Freedom of the Christian Legal Society and director of CLS's Washington, D.C., office. The center serves as a resource on church-state issues for members of the branches of government and the religious community. Sam graduated from the University of Southern California and the Harvard Law School, then became a partner in a Los Angeles law firm, specializing in complex business litigation. In 1977 he served as administrative pastor and coordinator of ministries at Grace Community Church in Los Angeles County. Sam is a member of the California Bar and the American Bar Association.

ACKNOWLEDGMENTS

Excerpt from "A Little School Against the Big Bureaucracy" by William J. Miller, *Reader's Digest,* August 1980.

BATTLE FOR RELIGIOUS LIBERTY
© 1982 Lynn R. Buzzard, Samuel Ericsson
Published by David C. Cook Publishing Co., Elgin, IL 60120
Edited by Janet Hoover Thoma
Cover design by Britt Taylor Collins

Library of Congress Cataloging in Publication Data

Buzzard, Lynn Robert.
  The battle for religious liberty.

  Bibliography: p. 286
  Includes index.
  1. Religious liberty—United States.
2. Church and state—United States.
I. Ericsson, Samuel. II. Title.
BR516.B87   1982   261.7′2   82-7284
ISBN 0-89191-552-4   AACR2
Printed in the United States of America
LC: 82-7284

CONTENTS

PART FOUR: THE CHRISTIAN RESPONSIBILITY

APPENDIXES

PART ONE

WHATEVER HAPPENED TO OUR RELIGIOUS FREEDOM?

1

Civil Rights
for Believers, Too!

This is an age of civil rights, a time when people of numerous and varied persuasions are demanding their liberties. At the same time, however, many Christians are wondering what has happened to their traditional religious freedom.

You might say, "I didn't know I was losing my religious freedom." But do you realize that in cities such as Los Angeles, Seattle, and Atlanta, the right to hold Bible studies in private homes has been questioned?

In Los Angeles Christians meeting in two different home Bible study groups were told to "cease and desist." The residences had not been zoned for "church purposes," said the Department of Building and Safety.

One of the groups volunteered to stop their singing, which had not been boisterous or rowdy, and to disperse the few cars that brought them to the residences. Still the department held fast. A supervisor even said that a "cease and desist" order would be issued against any religious meeting in a private home not zoned for church use, even if only one person outside the household was attending. A paraphrase of such an order would be: two Christians from different households can no longer meet to study the Bible unless they are in a church.

In September of 1980 the mayor of Los Angeles entered the discussion. "A Bible study would not be a permissible use in a single family residential area," he said.

The Christians were represented by Sam Ericsson, one of

9

your authors. Only months before, the Department of Building and Safety had closed down a residence my church had used two hours a week to minister to physically and mentally handicapped children. Our "violation": the children were praying and studying the Bible in a facility that had not been approved for such use by the city of Los Angeles.

At that time I had asked two inspectors if they would consider home Bible study meetings a violation of zoning ordinances.

Yes, they were both sure a person would havé to get a permit from the city.

"Do you realize," I had asked, "that the system you are proposing is closer to the Soviet than the American?"

"What can we say?" they had replied, shrugging their shoulders.

Both of these instances were satisfactorily resolved without court action. And eventually the mayor of Los Angeles announced that Bible studies in private homes would not be treated differently from other meetings. But our experience is not unique.

In a town near Boston, the building commissioner notified a clergyman that inviting more than four people to his home for a Bible study was a violation of the home occupations ordinance. And in Florida, a group of nine orthodox Jews, too poor to afford a synagogue, were told they couldn't meet and pray in their homes.

Bible studies and religious functions seem to be treated differently than bridge parties or political teas for candidates. This seems especially unusual when our society is currently condoning citizens' rights to do anything within the privacy of their homes.

The rights of Christian students and teachers are also being threatened. In the last two years Jeanne Brandon, Jill George, Bill Smith, and a small group of fellow students at Guilderland High School in New York State asked the principal if they could meet for prayer in a classroom before school started. The principal said, "No." A local court said, "No." New York's Court of Appeals said, "No." In fact, the court declared such practices would be "too dangerous to permit." The case (*Brandon* v. *Guilderland School District)*) was appealed to the United States Supreme Court, which refused to review the decision.

High school students in West Virginia, California, and other states have also been denied the right to hold Bible studies before school. In fact, the attorney general of Tennessee even declared that members of a high school football team could not gather before a game and pray.

Teachers have not fared much better. Their right to express divergent points of view in the "free marketplace of ideas," which has been traditional in American public schools, is constantly being questioned.

America's founding fathers would never have dreamed that any teacher would have to ask, "Can we still sing Christmas carols in the public schools?" as an issue of the *Music Education Journal* queried in 1976. Or that a teacher would wonder if religious art could be used on a bulletin board during the holiday season or a Christmas tree occupy the classroom or the school's lobby. After all, the Bible and the Isaac Watts Hymnal were reading textbooks in Virginia in colonial times.

Yet in 1971 the American Civil Liberties Union sent a letter to California school superintendents, declaring that "The observance in public schools . . . of such occasions as Christmas . . . as religious holidays is contrary to the separation principle."

And in 1977 a school board in Williamsburg, Virginia, banned religious holiday programs, religious music, and religious symbols in the public schools. The parents' and teachers' outcries were so great that the attorney general finally agreed that the school board's policies did not have to be so "widesweeping."

As Americans, we pride ourselves in our commitment to freedom, even for the bizarre and unusual. Our nation has been a haven for oppressed peoples; our concern for personal freedoms has grown as civil rights for minorities have been expanded. Constitutional guarantees of free speech, rights of association, privacy, and free exercise of religion are among our greatest liberties.

Why, then, are so many situations emerging in which the rights of Christians seem to be infringed or diminished? Why are religious organizations coming under increased governmental scrutiny, with attempts to regulate, license, supervise, and monitor their activities? In an age that grants the pornographer his right to freedom of the press and the homosexual his right to sexual preference, aren't civil rights for believers, too?

It's time for Christians to examine the scope of their rights and be sure that important liberties are not lost. It's time for us to accept responsibility for our society, and do more than just complain, because there are more cases involving religious liberty before our courts than ever before. There seems to be a systematic attempt to challenge traditional moral and Christian values. What is happening to the Christian in this age of "civil rights"? What factors are contributing to the courts' view of religious freedom?

We cannot give a full account of this critical shift in our society in this volume, but we will explain some of the central elements at work in our culture, which have combined to create real challenges to believers' liberties.

PLURALISM DETERIORATING INTO SECULARISM

America has long seen itself as a community open to diversity and variety. The Statue of Liberty has stood as a beacon to peoples of different languages, races, and economic standings. Today that pluralism is increasingly evident. We are not only a nation with racial and ethnic variety, but of clashing values and life-styles. It is no longer a matter of a few variations on a central theme, but profound and radical alternatives.

If there once was a Christian cultural dominance in our national life, it no longer exists. *Playboy's* hedonism, Marxism, and variants of humanism, utilitarianism, and existentialism are only a few of the alternatives that now compete in the marketplace of ideas. One need only watch an evening of television or attend a university in order to guess which value systems seem dominant.

Not only is the range of views greater, but the visibility of the alternatives has expanded. Homosexuals are not the only ones who have emerged from closets to urgently press their views. Today *Playboy* and *Hustler* sit on newsstands and in our family drugstores beside *Time* and *Fortune*. Pamphleteers stand at every stoplight and in every airport to greet us with a philosophy (and requests for a donation).

There is also substantial evidence that public institutions have succumbed to this laissez-faire morality. Not too long ago, the laws of almost every state provided criminal penalties for homosexual conduct; as recently as 1971, 20 percent of the states allowed penalties of twenty years or more. Only two states did not penalize such activity. The states also regulated pornography, outlawed most abortions, and made divorce difficult.

Now the law has radically shifted its role. It has decriminalized conduct it formerly prohibited (such as homosexuality), then given legal status to such conduct, and finally protected it. Recently, the Massachusetts High Court even struck down attempts to prohibit the use of children in pornography.

Much of this shocks our psychic equilibrium. To those whose world was comfortable and easily defined when Christianity was a more pervasive part of our society, these assults are unnerving.

Yet pluralism itself is valuable. Freedom to believe as one wishes is essential. Without it, even Christian choice is meaningless. And certainly we need not fear the competition of other ideas. "He who is in you is greater than he who is in the world," John declared in 1 John 4:4.

Christians did quite well in the hostile and pluralistic first century. Our faith does not need cultural censorship to assist its life-giving effectiveness. Indeed, Christian values may look especially attractive alongside the raw materialism and narcissism of modern alternatives. The radical options may in fact help all of us to clarify our beliefs with more precision. It may force us to "renew our minds" and center in on our fundamental commitments.

However, there is an ominous character to what is touted as "pluralism" today. It is hailed as freedom for diversity, but instead it seems to demand a conformity to a humanistic philosophy. It is a pluralism that encourages the expression of all kinds of views—but only if they coincide with the prevailing consensus. This philosophy is perhaps primarily manifested in public education and media circles. How long has it been since Christian values about family and sexuality received a positive reinforcement in a popular tv series? Or were given equal time in a high school text on sex?

One would have thought that pluralism would mean an equal opportunity for all people to express their views. If this is so, why do university officials and groups such as the American Civil Liberties Union (ACLU) encourage all sorts of student groups to form at universities—except religious groups? Why can you promote ideas if they come from Marx or Freud or some philosopher or scientist, but not if they come from the Bible?

Some Christians say that we do not have a genuine pluralism, but the increasing dominance of our public life by a hostile secular philosophy: secular humanism. This religion denies theistic presuppositions, rejects moral absolutes, and makes man and science the measure of all things. Humanists see religion as archaic, disruptive of community, damaging to psychological health, and something to be tolerated, at best—or ultimately removed from society by enlightened persons.

This humanism is as evangelistic and expansive as any religion the world has ever seen. Advocates promote its ideas subtly, but vigorously. It is a philosophy so total that it amounts to a religion, a system of values and commitments that shapes life. The secularist view of life is at war with all religious perspectives. It will seek to rout them out as superstition or ignorance. Sometimes it will attack religion, but more often it will simply laugh at or ignore it.

This philosophy is increasingly shaping our youth, our politics, and our education. The English historian E. R. Norman once suggested that pluralism is a word society employs to describe itself during its transition from one orthodoxy to another.

AN EXPANSIVE STATE

The continually expanding federal government is another factor that is contributing to a loss of religious freedom. Our culture increasingly deifies the expansive state. Government expands at dizzying rates. Much of that is inevitable in an increasingly complex world, but other forces seem to be at work as well. The whole notion that government ought to supervise, regulate, control, and monitor our affairs is one fostered by a form of liberal politics, which sees institutional and financial solutions to the complex human problems facing modern man. Government bureaucracies grow rapidly, filled with well-meaning people who intend to do us well. But some tend to agree with the skeptic who once suggested: if you ever discover someone is seeking you to do you good, run for cover.

A state that seeks to expand the territory that it supervises is a state likely to have its own ideas about what is good and valuable—ideas that may clash with a faithful and prophetic religious commitment.

A NEW THEOLOGY: A LORD OF HISTORY

J. B. Phillips wrote a book a few years ago called *Your God Is Too Small*. He challenged Christians to a larger vision of God and of his claim upon us. In some respects, the struggle between religious values and the state is increasing because Christians have discovered a bigger God—a God who is Lord. Christians are rejecting secularist John Locke's counsel that "the only business of the church is the salvation of souls, and in no way concerns the commonwealth."

We are recognizing that the term *Lord* is not just a term of endearment as in "Dear Lord Jesus" but an expression of sovereignty. To declare Jesus as Lord is to declare his dominion over every aspect of life: school systems, courts, even sanitary districts. To be sure, that lordship is not now manifested (and will not be until his return), but we declare it as a secret of the Kingdom.

When we recognize that Christian responsibility extends to all of human life, we inevitably clash with other values and other "lords," just as the Christians at Ephesus clashed with the government of Caesar and the worship of idols like Diana. Early Christians responded by openly declaring their allegiance to Jesus as Lord, even when it meant going to jail. Today Christians are again resisting the attempt of the world to insist that they "stick to religion" as if their faith only involved gospel songs, prayer meetings, and life after death. Instead Christians are refusing to "stay in their place," seeking instead to be salt and light to the earth.

Christians are learning that we can no longer rely on the school and the neighborhood to promote our values and assist in sustaining Christian faith. We will have to start teaching our children the faith, begin to develop sustaining communities that nurture our beliefs, and start preparing ourselves for intellectual and spiritual warfare for men's minds.

RELIGIOUS DIVERSITY

Another element that has contributed to a decrease in religious freedom is the variety of religious expression now present in our society. We used to know what a church was: it had a steeple, altar, organ, or some version of these. Now we have cults, mail order ordinations, tax frauds, religious communes, street solicitors, and airport hustlers. Courts are ill-equipped to deal with this range of religious concepts. Who are the truly religious? How can the courts ascertain the sincere from the fraudulent?

Some Christians have inadvertently contributed to diminishing religious freedoms by encouraging legal restrictions on unpopular groups. It would be good to remember that Christians have been—and in many countries still are—the odd and rejected group. Whatever legal principles we encourage to stop or limit other groups may well be applied to us.

SHIFTING CHURCH/STATE RELATIONS

There has been almost exclusive attention in the past couple of decades to the notion of "the separation of church and state." Most people probably believe that the United States Constitution mandates such separation. This concept is so engrained in public officials, school officials, and bureaucrats that there is an almost automatic, knee-jerk reaction to excise any vestige or hint of religion from public life. Thus a Santa Monica college in California insisted that Christian students may not sit on the school lawn and conduct a Bible study because it would violate "the separation of church and state" (*Campus Christian Fellowship* v. *Santa Monica College*).

This exclusive attention to one constitutional principle to the exclusion of other important liberties (free speech, free exercise of religion) is a major element in the exaggerated secularization of our public life.

PRINCIPALITIES AND POWERS

The apostle Paul spoke in Ephesians of "principalities and powers" and "spiritual hosts of wickedness," and suggested that we are not wrestling merely with flesh and blood. There is an evil character in our culture, which seeks to destroy good. The comic-strip character Pogo declared it in part when he said, "We have met the enemy and he is us." But the Bible goes one step further and suggests that evil is greater than our own individual sin. Satan stands behind it. How else can one explain the evils of racial hatred or the ovens of Auschwitz? The flood of drugs or pornography in our culture?

SO WHAT DO WE DO?

The classic response is to get frustrated, angry, and bemoan the evil around us. Or perhaps to sing another song, hoping for the end to come. Many truly concerned people feel despair and are overwhelmed by the increasingly difficult situation. However, there are constructive, effective, and biblically faithful alternatives. Christians *can* act to preserve their freedom.

Concerned Christians ought to recognize the scope of the issues before them, know their rights, and in certain cases, proudly claim—and even demand—them. Christians should know where to get help when they need it.

A sensitive and alert Christian community can assure the important freedoms of religion upon which our culture was built. The words of George Washington, as quoted by President Carter in his address to the nation, are crucial:

> You took the good things for granted—now you must earn them again. For every right that you cherish, you have a duty which you must fulfill. For every hope you entertain, you have a task that you must perform. For every good that you wish to preserve, you will have to sacrifice your comfort and your ease. There is nothing for nothing any longer.

2

Decisions
Make a Difference

In 1954 the United States Supreme Court handed down a decision that changed the face of American society: *Brown* v. *Board of Education*. This decision declared that school segregation was a denial of a fundamental constitutional right. All across America separate schools for blacks and whites were struck down. The decision made a difference.

In 1973 the Supreme Court again changed our lives. The Court's controversial decision on abortion, *Roe* v. *Wade,* struck down the laws of nearly every state and declared a woman's right of privacy, which prevented the state from prohibiting abortions during the first two trimesters. This has resulted in 10 million abortions since 1973, or 5,000 abortions per day. The decision made a difference.

Court decisions affect our freedoms—including our religious freedoms.

In 1980, a federal court (in *Florey* v. *Sioux Falls School District*) upheld the right of the public school system in South Dakota to use religious music in its Christmas program. The decision made a difference.

Over six years ago, a group of high school students in Huntington Beach, California, sought recognition to organize as a school group "to enable those participating to know God better . . . by prayerfully studying the Bible." The group wished to meet at lunchtime in a schoolroom to study the Bible. Over one hundred Edison High School students signed a written application for recognition as a student group.

The principal said, "No." The school district said, "No." And on March of 1977 a California court of appeal upheld the school district's denial. Recognition of the student group would amount to "sponsorship" of a religious activity by the state, the court said.

The decision made a difference. Christian students in California high schools may no longer organize and meet in school facilities.

Decisions make a difference. Courts shape our liberties.

But very few Christians ever get involved in legal matters or legislation. Many Christians have a deep suspicion of courts and lawyers. Attorneys are often perceived as crooked, expensive, obscure, picky, and pretentious. According to Scripture, Jesus was not too impressed with the lawyers of his own day either.

But make no mistake about it, the law shapes our freedoms and affects the lives of each of us. Courts and cases shape our values, rights, duties, and freedoms.

The very nature of our legal process assures that decisions affect not only the parties in the case itself, but the rights of many others. The principle is that of *stare decisis*—the concept of precedent. Decisions, unless reversed or modified, are followed by courts faced with similar situations. When Oliver Brown began the lawsuit on his daughter's behalf (*Brown* v. *the Board of Education*), he did not know it would result in the desegregation of schools across America. If Linda Brown wins, so do all others like her. If Huntington High School students lose, so do other Christian high school students in California.

That is why decisions make a difference to all of us. A loss of liberty in one case diminishes freedom for us all. A victory for liberty expands its scope for all. In every case, the court is applying a principle. Often, it is also modifying or even creating rules and standards. Many times these "rules of law" are more important than the disposition of the particular case, because they establish the guidelines and values that determine decisions in future cases.

Christians must gain a new appreciation of the significance of the legal process, because important issues face the courts today and in the next few years. The resulting decisions will affect our personal liberties and the scope of religious freedom in our nation for years to come.

Today courts are asked to determine if a minister of the

gospel is liable for malpractice for using spiritual principles, rather than referring the parishioner to a secular psychological counselor (*Nally* v. *Grace Community Church of the Valley*). Or courts decide if a Christian residence house at a public university can be denied the same standing as sorority and fraternity houses. Or courts determine if the state can set minimum standards for private religious education, controlling teacher selection and curriculum (*Ohio* v. *Whisner*).

These are just a few of the issues making their way into the judicial system. (Such cases are discussed in full in the third section of this book.) These cases will make a difference to the Christian layman, student, teacher, minister, or school administrator.

One might simply review the incredible impact of court decisions in such areas as civil rights, environmental law, and gay rights to realize how important courts are in shaping our liberties. Groups such as the ACLU and other legal activists have recognized the courts' vital role for years. We Christians ignore the judicial process at our own peril.

This is the reason Christians must consider taking issues that question religious rights to court. But what about biblical passages that seem to advise Christians to avoid the courts? The apostle Paul seems to suggest this in 1 Corinthians 6:

> When one of you has a grievance against a brother, does he dare go to law before the unrighteous instead of the saints? Do you not know that the saints will judge the world? And if the world is to be judged by you, are you incompetent to try trivial cases? . . . Can it be that there is no man among you wise enough to decide between members of the brotherhood, but brother goes to law against brother, and that before unbelievers? To have lawsuits at all with one another is defeat for you (vv. 1-7).

Your authors are committed to the implementation of 1 Corinthians 6 and Jesus' words in Matthew 18 about disputes among Christians (as described in the book, *Tell It to the Church*), but these texts do not seem applicable to issues of religious liberty.

A careful examination of the Corinthian passage and the context in which it occurs reveals a number of significant elements. The passage is directed at lawsuits between Christians and not lawsuits that concern nonbelievers or the government. The matters Paul has in mind seem to deal with contract, tort law, commercial disputes, and personal suits, those involving alleged wrongs by one party against another. They are not similar to suits that allege an infringement of constitutional rights or seek to limit the government from acting in an arbitrary and capricious manner. Both the litigants and the nature of the issues are different from the Christian concerns of today.

The very nature of law and government have substantially changed since New Testament times. Then, the courts were alien to any Christian or Jewish influence. The fundamental values of Roman law were not shaped by the Judeo-Christian tradition. And the government was a dictatorship, providing no opportunity for democratic involvement in making the law or challenging government powers. The context today is dramatically different, which gives Christians more reason to appeal to the secular court.

We have a voice in the law and in the appointment or election of judges. We elect representatives and often have powers of initiative and recall. The government is supposed to be responsive to the people and subject to the consent of the governed. To appeal to the courts is, at least in theory, not to appeal to a totally alien entity, but one which is part of our community.

As pagan as modern courts may often appear, Christian values and even specific biblical concepts have shaped much of the English common law out of which American law has evolved. Great jurists of history have been devout believers who sought to apply what they perceived to be the fundamental laws of nature and nature's God.

We might also look at direct biblical evidence that suggests that claiming our rights is indeed appropriate under some circumstances. Paul himself claimed his right to be tried by Roman justice and to appeal to the highest court in his land. "I appeal to Caesar," he demanded when he was brought before Festus in Caesarea.

A lawsuit that seeks to preserve constitutionally guaranteed freedoms of religion against challenge by individual or government threats is an attempt to maintain freedom for the gospel. Our nation was formed as a covenant; we, the people of the United States, established a government and conferred upon it limited powers at the same time that we specifically preserved other powers for the people. To insist that government stay within its powers and that it preserve and assure freedom is hardly the sort of activity Paul warned against in 1 Corinthians 6.

Finally, we have a cultural and social responsibility to assure that such liberties are not lost. It is one thing to accept a personal loss rather than pursue a long and perhaps costly and frustrating court battle. In such circumstances, accepting the loss may be the better part of practical and spiritual counsel. It is another thing, however, to decline to sue when the rights of our whole society are at stake, including those of our successors, our children, and descendants. The lawsuit is simply the device our society provides to ascertain the scope of liberty and to challenge improper governmental conduct.

Certainly in the process of such lawsuits it is important to test our attitudes to be sure that the factors Paul was concerned about do not infest us: bitterness, personal animosity, loss of willingness to negotiate and to suffer some loss. But it would be a tragedy if we—suffering under some false notion of spirituality—allowed precious freedoms to be lost. If someone strikes me on the face, perhaps the biblical counsel to turn the other cheek is precisely the conduct called for. But if I observe someone beating another, there is little biblical warrant for standing by and quoting passages about nonresistance to the suffering victim.

We believe that Christians may engage in lawsuits to preserve religious liberty. In fact the Christian community has a duty to establish such guarantees. We need to utilize those structures (such as the courts) that our society provides so that citizens can monitor and preserve their liberty.

THE IMPORTANCE OF LEGAL STRATEGY

Since decisions help shape the very course of law, it is important to bring those cases to court that have the best chance of succeeding. There is a legal aphorism: bad facts make bad law. Often cases with especially bad facts tend to press the court into a decision that produces a poor principle of law. Effective legal strategy means assuring that the cases brought to the courts involve valid constitutional issues, and that the legal counsel has developed an effective presentation of those facts and law.

Christians need to realize that there is still great potential for court decisions that will assure our freedom. Even though it is true that our legal system is increasingly infected by values and concepts that are foreign and even hostile to Christian perspectives, judges will not be totally unresponsive to important issues of freedom and religious liberty if they are made aware of them. In fact, some Supreme Court decisions in recent years have shown a recognition of the importance of religious liberties.

In *Wisconsin* v. *Yoder* in 1972, the Supreme Court upheld the rights of Amish parents over the attempts of the state of Wisconsin to force them to send their child to the public high school against their religious beliefs. In *Florey* v. *Sioux Falls* in 1979, the Supreme Court declined to review a decision of lower courts, which rejected attempts by the ACLU and others to stop the singing of "Silent Night" in public school Christmas programs. And in *Widmar* v. *Vincent* in 1982, the Court clearly protected the rights of Christian university students.

Some lower courts have also held in favor of the civil rights of Christians and others to distribute tracts, to raise funds, to preach and hold rallies, to meet on college campuses, and to resist IRS broad searches and seizures of church documents.

Christians can make a difference by effectively presenting the critical liberties and values that are at stake today to the courts. It is not too late for new court decisions to make a difference.

We also need to pray for those in authority. We easily criticize others; unfortunately we rarely pray for them. The task of leadership in the modern world is complex and awesome. Christians need to pray regularly, not only for the president, but for the Supreme Court, for other judicial officers, for House and Senate members, and for our local school boards. We need to add feet to our prayers by vigorous and positive participation in public life, in community service, and in our neighborhoods. We must be prepared to call our nation back to the covenants of freedom between the people and the United States government.

3

The Ability
to Say No!

Christians are discovering injustice. We are discovering, at least in small ways, what it feels like to be squeezed, penalized, and even at times ridiculed. We are sensing what it's like to have the "system" against us. And we don't like it!

Now we need to discover the capacity to say no! Aleksandr Solzhenitsyn said it. Patrick Henry said it. Lech Walesa says it—and freedom is enhanced. This capacity to stand against injustice is central to the concept of liberty as a fundamental inalienable right. No more taxation without representation, the colonists demanded. The capacity to say no was central to their declaration of liberty.

For us today it is also essential to say no before abuses become so drastic that a new government needs to be formed to overthrow the tyranny of kings or entrenched unrepresentative power. It is essential to say no, so our existing liberties may be preserved. So essential is this capacity that one founder of liberty in our nation suggested that a revolution would probably be necessary every hundred years just to maintain freedom. People must not lose the capacity to resist every form of oppression.

Of course, there is something impolite about saying no. We are taught early in life not to be too direct or uncooperative. Since our nation was born of civil disobedience and revolution, it is striking how we seem to resist any form of protest.

If civility teaches that *no* is impolite, there is a version of Christianity that teaches it is impious, at least as far as government is concerned. We admit that Paul's counsel to the Romans calls for believers to obey the government, for it is instituted by God with the purpose of restraining evil and supporting the good. However, Paul's counsel must be balanced with other clear and direct biblical commandments. There is the direct counsel, "We must obey God rather than men" (Acts 5:29). In addition, there are repeated and powerful demonstrations in Scripture of disobedience to government when that government was bent on evil or when it challenged the authority of God or when it became idolatrous and despotic. Government was in no sense immune from the judgment of the prophet or the revolution of a new family of kings in Israel.

Our difficult but essential task is to assess when government is to be obeyed and when it has so overstepped its authority and become so hostile to the gospel that it must be resisted. But even when one has decided to resist, it is not always clear how to do that. For example, is the resistance limited to noncooperation, or may it take active forms of political action, protest, use of power, or perhaps even revolution?

Christians should examine the basis for resistance. On what grounds, for example, should a Christian resist a governmental decree to cease public testimony? What types of licensing by the state are so egregious that they call for possible civil disobedience? Believers in many nations face these issues regularly. In the Soviet Union, Baptists must choose to be "registered" or unregistered and hence underground. They have divided, often bitterly, on that subject. Seven Siberian Pentecostals refused to serve in the Soviet army and to obey the government's restriction against teaching their faith to their children. At this writing they are spending their fourth year in the American Embassy in Russia, where they fled so they could emigrate to a country that was free.

You might say, "But our country is a democracy, not a dictatorship." Does the fact that the government is "ours" lessen our responsibility? Or does this give us more reason to take active roles in challenging honestly perceived abuses?

These questions raise issues that have created significant division within Christian communities. In the mid-nineteenth century, such issues divided Christians in the slavery controversy. In the 1960s our nation and Christian groups were similarly divided over the methods of civil disobedience that were used to achieve civil rights; shortly after that, there was the resistance to the Vietnam War. Now we see similar issues being raised regarding governmental power and control over religious organizations.

Some advocate a perspective that suggests that government is essentially of the devil, of this world and its principalities and powers; government is to have no power over the church and its ministries or over personal conscience. Some churches in California have refused to complete forms necessary to maintain their property tax exemption. A similar philosophy caused a Nebraska private school to refuse to give the state the names of students who were attending their private elementary and secondary schools. They insisted it was none of the state's business. They claimed a religious exemption, a free exercise right to be left alone. Their minister was finally jailed.

At the other extreme are groups so comfortable with government—at times perhaps eager for its favors—that they rarely ask questions about the impact of complying with every government officials' request.

Above all, Christians must learn to say no to injustice. A biblical commitment to justice must go beyond merely seeking to assure that "Christian rights" are protected. Justice is more than our rights. The Old Testament prophets stood up in the city squares and the kings' courts to demand that justice reign at the very center of the nation's life—its business, its politics, its international relations, its family life. They called for justice "at the gate"—a sort of local, commercial, small claims court.

Justice for the biblical prophet was not simply the current interest of the local synagogue's social concerns committee. It was part of God's very character and his call for righteousness. He is a God of justice who shows no partiality (Psalm 82). Justice is his continuous work (Deut. 10:17, 18), his active intervention in the affairs of man (Psalm 72). And God pleads that his people act for justice, which is not simply a concept, but involves action. "Do justice" is the plea of Micah. Amos wants to see justice roll down like waters—a flood that will refresh, renew, nurture, and clean society.

The prophets are particularly concerned that justice be shown to the poor, the oppressed, and the widow—helpless people who are unable to secure their own rights. The people of God are to speak up for the weak. But sometimes they are so weak, they are unaware of the injustice that needs correcting.

Our credibility to plea for our own justice will perhaps be assessed by the extent to which we speak for justice, human rights, and equal treatment for others. And as we ourselves begin to taste some episodes of injustice and resistance from the structured authorities of this world, we may become more sensitive to those who feel discrimination in destructive and permanent ways.

LOOKING AHEAD

Now that we have an overall view of the legal problems in our country today, we will turn to the specifics of law. This book is intended to be a handbook for Christians so they can understand their rights and resist unjust limitations upon their religious liberty. The next section of the book will acquaint you with the legal basis for religious liberty and the basic terminology used by the courts. The final section is a discussion of the rights of Christian teachers, students, pastors, and laymen.

Chapters within this final section address specific issues: a parent's right to influence school curriculum, the right to evangelize in a public forum, an employee's right to witness on the job, a student's right to invite a Christian person to speak on campus. When a particular problem arises, that chapter can be referred to, so a Christian can defend his or her rights.

The authors are not suggesting that a lay person can take his own cause to the courts. Obviously you will need the assistance of an attorney for such action. However, this book can help you understand your rights and know when an issue is important enough to be pursued in the courts.

PART TWO
THE ESSENTIALS OF RELIGIOUS LIBERTY

4

The Best Hope
for Our World

And sovereign law, that state's collected will
O'er thrones and globes elate
Sits empress, crowning good, repressing ill.

Daniel Webster, 1851

The United States Constitution is "the most wonderful work ever struck off at a given time by the brain and purpose of man," declared nineteenth-century British statesman William Gladstone. Other European notables—Edmund Burke, William Blake, the Marquis de Lafayette, and Alexis de Tocqueville—joined Gladstone in declaring the American experiment to be "the last best hope for the world." Englishman J. Arthur Partridge insisted that "next to the Christian religion . . . the American government and Constitution are the most precious possessions which the world holds or which the future can inherit."

Too few Americans have ever read the Constitution, which embodies ideas that are scarcely less than radical and revolutionary. At the heart of this document, hammered out by the Constitutional Convention in 1789, was a concept of liberty: a commitment to the principle that the rights of man were not derived by a grant of royal power, as in the celebrated document of English liberty, the Magna Charta. These rights were, as the Declaration of Independence had declared, "inalienable."

Why? Because they were derived from "Nature and Nature's God." These rights were centered in God, not man. These liberties were given by the Creator, and no man might legitimately infringe upon them. This commitment to a religiously rooted concept of freedom is crucial to our understanding of the nature and source of human rights. If this source is rejected, our freedom is threatened.

The Constitution is, in some ways, a political manifestation of a conviction that there is a "higher law" to which a people are accountable, a law that even the people cannot violate. This higher law will be followed even when it seems against man's short-term self-interests and the pressures of majorities.

Law has even been defined as something men create in their best moments to protect themselves against themselves in their worst moments. A constitution is a commitment to establish certain limits on the powers of both the government and the people. The United States Constitution insists that freedom persist when there may be strong temptations to limit it. Our Constitution provides a check on the possibility that the government would ignore the rights of the people.

The Constitution was, in part, an attempt to create a government with the necessary powers to effectuate a national government. The Articles of Confederation had proven unworkable. But the Constitution was, as Madison insisted, the "superstructure" for the basic concept of the rights of man, which had been declared in the proclamation of July 4, 1776. Along with the basic Constitution, the delegates passed the "Bill of Rights"—the first ten amendments—which specified some of the basic liberties government could not take away, such as freedom of speech, press, and religion.

Historian H. G. Wells described the Constitution as "indubitably Christian." Wells is not alone in his conviction that much of the philosophy that led to the noble American experiment was informed by Christian notions. In 1886 J. Arthur Partridge spoke of the American commitment to rights and freedoms as "founded upon the rock of religion. . . ." In fact, the whole colonial enterprise began with profound convictions about God's provision for the "new Israel." William Bradford in his history *Of Plymouth Plantation* demonstrated this religious commitment in his notes of May 19, 1643: "Whereas we all came into these parts of America with one and ye same end and aime, namely, to advance the kingdome of our Lord Jesus Christ, and to injoye ye liberties of ye Gospel in puritie with peace. . . ."

As the Revolution neared, the *Boston Gazette* reported the proceedings of a town meeting in Petersham, which included the following resolution, illustrating how necessary Christian underpinnings were to a new nation of liberty:

> Resolved, that it is the opinion of this town, that a despotic arbitrary government is the kingdom of this world, as set forth in the New Testament, and is diametrically opposed to the establishment of Christianity in a society, and has the direct tendency to sink a people into a profound sense of ignorance and irreligion.

Christian convictions about the fallen nature of man contributed to the strict limits on government provided for in the Constitution and the division of power, which limits abuse and provides for checks on political power. As Alexis de Tocqueville warned, liberty is unlike despotism; it cannot govern without faith. This same conviction caused Daniel Webster to declare that it was the settled conviction of all the people that "pure morality and true religion are indispensable" in the support of a useful and wise government. Philip Schaff, a noted nineteenth-century church historian, echoed the same thought a generation later when he wrote, "Republican institutions in the hands of a virtuous and God-fearing nation are the best in the world, but in the hands of a corrupt and irreligious people, they are the very worst, and the most effective weapon of destruction. . . ."

Christian values clearly formed the character of our nation, its commitment to inalienable rights, and the development of a constitutional government. No understanding of our liberty is adequate without recognizing the role of the Constitution in American history and law. A commitment to its principles is equally essential for the preservation of our liberty.

JUDICIAL REVIEW

But who shall define and enforce these guarantees and fundamental liberties? Who shall assure that Congress or the president shall not in moments of passion deprive the people of their rights?

The Constitution does not specifically answer these questions, though they were discussed at the Constitutional Convention. The answer, developed over the years by our political system, is now clear: the Supreme Court is the guardian of the Constitution. As a result of this power, many consider the Supreme Court of the United States to be the most powerful judicial body in the world.

In legal language, the Supreme Court has the ultimate power of "judicial review"—the power to review and ascertain whether or not a given policy, statute, or practice of government conforms with the requirements of the Constitution. If not, that statute or act is invalid. The full history of the development of this power by the Supreme Court is a fascinating story of constitutional philosophy.

The key element was the decision of the Court in *Marbury* v. *Madison* in 1803. This is perhaps the most important case in all of constitutional law, because the Court declared an act of Congress, the Judiciary Act of 1789, unconstitutional. While the basis of that decision is still debated in constitutional law classes, the decision established the principle that the Supreme Court has the power to review federal, state, and local legislation and the acts of federal, state, and local officials to determine if they violate the Constitution. This power of judicial review extends to all courts, so that even lower federal and state courts may rule on the constitutionality of governmental acts.

Well-publicized decisions of the Supreme Court, involving police search and seizure practices, rights of indigents to legal counsel, and segregation, have seen the Court exercise its power to declare certain laws and government practices to be unconstitutional. Politicians, lawyers, and interested parties eagerly await decisions of the Supreme Court for the last word. There is no appeal except through a constitutional amendment.

WHO WILL GUARD THE GUARDIANS?

Some have suggested that the Supreme Court's power of judicial review creates a government of nine ("nine old men," some were inclined to say before the appointment of Judge Sandra Day O'Connor) who have too much power and legislate their own values and norms. Some people even feel that the justices contradict the expressed will of the majority of the people or, at times, of the legislatures of the states and the Congress.

Often the criticism suggests that the Court needs to construe the Constitution more narrowly (or strictly) rather than read its own political or economic philosophy into it. (Persons who hold such perspectives are often referred to as "strict constructionists.")

Many conservatives believe the Supreme Court ought to apply the Constitution more in terms of the meaning—or intent—of the founders and authors, and not engage in attempts to "liberalize" it to conform to allegedly more modern views. The Courts' striking down of abortion laws, pornography statutes, and other local and state statutes has preempted the role of local government and substituted the Court's views of what the law ought to be for the decision of the people's elected representatives. Some believe that the Court has used the Constitution and its power of judicial review to create its own vision of society, often finding in the Constitution new "rights" not intended by the writers.

There is indeed a wide range of perspectives on how the Court ought to conduct its review. Should these nine justices be bound by the intent of the framers or should the words of the Constitution govern? If the words are the determining factor, then who shall supply their meaning—especially when the Constitution may be, as Harvard law professor Laurence Tribe suggests, "intentionally incomplete." This creates both an opportunity to expand citizens' liberties and to abuse individual rights if the fundamental values and processes that nurture liberty are forgotten.

Concerns about the Court abusing its power arose during the Constitutional Convention. Seeking to encourage ratification of the proposed constitution, Alexander Hamilton suggested that such concerns were ill-founded. The Court, Hamilton believed, constituted no threat because it had "neither force nor will, but merely judgment," and was therefore the "least dangerous branch."

In a day when courts are far more active, and perhaps more imaginative in forging new rights and striking down long-held practices (such as school prayers, abortion prohibitions, or obscenity laws), the Court is not at all without force or will and hardly the least dangerous arm of the federal government. More severe critics even suggest it is the most dangerous, because of its power and its lack of accountability to the people. Only five justices constitute a majority of the Court (which is needed for an official decision); therefore five justices can dramatically affect national policy and law.

The issue of who shall guard the guardians is one Professor Laurence Tribe describes as "acute"—especially when, as noted educator Louis Hartz suggests, fundamental values and beliefs are no longer widely shared in the United States. Hartz observed that "when half a nation believes in Locke and half in Filmer or Marx, the result is not law but philosophy." It is difficult to know what source the Court will use to find the principles that guide its interpretations.

However, the power of judicial review may be essential. When appropriately exercised, it assures liberty by thwarting the attempts of other government branches to deny rights guaranteed in our Constitution. The Court must exercise judicial restraint so it does not exceed the limits that a free people place upon all governmental powers.

Those who seek to assure freedom should recognize the Supreme Court's overwhelming power and its central role in assuring constitutional liberties. We need to remember the statement of Supreme Court Justice Robert Jackson: "We are not final because we are infallible, we are infallible because we are final."

5

Getting the Court's Attention

May a group of Christian students meet at a public university and use campus facilities? May you hand out tracts in a shopping center? May a church be forced to hire someone as janitor without regard to religious values? For the last word, ask the Supreme Court. It has the final word on civil liberties and rights guaranteed under the Constitution.

You may have earlier consulted an attorney, or sought to draft a statute, or created a policy for a school board. All of these actions affect practices, and in some sense affect constitutional law. But the final word is with the Supreme Court.

But how do you get the Court to hear you? Almost every party who believes he has stated an important constitutional claim hopes the Supreme Court will ultimately establish a new precedent, a new rule of law. Getting a Supreme Court hearing is not easy. Your chances of ever reaching the Supreme Court are small. With few exceptions, one cannot go directly to the Court, but must rather begin in the lower courts. The Supreme Court is primarily a court of appeal, which reviews the decisions of lower courts.

While the Supreme Court has great powers to review government practices, the Court is able to decide only a relatively few cases each year out of the hundreds that are filed. (An even smaller number actually involve new precedents in the area of fundamental constitutional rights.) In the vast majority of cases, the final decision will be made by a lower state or federal court.

36

These courts are also charged with interpreting the Constitution and protecting liberties. And their decisions do make a difference. For example, in *Yogi* v. *Malnak* a lower court refused on constitutional grounds to allow the teaching of transcendental meditation in New Jersey public schools. And the Supreme Court declined to review that decision.

Lower courts are also important, because they shape the constitutional arguments that the Supreme Court will review. Cases begin in the lower courts, and there the constitutional issues will first be argued. However, lower court decisions do not have the sweeping impact of a Supreme Court ruling. Nor are some lower courts as sensitive to constitutional issues as one might wish.

Let's imagine that one's goal is to obtain the highest review possible, in order to establish a firm principle of constitutional law. Then the Supreme Court is your goal. What does it take to get there? How does the system work?

First, there are some basic requirements before any court will consider a claim:

1. There must be a case or controversy. The Supreme Court, as other courts, does not hear hypothetical issues. It decides cases, actual controversies concerning specific facts and individuals. American law is case law. Constitutional principles come from specific facts, which often are crucial in shaping the decision. Technically a decision in any case is only a rule of law for that set of facts, but situations are sometimes sufficiently similar to warrant the same decision.

Whether or not one has a legal right to distribute religious literature in a shopping center mall must be determined by the facts of the particular case. Important elements might be the size of the shopping center, whether other events of a public nature take place there, and whether the management encourages the public to be there. Other considerations would be: did the distribution create a traffic flow problem? And were there alternative opportunities for this distribution? These facts plus constitutional rights of free speech and the rights of property owners will guide the Court's decision.

2. The controversy must be a legal one. The problem must be legal in nature, and lead therefore to a lawsuit. It may be a civil suit, in which a party seeks an injunction or other relief against another party. In the illustration above, the shopping center owner might seek an order barring the distribution. Or the pamphleteer might seek an order to keep the management from interfering with the distribution.

The case may be a criminal one, where the state seeks to prosecute a person (maybe our literature distributor) for violating an ordinance, such as one against trespassing or littering. The pamphleteer may then seek a court ruling: the statute as applied to his activity is an impermissible interference with his rights of free speech and free exercise of religion.

3. The party must meet the "standing" requirement. The party bringing suit must have "standing"—that is, the party must be sufficiently involved in the case to be threatened by its outcome. In the illustration above, the pamphleteer would have standing, but a local church or pastor would probably not have sufficient standing.

Often in lawsuits that allege a violation of the separation of church and state, the suit is brought by a person who simply claims standing as a taxpayer and challenges an impermissible spending of public funds. The court has generally rejected taxpayer status as insufficient.

However, there are exceptions. They have often been found in suits alleging that a use of government funds has impermissibly aided religion in violation of the Establishment Clause of the First Amendment. In 1966, in *Flast* v. *Cohen*, the Supreme Court granted the suit of a taxpayer who alleged that the Elementary and Secondary Education Acts of 1965 (which provided some federal financial aid to private religious schools) violated the First Amendment. But in 1982 the Court held that a group of taxpayers did not have standing to challenge the sale of government property to a religious organization (*Valley Forge Christian College* v. *Americans United for Separation of Church and State*).

4. The issue must meet the "ripeness" requirement. In some ways this requirement is a restatement of the requirement of a "case." But it goes a step further and requires that for court adjudication, the threat to one's rights must be imminent and not merely expected or anticipated sometime in the uncertain future.

Even if a controversy meets these tests, a lawsuit over a valuable legal right may *not* result in a constitutional decision by the Supreme Court, or even in a constitutional ruling by a lower court. Why not?

In the first place very few cases reach the Supreme Court.

The Constitution provides for a direct suit in the Supreme Court only in specialized cases, such as disputes between states themselves. All other cases begin in state or federal courts (U.S. district courts), usually referred to as trial courts. The process begins with a trial and decision by a lower court. Such a court may or may not decide the constitutional issues raised in the lawsuit. There may then be an appeal.

In state courts the appeal may involve a number of levels, ultimately reaching the highest state court (usually referred to as the state supreme court). In federal courts, the appeal is to a circuit court of appeal. There are twelve such circuits in the United States, each circuit covering a number of states.

After the trial and appeal courts rule, the parties may seek a hearing by the United States Supreme Court. This may occur by one of three processes:

1. Certification: A process by which a lower federal court "certifies" a question of law to the Supreme Court, which may answer the question or take the case itself. This process is rarely utilized and depends on the lower federal court requesting such action.

2. Appeal: In this context the right of "appeal" refers to those situations where the party seeking review has a right to a review by the Supreme Court. The only two situations where this right of appeal exists are when a state court has upheld the constitutionality of a state statute against a claim that the statute violates the United States Constitution or when a state court has held a federal statute to be unconstitutional. Both of these situations involve actual or potential conflict between the federal and state judiciary, and therefore review by the Supreme Court is almost essential. (The Court may still functionally ignore a full decision by holding that the constitutional issue is not clearly presented or the appeal is without merit.)

3. Petition for writ of certiorari: The vast majority of cases are referred to the Supreme Court by a party filing a petition for a *writ of certiorari,* which asks the Court to review the case and indicates why the petitioner believes the case raises important issues that deserve the high court's consideration.

In all these cases, a review by the Supreme Court is discretionary. The requests for such review are so great that the Court has to limit the number of cases it will hear. The Supreme Court often simply denies the "writ." While commentators sometimes refer to such refusals as an indication that the Supreme Court has agreed with or affirmed the lower court decision, such is not necessarily the case. It may also mean that the Court did not find the issue important enough or the legal facts properly framed. The court rarely indicates the reasons for the denial of a *writ of certiorari.*

The decision to hear a case under the certiorari procedure depends on the "rule of four." If four justices support a review, it is accepted.

But even if the case is accepted, it still may not result in the great constitutional statement the parties may wish. Even the winner may be disappointed. The Court may decide the case *not* on constitutional grounds but on some other basis—on "independent grounds." The Court often seeks to avoid making constitutional law, and will first consider other bases for a decision. One example is the recent case between the National Labor Relations Board (NLRB) and a group of Catholic bishops. The bishops questioned if the Labor Relations Board had the power to require Catholic schools to allow an election to determine union representation among their teachers. The Catholic bishops had raised many constitutional questions about government interference with the religious mission of the schools. The Court sided with the Catholic bishops, but did so without comment on these constitutional questions. Instead the Court interpreted the federal statute that gave the NLRB its power as *not* authorizing such power over employees of religious schools.

The Court may also decide the question on very narrow grounds—that is, confine its holding to the specific facts in *that* case, and thus deliberately seek to avoid establishing broad principles. The Court took precisely this approach when it decided that President Carter had the power to negotiate the settlement of the Iranian crisis, including the assignment of all claims against Iran to an international arbitration panel.

The following summary of developments in a well-known case, *Florey* v. *Sioux Falls School District,* illustrates the complexity and scope of a local issue that is pursued through the legal system on constitutional grounds:

December 1977	Justin Florey participated in a kindergarten Christmas program at Hayward Elementary Public School in Sioux Falls. Justin's father, Roger Florey, complained to the school district's superintendent that the program had excessive religious content.
	As a result of Florey's complaint (and others), a citizens committee was formed to develop and implement rules concerning the relationship between religious beliefs and school functions. (Some of the committee included: the school district's director of music; an attorney; Jewish, Catholic, and Protestant clergy; and a member of the Civil Liberties Union.)
November 13, 1978	After public hearings, the school board initially adopted the policy and rules recommended by the citizen's committee (see chapter 14 for actual policy statement).
November 17, 1978	Affidavit of Roger R. Florey taken, in which he claimed that both he and his son suffered and continued to suffer irreparable harm because of Justin's exposure to and participation in Hayward Elementary School's religious exercises. Florey also claimed irreparable harm and loss of his constitutional right.
November 28, 1978	Plaintiffs Florey and American Civil Liberties Union (ACLU) filed action for

declaratory and injunctive relief. In their complaint they alleged the policy and rules adopted by the school board violated the Establishment Clause of the First Amendment.

November 28, 1978   Plaintiff's brief filed.

December 4, 1978   Guidelines from the Citizens Committee on Church/State Relationships to the Sioux Falls Board of Education was officially adopted.

December 7, 1978   District court heard evidence on the motion for preliminary injunction against the Board of Education.

December 13, 1978   District court denied motion for preliminary injunction based on the grounds that the traditional criteria had not been satisfied. Court also concluded that the granting of a preliminary injunction in the middle of the Christmas season would not be in the public interest.

December 30, 1978   Plaintiff's reply brief filed.

Defendant's responsive brief filed.

Defendant's summation.

Plaintiff's summary of evidence.

February 14, 1979   Memorandum opinion handed down by the United States District Court in South Dakota, Judge Andrew W. Bogue presiding. The court denied the Plaintiff's request for relief and also denied plaintiff's prayer for permanent injunction against the school board. The court held that the policy, rules, and the implementation thereof did not result in any particular relationship between the school and any religious authority.

March 6, 1979 — Plaintiff filed a notice of appeal regarding both orders, which were denied.

May 16, 1979 — Plaintiff filed brief with the United States Court of Appeals for the Eighth Circuit. Plaintiff alleged that the school board's policy allowed schools to observe both the secular and religious basis of Christmas. Plaintiff claimed that such practices violate both the Establishment and the Free Exercise Clauses of the First Amendment.

May 21, 1979 — William P. Thompson, stated clerk of the General Assembly of the United Presbyterian Church of the United States of America, filed a motion for leave to file brief as *amicus curiae* (an interested nonlitigant).

May 31, 1979 — Order permitting those listed below to file *amicus curiae* briefs:
1) Unitarian Universalist Association
2) National Jewish Commission on Law and Public Affairs
3) Anti-Defamation League
4) General Assembly of the United Presbyterian Church
5) American Jewish Congress

June 12, 1979 — Appellant (plaintiff) filed motion to advance hearing.

September 11, 1979 — Case submitted to United States Court of Appeals who took it under advisement and made no immediate decision.

April 22, 1980	United States Court of Appeals (a three-judge panel) decided the case, 2-1, in favor of the school board. The court upheld the right to include religious literature, music, drama, and the arts in the curriculum and in school activities, provided the material is presented objectively and is intrinsic to the learning experience. Also the court held that the emphasis on religious themes in the arts, literature, and history should be only as extensive as necessary for a balanced study. Such studies should never foster any particular religious tenets or demean any religious beliefs.
May 2, 1980	Appellant filed petition for rehearing and suggestions for rehearing en banc (*en banc* means the whole court of appeals, rather than just the three-judge panel).
May 20, 1980	Appellant's petition for rehearing and suggestions for rehearing en banc were denied.
September 17, 1980	Petition for writ of certiorari filed seeking review by the Supreme Court.
November 10, 1980	Supreme Court of the United States denied the appellant's petition for a writ of certiorari.

One can see that it is a complicated, time-consuming, and often expensive process to establish constitutional principles in the Supreme Court. Because it is so difficult to obtain a Supreme Court hearing, cases that raise constitutional issues of fundamental liberties must be carefully planned and litigated. Effective litigators plan such cases from the very earliest stages, anticipating what facts, arguments, and principles of law are most likely to obtain a hearing at all levels.

6

Those Vital Sixteen Words

Congress shall make no law respecting an establishment of religion or prohibiting the free exercise thereof.

First Amendment
The United States Constitution

Our religious liberties are based on sixteen words. These few words form the battleground upon which the issue of freedom of faith will be waged. However, the two words most associated with the First Amendment's clause about religion are the words *wall* and *separation* in the expression "wall of separation." Neither of these words occur in the First Amendment. Nor does the commonly used phrase "wall of separation" occur in any court opinion prior to the 1940s.

It was Thomas Jefferson who coined the phrase *wall of separation,* which has so shaped our constitutional law. Jefferson had written to the Danbury Baptists in Connecticut who attacked him during his presidential campaign, calling him an infidel and an atheist.

> Believing that religion is a matter which lies solely between man and his God, and that he owes account to none other for his faith or his worship, that the legislative powers of government reach actions only, and not opinions, I contemplate with sovereign reverence that act of the whole American people which declared that their legislature should "make no law respecting an establishment of religion, or prohibiting the free exercise thereof," thus

45

building a wall of separation between church
and state.

Jefferson was a man of the Enlightenment Era of the eigh-
teenth century, with the rationalism and anticlericalism of that
philosophic bent. His religious views were hardly evangelical, or
in accord with most of his contemporaries. When he envisioned
a wall, he saw it largely as a wall to protect the government from
the church and the clergy. Later he softened his stance on this
issue. He provided for a chapel and the teaching of religion at
the University of Virginia, and supported the teaching of morals
in the outpost schools of the Northwest Ordinance.

The words *the wall of separation between church and state,*
which are so often quoted to restrict Christian involvement in
government and education, are not a part of the United States
Constitution or its First Amendment. In fact, Thomas Jefferson
was in Europe at the time the First Amendment was written.

However, the sixteen words that are in the Constitution do
form a significant basis for our religious liberties: our rights to
worship, to believe, to promote our faith, and to raise our
children in accord with our deepest convictions.

On the face of it, the Religion Clause contains two
somewhat distinct prohibitions on government:

(1) Congress shall make no law respecting an
establishment of religion . . .
(2) . . . or prohibiting the free exercise
thereof.

These two provisions have come to be referred to as the
Establishment Clause and the Free Exercise Clause. The sixteen
words of the Religion Clause are simple enough, but what do
they mean?

A LOOK AT THE LANGUAGE

The reader unfamiliar with American legal history might be
surprised to note that the prohibition relates to the Congress:
"Congress shall. . . ." Note that the Constitution does not say
the states. It is the national government, not the state governments, that was prohibited from passing a law respecting an
establishment of religion or prohibiting the free exercise thereof.

At the time of the passage of this amendment, five states had established churches, which were officially endorsed and/or supported by the state governments. In addition to formal established or preferred churches, numerous state laws contained religious requirements for voting, laws prohibiting blasphemy, and many other statutes that provided privileges or penalties related to Christian values, beliefs, and morals. The First Amendment did not touch any of these, because its power was limited to acts of Congress. The framers did not intend to expunge Christian influence from the nation, or even establish a climate of neutrality towards religion.

Since many states had laws favoring religion generally and often certain churches in particular, the Religion Clause may have been intended to preserve the state's prerogatives in this area. The states wished to limit the power of the national government over their affairs. Further evidence supporting this "states' rights" concern is found in the clause's use of the word *respecting*. Strictly interpreted, the clause does not merely prohibit the national government from passing laws creating or favoring one religion over another, but any law at all regarding or respecting the establishment of religion. This clause protects the state establishments from national interference.

Some reviewers of the language and the debates of the Constitutional Convention have also noted that the wording does not prohibit *the* establishment of religion, but *an* establishment of religion. Michael Malbin in his volume, *The Intent of the Framers,* insists that this wording was deliberately chosen. The colonists meant to prohibit official activities that tended to promote one sect over another, rather than prohibiting nondiscriminatory aid to religion. Justice Joseph Story, in his commentary on the First Amendment, concurs with Malbin's analysis. It was a particular religion (in the sense of one sect or church denomination) that was not to be established. It was not a prohibition of favoritism toward religion itself.

A reading of the debates at the Constitutional Convention reveals a concern that the provisions and language of the Religion Clause not disturb the pattern of general support for religion in public life. Concern was even expressed that the language proposed by Madison might be misinterpreted as a prohibition of support of religion. Or as Benjamin Huntington of Connecticut put it, the language might "patronize those who profess no religion at all." Constitutional Convention members Samuel Livermore and Elbridge Gerry concurred.

The drafters of the Constitution were undoubtedly concerned about much more than state rights. Americans knew the dangers of tyranny in established religion; more than a few of them had experienced persecution for beliefs contrary to the official religion of their former countries. Many also knew the consequences of the doctrines of an empowered clergy being forced on a people. There were indeed some leading members of the government who were vigorous defenders of a more broadly conceived concept of separation.

Leaders like Thomas Jefferson and James Madison were less enthusiastic about religion in public life and favored a stricter "separation" between church and state. But it would be difficult in light of the concerns expressed in the debates over this amendment and the actual practice of the various states to argue that the framers intended to eliminate all vestiges of religion from public life.

The concept of a thoroughly secular state divorced from a moral-religious presupposition was largely unknown and certainly outside the intentions of the founders of our nation and drafters of the Bill of Rights in 1789. As contemporary theologian Rousas Rushdoony has commented, "To read the Constitution as a charter for a secular state is to misread history and misread it radically." In fact, Mark DeWolf Howe, former professor of law at Harvard University, observed that far from seeking to inhibit religion, "the most important purpose of the First Amendment was the advancement of the interests of religion."

Words may speak eloquently of freedom and religious liberty, but as we learned from George Orwell's *Animal Farm* and *1984,* words have funny ways of losing their meaning in the hands of manipulators. Nothing illustrates this more clearly than the Constitution of the Soviet Union, which guarantees "freedom of religious worship." Georgi Vins and countless other believers who have been imprisoned for living their religious beliefs have found these four words to be meaningless.

The sixteen words in our Constitution must not be simply proclaimed and cherished, but their assurance of liberty must be vigorously defended. The interpreters—whether they are political philosophers, government agencies, or religious leaders—must be watched carefully to assure these freedoms are not sold for a mess of cultural porridge.

This is all the more so since these sixteen words, as Chief Justice Warren Burger said, were "not the most precisely drawn portions of the Constitution." These words gain their strength and their liability from their simplicity. Their intent, as Burger observed, "was to state an objective, not to write a statute." In recent years the Court has begun to inquire into the meaning of these clauses and how they ought to be applied in contemporary American society.

SUPREME COURT INTERPRETATION

The Supreme Court did not face the issue of the meaning and application of the Religion Clauses until modern times. The Free Exercise Clause was not addressed until 1878, with very little Court interpretation until recent years. And the Establishment Clause was not examined until the 1940s—a full one hundred and fifty years after it was written. Much of the reason for the lack of cases related to these constitutional provisions stemmed from the religious consensus that existed within American society, which led to many informal and some formal relationships between Christian religion and moral values and the state.

As Justice Joseph Story commented: "Probably at the time of the adoption of the Constitution . . . the general, if not the universal sentiment in America was that Christianity ought to receive encouragement from the State. . . . An attempt to level all religions, and to make it a matter of state policy to hold all in utter indifference, would have created universal disapprobation if not universal indignation."

But the rise of a more secular society, the growth of segments of the Christian community that did not share so fully (by choice or otherwise) in the government's favor, and the rise of other religious groups has created a flurry of cases. While most Americans are aware of the decisions regarding school prayer and Bible reading, those decisions were only the first in what seems to be a growing tide of issues facing courts.

In 1980, two federal trial courts held that the Establishment Clause barred or severely limited Christian students from organizing a meeting at the campuses of two public universities (University of Missouri at Kansas City and Western Washington

University). The courts declared that allowing students to use the rooms was constitutionally impermissible because it would aid religion. Another United States district court (in *Brandon* v. *Board of Education*) held that allowing students at a New York high school to meet in a classroom before school for prayer was "too dangerous to permit."

These examples illustrate the long road we have traveled: from a concern by the authors of the Bill of Rights that their language not result in hostility to religion to a time when religious belief seems too often to be a handicap.

HOW HAVE WE COME SO FAR?

A major cause of this shift comes from a seriously flawed reading of history. Mark Howe, former law professor at Harvard, declares that the "Court has dishonored the art of the historian. . . ." When the Court decided the seminal *Everson* v. *Board of Education* case in 1947 (which questioned whether state tax money could be used to transport children by bus to parochial schools), it set the tone for interpreting the First Amendment in sweeping language. Justice Hugo Black wrote the opinion for the Court, in which he purported to rely upon the intent of the framers and the history of their period.

However, the Court drew heavily upon Thomas Jefferson's letter to the Danbury Baptists and the beliefs of James Madison, who was perhaps the most extreme of the separationists. He vetoed a bill to grant a charter of incorporation to the Episcopal Church in Washington, D.C., opposed the appointment of chaplains to the military services, and objected to the presidential proclamation of days of thanksgiving. Madison clearly did not reflect the majority sentiment of the nation, nor was his recommended language for the religion clause adopted by the delegates.

Laurence Tribe notes that the Court's view of history (expressed by Justice Black) is suspect. But "what is indisputable is that with remarkable consistency, later courts have accepted the perspective [of Justice Black] as historical truth." Constitutional commentators, many with little interest in evangelical faith, have dubbed the Court a poor historian when it declared the founders intended to create a "wall of separation," which was intended to reject aid even to religion in general. Such interpretations are "superficial."

If the concept of separation or wall was present in the minds of most of the authors of the First Amendment, it was probably the type of "wall" espoused by Roger Williams. Williams, like Jefferson, envisioned a necessary barrier, but unlike Jefferson, Williams felt the wall was to protect the church and not the government. Williams wrote:

> . . . when they have opened a gap in the hedge or wall of separation between the garden of the church and the wilderness of the world, God hath ever broke down the wall itself, removed the candlestick, and made His garden a wilderness, as at this day. And that therefore if He will eer please to restore His garden and paradise again, it must of necessity be walled in peculiarly unto Himself from the world . . .

Rather than saving the state from the ecclesiastics, Williams saw the need for protecting the church from the state, which would corrupt it. Mark DeWolf Howe's volume, *The Garden and the Wilderness,* is drawn from Williams's image. This book contends that to the extent the framers had a wall in mind, it was inspired more by the faith of Williams than by the doubts of Jefferson. Rather than a mere political principle, it is in fact a theological principle centered on an evangelical faith.

Everson set the stage for a whole tradition, which has formed not only the official decisions of the Supreme Court but shaped popular opinion about the "separation of church and state" for the past thirty-five years. Not that the decisions themselves have always been erroneous, but to ground them, as Michael Malbin put it, "in an incredibly flawed reading of the intentions of the authors" is fallacious. Leonard Manning in his *Law of Church State Relations* comments, "Undoubtedly the Court has the right to make history, but it does not have the right to remake it."

When the Supreme Court in a modern case such as *McCollum* analyzed the meaning of the Establishment Clause, it spoke not of the general support of religion, but of Jefferson's restrictive wall. Justice Frankfurter's concurring opinion declared: "Separation means separation, not something less. Jefferson's metaphor . . . speaks of a 'wall of separation', not just a fine line easily overstepped. 'The great American principle of separation,' . . . is one of the vital references of our constitutional system."

In dissenting from the *McCollum* decision, Justice Stanley Reed warned that "a rule of law should not be drawn from a figure of speech."

At times, the Court itself seems to withdraw from the rigors of a high and impregnable wall, as Justice William Douglas did in rendering the decision of the Court in *Zorach* v. *Clausen* (which upheld the constitutionality of a public school's off-campus, released-time, religious education programs):

> The First Amendment . . . does not say that in every and all respects there shall be a separation of church and state. . . . We are a religious people whose institutions presuppose a Supreme Being. . . . [The State] respects the religious nature of our people and accommodates the public service to their spiritual needs. To hold that it may not would be to find in the Constitution a requirement that the government show a callous indifference to religious groups. That would be preferring those who believe in no religion over those who do believe.

Yet this perspective in *Zorach* has been overwhelmed by rigid separation. The costs to religion and to the state are only now becoming apparent.

7

The Establishment Clause

Congress shall make no law respecting an establishment of religion . . .

First Amendment

If one wishes to argue before the Supreme Court that a city has the right to erect a creche in the city hall at Christmastime—or that students have the right to conduct a religious assembly—one must speak the language of the Court and learn to apply its principles. For this reason we will trace some of the Supreme Court's Religion Clause decisions.

The Court's first encounter with the Establishment Clause of the First Amendment was in 1947 in *Everson* v. *Board of Education*. Prior to *Everson,* some cases had raised establishment questions, but the court had decided the cases on other grounds.

The issue in *Everson* was whether state tax money could be used to reimburse parents for the cost of transporting children by bus to parochial schools. The *Everson* opinion is central to understanding the modern Court's view of the Establishment Clause for two basic reasons:

1. It applied establishment prohibitions to the states. As you will recall the language of the First Amendment only spoke of Congress. In *Everson,* however, the Supreme Court held that the Establishment Clause was also to be applied to the states. The Court in *Cantwell* v. *Connecticut* (a 1940 case involving free exercise) held that the Fourteenth Amendment of the United States Constitution "rendered the legislatures of the states as incompetent as Congress" to enact laws that violated the Establishment or Free Exercise Clauses. Now in *Everson* it applied that principle.

The Fourteenth Amendment contains the Due Process Clause ("nor shall any State deprive any persons of life, liberty or property, without due process of law"). The Court has held that the liberty spoken of in that clause includes many of the liberties included in the Bill of Rights. *Cantwell* and *Everson* established that the Religion Clause could be applied to the states as well as the federal government.

Now all levels of government are prevented from acts that violate the Establishment Clause or the Free Exercise Clause. Thus any "state action," as lawyers refer to it, must conform to these constitutional guarantees. Acts of Congress, state legislation, acts of government officials, government administrative agencies—all are constitutionally bound. This includes not only formal legislation, but also acts of officials of the government such as policies of a zoning board, some actions of a public school teacher, the tax board of a county, and the state or local library. At times, even action by private persons or organizations may be "state action" if public monies are used or other linkages to government are significant.

Everson has greatly expanded the scope of authority of the Religion Clause of the First Amendment and offered broad assurances of religious freedom.

2. The "Separationist" Perspective: The second key element in *Everson* was the pattern set for viewing the First Amendment in sweeping language. Justice Hugo Black, who delivered the opinion of the Court, drew heavily on Thomas Jefferson and James Madison. He read the establishment prohibitions as analogous to Madison's efforts in Virginia to resist a tax levy, which would have supported the established Episcopal Church.

Black indicated that the Establishment Clause was to be given a "broad interpretation." It was intended to erect a "wall of separation between church and state," and this wall "must be kept high and impregnable"—not even the "slightest breach" could be approved. Justice Wiley Rutledge in a concurring opinion was even stronger. He argued that the clause was intended "to uproot all such relationships" between church and state and not simply formal relationships of established churches. "It was to create a complete and permanent separation of the spheres of religious activity and civil authority. . . ."

The very next year the Court (again with Justice Black delivering the opinion of the Court) decided *McCollum* v. *Maryland,* a case involving a released-time program in Champaign, Illinois, where religious teachers were allowed to come into the public schools weekly for a period of thirty minutes of optional religious instruction. The teachers came from a variety of churches; pupils were allowed to receive the religious instruction of their choice—or none at all—based upon their parents' requests.

The Court held that the practice violated the prohibition of establishment. It rejected a claim that the clause only prohibited government assistance. A concurring opinion by Justice Felix Frankfurter concluded "we renew our conviction that we have staked the very existence of our country on the faith that complete separation of church and state is best for the state and for religion. . . . 'good fences make good neighbors'."

Thus *Everson* and *McCollum* set a pattern of interpretation often described as "separationist." While there were exceptions to the "high and impregnable wall," the Court seems to hold this basic view.

AN IMPERMISSIBLE ESTABLISHMENT OF RELIGION

What does the Supreme Court mean when it declares that an act is an impermissible establishment of religion? In a series of cases, the Supreme Court has developed a test to determine if such an establishment of religion has occurred. This test is often referred to as the *"tripartite test"* and was explicitly spelled out in *Lemon* v. *Kurtzman.* It is critical to understanding the questions the court will use to assess the constitutionality of any challenged act or practice.

In 1977, the Supreme Court in *Wolman* summarized the test: "In order to pass muster, the statute must have a secular legislative purpose, must have a principal or primary effect that neither advances nor inhibits religion, and must not foster excessive governmental entanglement with religion."

The three parts of the test are:

1. Purpose: The purpose or intent of the statute or governmental regulation must have a legitimate secular end, and may not be to aid or inhibit religion.

2. Effect: The primary effect, notwithstanding the purpose, must not be to aid or inhibit religion.

3. Entanglement: The result must not excessively entangle the government in the affairs of religion.

In order for a statute or governmental act (or policy or regulation) to be permissible and avoid running afoul of the Establishment Clause, it must pass all three of the tests.

PURPOSE TEST

The "secular purpose" requirement evolved from cases involving state or federal statutes that provided governmental financial assistance to religious organizations; but this requirement is now broadly applied. What was the *intent* of the legislature (or school board or government agency) in establishing a law or policy? If the very *purpose* was to aid religion, the Establishment Clause has been violated. But how is the purpose ascertained by the Court? Not primarily by examining the hidden motives of the Congress or legislature, but by reviewing the statute itself and the legislative hearings that led to the bill's enactment.

Often the statute will state a purpose. If a legitimate secular purpose has been indicated, the Court will rarely look behind this statement. Thus in many cases involving state and federal aid to parochial schools, Sabbath laws (requiring business closure on Sundays), and cases involving military chaplains and conscientious objector exemptions, the Court has not found any *purpose* violations.

On rare occasions the Supreme Court has looked behind the language of a statute and found an impermissible purpose to advance religion. In 1968 in *Epperson* v. *Arkansas*, the Court found that Arkansas's antievolution statute embodied an impermissible purpose. The Court believed the statute was simply a successor to an earlier Tennessee "monkey law," which was overtly religious. Justice Abe Fortas in a footnote declared, "It is clear that fundamentalist sectarian conviction was and is the law's reason for existence."

More recently, the Supreme Court (by a 5-4 decision) rejected a Kentucky statute that authorized the permanent posting of the Ten Commandments in classrooms of the state's public schools. The legislation contained a statement that the purpose was to encourage an awareness of the cultural sources of western civilization and law—an arguable secular purpose. The Court rejected the statute, holding that the real purpose was a sectarian one. Unfortunately the *purpose* test inevitably thrusts the Court into assessing motives—a difficult and dangerous area for judicial analysis.

The principle of the purpose test is clear: no government action may have as its purpose the promotion or inhibition of religion. It is worth noting that purposes of inhibiting religion are just as impermissible as those promoting religion.

PRIMARY EFFECT TEST

It is not sufficient that an act merely have a legitimate secular purpose. It also must not have the primary effect of aiding or inhibiting religion. Note that the test does not prohibit *any* effect that aids or inhibits religion. If that were required, police could not protect church property and tax exemptions could not be allowed for contributions to religious organizations. Legislation that did not have some effect to either aid or inhibit religion would be hard to imagine. The test does not prohibit all such effects but prohibits a *primary* effect that aids or inhibits religion. Obviously the word *primary* is susceptible to varied interpretation. The Court has sometimes spoken of *direct* effect or *substantial* effects, and at other times used antonyms such as *indirect, incidental, remote,* or *independent* to describe effects that are permissible.

Cases where this issue has been central have involved aid to parochial schools—elementary, secondary, and collegiate. In *Tilton* v. *Richardson* and in *Committee for Public Education* v. *Nyquist,* the Court went beyond *primary* effects to invalidate programs where the nonsecular effect was merely possible. Laurence Tribe has suggested that under more recent and stricter Court decisions, the nonsecular effect must be "remote, indirect, and incidental" to survive constitutional challenge. This would seem especially true where government money is involved, such as aid to parochial education.

A thorough review of the way the Court has struggled with the scope of permissible effect would take many pages. Volumes have been written analyzing the Court's path through this maze. But it is important to realize that the courts will review the effect of any policy or statute that bears on religious rights.

We must also recognize that the prohibition is not only against state action that "aids" religion, but against "inhibiting" religion. Several cases have involved statutes that have alledgedly had the effect of inhibiting religion. In *McGowan* v. *Maryland* the claim was made that a statute requiring Sunday closing of businesses (even though it had a secular purpose of establishing a uniform day of rest) was advantageous to Sunday-observing groups and inhibited Sabbatarians. The Court rejected the claims, indicating the inhibiting effect was incidental. However, in a secular society, more and more situations are arising where Christians can allege the impermissible effect of inhibiting religion.

EXCESSIVE ENTANGLEMENT TEST

The third part of the tripartite test examines whether or not the implementation of any statute or policy will result in impermissible entangling of church and state. As James Madison said, "[the national government] has not a shadow of right . . . to intermeddle with religion."

The concern about entanglement emerged initially in a church property dispute. The Court indicated the danger of assessing church doctrine and involving courts in internal church disputes. In such cases there is an impermissible theological entanglement.

Administrative Entanglement

The entanglement test is primarily applied, however, where the entanglement is administrative. In a number of cases (frequently involving financial assistance to religious schools) the courts, while finding no impermissible *purpose* or *effect,* have struck down statutes because of the entangling of the institutions. The Court has spoken of the government's impermissible "comprehensive, discriminating and continuing" surveillance of the programs, the use of funds, accounting decisions, etc. For example, some statutes have attempted to provide financial assistance to religious schools but limited this assistance to the teaching of "secular" subjects only. The government would then have to review the curriculum and accounting procedures. Courts have found such arrangements to inevitably involve government entanglement with the religious institutions.

Therefore they violate the Establishment Clause.

Again the test is not totally clear. Justice Byron White once referred to it as "curious and mystifying." It does, however, express the Court's concern that government and religious organizations must avoid relationships in which the government supervises religion.

Political Divisiveness as Entanglement

At times, the Court has found an additional type of "entanglement," which involves the creation of an atmosphere of political divisiveness. What has apparently concerned the Court is the potential for a program (for example, aid to parochial schools) to create politically warring factions in a community and an environment in which people "find their votes aligned with their faith." Justice John Harlan warned that "political fragmentation on sectarian lines must be guarded against." This test has been applied in contexts where religious groups have sought some form of government aid.

Recently there has been an interesting twist given to the entanglement prohibition. Traditionally, the entanglement test was used to prohibit government *aid* to religious institutions. The argument has been successfully made in a number of courts that the entanglement prohibition may also limit government *regulation* of religious institutions. For example, a recent decision of a United States district court in California held that private religious schools were exempt from participation in state unemployment plans. The secretary of labor had held that teachers of secular subjects in such schools must be included and taxes collected for them. The schools successfully argued that such an involvement of the government would require the sort of supervisory entanglement the Supreme Court had declared a violation of the Establishment Clause. Similar issues have been raised with state regulation of private Christian schools, such as state licensing and curriculum supervision.

In many cases the tripartite test does not yield an obvious conclusion. There are a number of flexible points, such as what is a "secular" purpose? What is a "primary" effect as opposed to an "indirect" or "incidental" effect? What is "excessive" entanglement? Nevertheless, the test is a central tool of constitutional analysis; those concerned with religious liberty must be familiar with its use.

ACCOMMODATION AND
BENEVOLENT NEUTRALITY

If the tripartite test were applied with a strong "separationist" posture, it might create a de facto hostility to religion. Widespread practices that indicate some governmental favor toward religion (such as chaplains paid by the government, property and income tax exemptions for churches, religious language on government currency, and prayers in the United States Congress) could be struck down.

In actual fact, the United States Supreme Court has not applied the strict principle of "impregnable walls of separation." It has been as flexible as Chief Justice Warren Burger suggested when he said, "There is room for play in the joints productive of a benevolent neutrality which will permit religious exercise to exist without sponsorship and without interference."

Burger expressed the same concern in *Lemon* v. *Kurtzman:* "Judicial caveats against entanglement must recognize that the line of separation, far from being a 'wall', is a blurred, indistinct and variable barrier depending on all the circumstances of a particular relationship." Outside the public school context, the Court has shown a willingness to utilize a more flexible standard than "separation," which is sometimes expressed in the policy of *benevolent neutrality* and *accommodation.*

Judge Alphonso Taft, the father of the Supreme Court justice and president said, "The government is neutral, and, while protecting all [religions], it prefers none and it disparages none." Justice Tom Clark in *Abington* v. *Schempp* declared similarly, "in the relationship between man and religion, the State is firmly committed to the position of neutrality."

But the Court has gone further than to enunciate a concept of neutrality. If strictly applied, neutrality would void the very special protections afforded religious expression in the Free Exercise Clause. Justice Arthur Goldberg seemed to recognize the dangers of an artificial neutrality in a concurring opinion in *Abington* v. *Schempp.* He warned that an untutored devotion to the concept of neutrality could lead to "a brooding and pervasive devotion to the secular and a passive, or even active, hostility to the religious." Such results, Goldberg argued, are prohibited by the Constitution. The neutrality is a "free exercise neutrality," which is not blind to the religious character of most of the people nor requires state hostility to religion. Thus the courts have spoken of *benevolent neutrality* or the principle of accommodation of religion—*accommodating neutrality.*

The doctrine of accommodation was expressed in *Zorach* v. *Clausen,* which involved another released-time, religious program and was decided just a few years after *McCollum.* Students were released for an hour a week to attend off-campus religious instruction. Attendance records were kept by the religious institution for the school. Certainly the purpose of the statute was religious in motivation, and its effect was certainly to aid religion. Yet the Court upheld the policy. Justice Douglas, writing for the Court, seemed to speak in different tones from Justice Hugo Black's images:

> The First Amendment, however, does not say that in every and all respects there shall be a separation of Church and State. . . . Otherwise the state and religion would be aliens to each other—hostile, suspicious and even unfriendly. . . . We are a religious people whose institutions presuppose a Supreme Being . . . When the State encourages religious instruction or cooperates with religious authorities by adjusting the schedule of public events to sectarian needs, it follows the best of our traditions. For it then respects the religious nature of our people and accommodates the public service to their spiritual needs. . . . [We] find no constitutional requirement which makes it necessary for government to be hostile to religion and to throw its weight against efforts to widen the effective scope of religious influence. . . .

The very tension between the refusal in *McCollum* to allow an accommodation and permitting it in *Zorach* indicates that the accommodation doctrine will not always prevail. In fact there seem to be three different kinds of situations: those where an accommodation is *required,* those where it is *permissible,* and those where it is *prohibited.* Or in other language, situations where the government *must,* where it *may,* and where it *may not* accommodate religion.

Required Accommodation

There are some situations where accommodation is required in order to preserve free exercise protections and not impermissibly infringe on important religious liberties or create penalties for religious freedom.

In *Wisconsin* v. *Yoder,* the Court held that the state must accommodate the religious beliefs of the Amish who objected to enrolling their children in high school as required by state law.

In *Sherbert* v. *Verner,* the Court held the state unemployment compensation plan must accommodate its requirements to the religious convictions of a Sabbatarian, Adell Sherbert, who opposed Saturday employment. The state of South Carolina had denied unemployment benefits to Adell Sherbert, who was discharged for her failure to accept work on Saturday. The Unemployment Compensation Act provided that unemployment benefits were not available if a person would not accept suitable work. But the Supreme Court held that the denial of benefits to her interferred with her free exercise of religion.

Permissible Accommodation

More common than the situations requiring accommodation are those where the state may, but is not required to, accommodate religious interests.

In *Walz* v. *Tax Commission,* a case involving a challenge to the tax exemption given to church properties, Justice Warren Burger wrote the opinion of the Court, which upheld the constitutionality of the exemptions. The Court said that the state could have an interest in encouraging religious values—and avoiding threats to those values—through property taxes. The Court then declared that accommodation was permissible even in situations where it was not mandatory: "The limits of permissible state accommodation to religion are by no means coextensive with the noninterference mandated by the Free Exercise Clause."

The *Walz* Court did not hold that New York was required to provide tax exemptions, but that it may, thus indicating that government may sometimes choose to accommodate religious interests without necessarily violating the establishment prohibitions.

Justice Warren Burger in *Walz* also indicated his concern that the Establishment Clause not be interpreted to create hostility to religion. He declared that the Free Exercise and Establishment Clauses must be accommodated to prevent "the kind of involvement which would tip the balance toward government control of churches or governmental restraint on religious practices." Burger declared that "perfect or absolute separation" is simply not possible, and that the First Amendment sought to mark the boundaries of excessive entanglement.

Prohibited Accommodation

There are certain situations where accommodation is prohibited. *McCollum* (in which religious teachers came into the public school for an optional, thirty-minute religious instruction class) illustrates this type of situation where establishment concerns overwhelm potential accommodation interests. In practice, most of the situations where this has been found have been educational contexts, involving both religious practices in public schools and financial aid to religious schools.

The Court continues to review the dimensions of accommodation and the degree of benevolence in its neutrality. It is clear, however, that in certain key cases, the Court has found and applied a principle of accommodation, which seeks to assure that the Court's concern with establishment does not create blindness to the religious interests of the people.

8

Free Exercise Clause

. . . or prohibiting the free exercise thereof. . . .

First Amendment

In a world where Christians are still persecuted for their beliefs, no constitutional guarantee is perhaps more precious than the guarantee of the free exercise of religion. Christians who know their biblical and secular history should value this religious freedom as a prized possession. Far too often we have seen one religious group persecute another or the secular state persecute or discriminate against Christians.

The very faith we profess as Christians assumes a freedom of faith and conscience. We believe that salvation is by grace and calls for personal acts of commitment to our Lord. We believe in the Holy Spirit's guidance and the duty to follow the dictates of our conscience. Faith comes by the Word of God. All of these flourish only in a free environment. For religious reasons as well as reasons of politics and pragmatics, Christians should enthusiastically endorse the guarantees contained in the First Amendment concerning the free exercise of religion.

Of course, such freedom must include the freedom to be wrong, even perhaps eccentric. Too often people have spoken in favor of freedom, but only meant freedom to hold beliefs and opinions like their own. As Justice Jackson said in *U.S.* v. *Ballard* (1944), ". . . the price of freedom of religion or of speech or of the press is that we must put up with, and even pay for, a good deal of rubbish."

Real freedom means diversity and error, includes the bizarre as well as the normal, encompasses traditionalists and innovators alike. It may even include the repulsive. Nevertheless, within broad limits, the freedom must extend to all.

The commitment to free exercise has received many of its court tests in the context of unpopular groups. Historically, the Mormons and the Jehovah's Witnesses were principal litigants in testing the scope of the Free Exercise Clause. One observer has even suggested that the Jehovah's Witnesses knocked on the door of the Supreme Court almost as often as they knocked on their neighbors' doors. They were the ones who did not share the mainstream religious practices, therefore they sought to insure that the free exercise guarantees also protected their faith and practices. Today, other nontraditional groups are testing the scope of free exercise rights—groups such as the International Society for Krishna Consciousness, the Unification Church, the Church of Scientology, and others who have seen the law restrict their activities.

However, in an increasingly secular society, there may be frequent occasions for more traditional religious groups to make claims based on the Free Exercise Clause. Whenever you have government regulations and policies that inhibit religion or coerce practices contrary to religious convictions, then free exercise claims are going to emerge.

But what does the Free Exercise Clause protect? How is it applied?

Imagine that as a parent you object to the use of certain novels in the junior high school. Does the Free Exercise Clause require the school to exempt your child?

Or may your church's private Christian academy claim a free exercise right to be exempted from a state requirement that all children complete a sex education class, or use a state approved textbook for biology?

How will the Supreme Court assess your case?

Unlike the Court's evaluation of an Establishment Clause claim, there is no clear test to determine a valid free exercise claim. This is partly due to the fact that relatively few free exercise claims had come before the Court until very recent years. The Court has given much attention to the Establishment Clause, but relatively little to the Free Exercise Clause.

LIMITS TO FREE EXERCISE
It is clear that free exercise is not an absolute guarantee.

One may not escape prosecution or penalty for stealing, for sacrificing humans, or for shooting heroin, simply by claiming that the act was done for religious reasons. There are limits to the scope of free exercise liberties, and part of the Supreme Court's task has been to develop a means of determining those limits.

The Belief-action Distinction

The Court first sought to determine permissible from impermissible free exercise by distingishing between belief on the one hand and action on the other. In 1878 George Reynolds, who was a resident of the territory of Utah, was convicted of the practice of polygamy. He argued that his polygamous practices were part of his religious duty and convictions, and that the Free Exercise Clause prohibited his prosecution.

Chief Justice Morrison Waite, writing for a unanimous Court, rejected Reynolds's argument. Waite turned to Jefferson and his bill for establishing religious freedom in Virginia. Jefferson had said, "It is time enough for the rightful purposes of government for its officers to interfere when principles break out into overt acts against peace and order."

Drawing on Jefferson, Waite declared that the Free Exercise Clause deprived the Congress of legislative powers over "mere opinion, but it was left free to reach actions which were in violation of social duties or subversive of good order." The Court thus drew a distinction between religious belief, which was entitled to absolute protection, and action, which was not so entitled. The chief justice illustrated his point by insisting that the government certainly would have the power to prevent human sacrifice.

The belief-action distinction has been modified since *Reynolds* to provide for further protection for some kinds of action, but the basic concept of restricting action that violates social duty or good order remains. For instance, the courts frequently issue orders requiring life-saving blood transfusions for minor children over the objections of their parents' religious beliefs. Nor may one totally avoid educating one's children merely because it is against religious beliefs.

Some such distinction seems necessary, but there is obviously great danger. If only belief is protected, that is hardly free *exercise*. Belief that can not be acted upon is not worth much. Certainly from a biblical perspective, belief includes action and obedience. "Faith apart from works is dead" (James 2:26).

The first modern case on free exercise indicated that the Court was willing to protect action as well as belief. Newton Cantwell and his sons, all ordained Jehovah's Witness ministers, were arrested in New Haven, Connecticut, for unlicensed door-to-door solicitation in a Catholic neighborhood. They had also played records on street corners, which were offensive to the Catholic community because they attacked the Catholic church and organized religion as instruments of Satan.

The Cantwells were charged and subsequently convicted of violating a state statute, which prohibited solicitation of money for a religious or charitable cause without prior approval by the secretary of public welfare (who determined whether the cause asserted was genuinely religious).

The Supreme Court voided the convictions under the Free Exercise Clause. The Court first held that the state of Connecticut was subject to the protections of the Free Exercise Clause. (*Cantwell* was the first case to apply the Free Exercise Clause to the states through the Fourteenth Amendment's Due Process Clause.) Justice Roberts, speaking for the Court, wrote more affirmingly of the freedom to act than had the Court in *Reynolds:*

> Thus the Amendment embraces two concepts—freedom to believe and freedom to act. The first is absolute but, in the nature of things, the second cannot be. Conduct remains subject to regulation for the protection of society. . . . In every case the power to regulate must be so exercised as not, in attaining a permissible end, unduly to infringe the protected freedom.

The Court went on to indicate that the state had the power to regulate the times, places, and manner of solicitation on the streets and assure the peace and safety of the community. The Court held, however, that the statute under which Cantwell had been convicted was impermissibly broad and thus unconstitutional. Cantwell and his sons were cleared of all charges.

In 1943 the Court in *West Virginia State Board of Education* v. *Barnette* further confirmed the protection of action. Walter Barnette, a father of school children, complained that the state's compulsory flag salute violated his free exercise rights since his Jehovah's Witness faith prohibited such salutes. The penalty for failure to salute was expulsion, and then prosecution of the parents for failure to send the children to school as required by law.

The Court sustained Barnette's free exercise claim. Justice Robert Jackson declared, "Here we are dealing with a compulsion of students to declare belief." The Court recognized that conduct itself is a form and expression of belief. While certain freedoms are always infringed in a society, "freedoms of speech and of press, assembly and of worship may not be infringed on such slender grounds. They are susceptible of restriction only to prevent grave and immediate danger to interests the State may lawfully protect."

Jackson then issued what has become a widely quoted statement—the "fixed star": "If there is any fixed star in our constitutional constellation, it is that no official, high or petty, can prescribe what should be orthodox in politics, nationalism, religion or other matters of opinion or force citizens to confess by word or act their faith therein."

It is important to note that Barnette did not hold that the flag salute practice must cease. The policy in and of itself was not an infringement of free exercise, only when it was applied to Barnette and those with similar convictions. Thus within limits religious-based exemptions are available—for example, in the context of jury duty, taking oaths, and military conscription.

The Court in these decisions clearly began to establish an important free exercise right. But how does it decide whether to grant an exemption? While there is no clear test, a pattern of analysis has been regularly followed.

THE PROCESS OF WEIGHING INTERESTS

Cantwell and *Barnette* laid the initial groundwork for a three-stage process, which the Court now seems to apply in free exercise cases. There are essentially three questions which the Court asks if a free exercise claim arises:

First: Has the statute or government action created a burden on the free exercise of religion?

Second: Is there a sufficiently compelling state interest to justify this infringement of religious liberty?

Third: Has the state in achieving its legitimate purposes

used the least intrusive means possible so that the free exercise is not infringed any more than necessary to achieve the legitimate goal of the state?

BURDEN ON FREE EXERCISE

Imagine a parent who objects to a compulsory vaccination program being conducted through the public school. Or suppose an employee objects to an employer's requirement that he or she work on Sunday. Has a burden been placed on that person's religious liberties?

The first question the Supreme Court will ask is whether any burdens have been put on religion at all. Does the statute require something that is contrary to the complaining party's religion? The courts will often look at two elements: the sincerity of the religious belief and the centrality of those beliefs.

In the illustration above, the Supreme Court will first inquire whether a sincere religious belief is opposed to vaccinations, and then whether that belief is central to the person's religious faith.

It is important to note that the Court does not inquire into the truth of religious beliefs. In a case involving persons who sought money through the mail, claiming they were divine messengers (*United States* v. *Ballard*), the Court held that the truth of their claim could not be submitted to a jury. Freedom of thought and religion, Justice Douglas declared, includes the right to believe that which cannot be proven. "Heresy trials are foreign to our Constitution. The religious views espoused by respondents might seem incredible, if not preposterous, to most people. But if those doctrines are subject to trial . . . then the same can be done with the religious beliefs of any sect."

The Court does inquire into the sincerity of the person's belief. Such an inquiry may undoubtedly involve the believability of the religious claims, but it needs to be made in order to avoid the mere claim of religious belief to escape a mandatory regulation. The problem, as Laurence Tribe observes, is how to preserve a generous accommodation of religion while "assuring that religion is not invoked as a cheap excuse for every conceivable form of self-indulgence." A court has, for example, rejected the claim of a "peyote preacher" (*In re Grady*) who sought to be exempt from laws prohibiting the use of peyote (a stimulant drug derived from mescal buttons). A court determined that he was not a bona fide and honest user of peyote.

In its inquiry into the sincerity of beliefs, the Supreme Court has occasionally looked at historical evidence. In *Wisconsin* v. *Yoder,* the Supreme Court noted the Amish people's longstanding objection to enrolling their children in public high schools, and took that as evidence of the sincerity of the religious belief.

In a somewhat bizarre case, a United States district court noted that a group seeking religious exemption from federal drug regulations (*United States* v. *Kuch*) referred to its members as "Boo-hoos." Further, the seal of this "church" was a three-eyed toad, and the "church" motto was "Victory over Horseshit." The court denied the exemption.

Likewise the Court denied the claim of a party who refused to appear in court on Saturday, alleging he was a Sabbatarian (*Dobkin* v. *District of Columbia*). The Court noted that the man regularly conducted business on Saturday. As these cases illustrate, courts do not inquire directly into the truth of the claim, but they may consider evidence of the sincerity of the claim.

A mere personal conviction, preference, or ethical principle will not usually be sufficient to claim a free exercise privilege. However, the Supreme Court has recently ruled that a "religious" right need not emerge from a religious system with a traditional belief in God. In some situations, a deeply held belief that functions like religion will suffice (for example a conscientious objector's aversion to war).

The Court may also inquire into the centrality of the religious belief. Does the practice the government is prohibiting or regulating go to the core of the belief, or is it peripheral and incidental? In *Wisconsin* v. *Yoder,* the Court noted that the Amish people's convictions against becoming involved in the public high schools were central to their way of life and faith.

For instance, if you claimed exemption from a vaccination program, the Court might inquire: how central is this objection to your faith? If you were a member of a church with a history of such objections, that would be evidence of sincerity and perhaps centrality.

In the important Supreme Court decision involving exemption from Saturday work requirements (*Sherbert* v. *Verner*), the Court inquired as to the centrality of the Seventh Day Adventists' prohibition against working on the Sabbath, and concluded it was a "cardinal principle." In an interesting California case, *People* v. *Woody,* the Court examined the claim of a Native American group, who wished to be exempt from state criminal statutes prohibiting the use of peyote during their religious ceremonies. Whereas the "peyote preacher" referred to earlier lost his case, the Court found that the use of peyote in these ceremonies was not only long-standing but a "cornerstone of the Navahos' religion." To prohibit it would, in the Court's words, go to "the theological heart of Peyotism." One can see that the issue of centrality is not assessed on an objective basis, but in terms of the opinions and beliefs of the person seeking the exemption.

The extent to which a particular government regulation offends the religious beliefs and practice of a person has become crucial in a number of recent cases. For example, religious schools, which have sought exemptions from broad state standards regarding curriculum or teacher certification, must show that the standards offend their sincerely held beliefs, and that these beliefs are central to their faith and religious mission. If they fail to show centrality, they are not likely to succeed.

COMPELLING STATE INTEREST

Suppose your religion involved snake handling, and a state law prohibits such activities. Will you be successful in claiming an exemption based on the Free Exercise Clause?

Or consider a state policy of the Department of Children's Services, which prohibits corporal punishment in any state licensed facility. A church-owned orphanage insists that to "spare the rod spoils the child," and claims a free exercise right. How will the Court evaluate the competing interests?

The second step in the analysis of a free exercise claim is to inquire whether there is a sufficiently compelling state interest to warrant the intrusion into religious liberty.

Before any fundamental liberty—speech, assembly, religion—may be infringed upon, the state must show that its purposes in limiting the freedom relate to a legitimate state function. Free speech does not include the freedom to holler "Fire!" in a crowded theater. Speech is a protected right, but there is a legitimate state purpose in protecting life and peaceful order.

Legitimate state powers and concerns are health and safety,

military defense, and the educational development of the public, to name a few. These powers derive from the people in a constitutional structure. The Bible also teaches that government has legitimate functions to suppress evil and support good. Thus all government power is not to be rejected.

The *compelling state interest* principle requires that the government establish that its purposes are *legitimate* ones for the state and that they are *compelling*. On the other hand, the person seeking exemption from the government regulation will seek to show that the state is not pursuing a legitimate purpose, or more likely, that the purpose, though legitimate, is not compelling compared to the infringement of liberty.

This test has been called a *"balancing test"*—weighing the interests of the state against the religious liberty. Which is more compelling under the particular set of facts? Which ought to take precedence?

At times, the decisions seem relatively simple. The state's interest in preserving life is compelling compared to the parent's objection to a transfusion for a minor child. In many cases, however, the balancing of interests will be less clear. The greater the state's legitimate interests, the more central the religious belief will have to be to overcome it.

LEAST INTRUSIVE MEANS

Suppose that in its concern to prevent fraud in religious solicitations, a state passes a law that requires all religious groups to obtain a solicitation permit and to complete financial reports, which will be the basis for an "effectiveness" rating by the state. How will the Supreme Court review this policy of the state?

The final step in the analysis requires the state to show that the *means* or *manner* in which it is achieving its legitimate state objective is the *least intrusive means*. The state must show that it has chosen a way to achieve its legitimate state end that imposes as little as possible on religious liberties.

For example, in 1939 Miss Schneider, a Jehovah's Witness, was canvassing door to door for the Watch Tower Bible and Tract Society (*Schneider* v. *Town of Irvington*). She was convicted of violating an ordinance that required a permit from the chief of police to canvass, solicit, or distribute literature door to door. The Supreme Court reversed her conviction, noting that the state purpose of preventing fraudulent appeals was legitimate, but that other means were available. Instead of these permits, the town might simply prosecute frauds. The fact that these other means were "less efficient and convenient" did not affect the Court's decision.

The Supreme Court, in the *Cantwell* case already noted, invalidated New Haven's license requirement as a "forbidden burden upon the exercise of liberty," noting that less drastic means of insuring peace and tranquility existed. That is why Cantwell and his sons were cleared of charges.

The Court went even further in *Sherbert* v. *Verner,* the case that involved opposition to Saturday work. In *Sherbert* the issue was whether or not unemployment benefits could be denied to a Sabbatarian, who refused to accept work that involved Saturday hours. In this case, the Court not only held that free exercise might exempt someone from a state-imposed burden, but also prevents discrimination in the distribution of benefits. The Court declared:

> Here it is not only apparent that the appellant's declared ineligibility for benefits derives solely from the practice of her religion, but the pressure upon her to forego that practice is unmistakable. The ruling forces her to choose between following precepts of her religion and forfeiting benefits, on the one hand, and abandoning one of the precepts of her religion to accept work, on the other hand. Governmental imposition of such a choice puts the same kind of burden upon the free exercise of religion as would a fine imposed against appellant for her Saturday worship.

While the Supreme Court continues to struggle with the appropriate scope of religious-based exemptions, it has shown great deference to religious conviction and a commitment to assure within broad limits the opportunities for religious belief and practice with minimal government intrusion. In the context of an increasingly active state, which involves itself in almost every arena of human activity, this deference to religion seems crucial to preserve the full play of religious conviction. Unfortunately difficult problems arise in a pluralistic society. How do courts define religion? What ideas ought to be protected as religious? What of deeply held convictions of conscience, which are not religiously motivated? These are issues the Supreme Court is just beginning to address.

It is also important to note that the Court has been especially sensitive to religious convictions, and that the Court hardly deserves the kind of criticism Christians have often directed toward it. The Court has frequently sided with religious freedom against government regulation.

CONFLICT BETWEEN ESTABLISHMENT AND FREE EXERCISE

Some cases involve both establishment and free exercise issues, and then one clause of the First Amendment seems pitted against the other. For example, whether or not Christian students may form a recognized student club and meet on the campus of a public university raises both free exercise and establishment questions. The students allege the issue is one of free exercise (as well as free speech, equal protection, rights of assembly). The opponents may allege that the issue is one of establishment—allowing the students to organize and use public facilities is an "aid" to religion.

As Justice Burger wrote in *Walz* v. *Tax Commission* (which dealt with tax exemption for church properties), "the court has struggled to find a neutral course between the two religion clauses, both of which are cast in absolute terms, and either of which, if expanded to a logical extreme, would tend to clash with the other." A major confrontation between the two clauses exists in government-sponsored chaplaincy programs. Programs like these caused Justice William Brennan in *Abington* to observe, "There are certain practices, conceivably violative of the Establishment Clause, the striking down of which might seriously interfere with certain religious liberties also protected by the First Amendment."

In numerous instances, the Court has sided with the free exercise concerns of religious freedom. In *Cruz* v. *Beto,* the Court implicitly approved the state of Texas's payment of prison chaplains' salaries as reasonably necessary to permit those in custody to practice their religion.

In cases involving government aid to private religious

schools, however, the Establishment Clause seems to have taken precedence. In numerous cases the Court has rejected neutrally applied aid to schools on establishment grounds, and hardly considered the free exercise claims. In *Meek* v. *Pittenger,* the majority again rejected such aid. Vigorous dissents were written by Justice William Rehnquist and Chief Justice Warren Burger. Rehnquist complained that the majority's views threw the weight of the Court "on the side of those who believe our society as a whole should be a purely secular one." And Burger hoped "that at some future date, the Court will come to a more enlightened and tolerant view of the First Amendment guarantee of free exercise of religion, thus eliminating the denial of equal protection to children in church-sponsored schools."

Professor Laurence Tribe argues that the free exercise principle "should be dominant in any conflict with the anti-establishment principle." Such dominance would be the result of commitment to religious tolerance rather than "thwarting at all costs even the faintest appearance of establishment."

OTHER CONSTITUTIONAL
PROTECTIONS OF LIBERTY

While the Religion Clauses of the First Amendment speak specifically to the issue of religious freedom, they are by no means the only constitutionally provided liberties that relate to religious freedom and expression. Chief among the other constitutional provisions are the guarantees of free speech and expression contained in the First Amendment, rights of assembly and association also contained in the First Amendment, and a rather large and expansive collection of rights associated with the Fourteenth and Fifth Amendments, including the guarantees of due process and equal protection. A detailed analysis of these constitutional provisions and Court decisions will not be provided in this book, but these guarantees are considered as they apply to the specific religious issues discussed in the next section.

PART THREE
A HANDBOOK OF YOUR RIGHTS

Part 3

Introduction

This section provides a brief survey of the state of the law as it relates to specific religious liberty issues. Because the issues are quite complex, a truly complete study of every issue is not possible in this book. Legislation and court decisions are also constantly changing the state of the law.

We do not intend to provide specific legal counsel as to how to proceed with a case, but instead to give you some general guidelines for understanding the issues of today. Even when an issue appears settled, it can be thrown into doubt by a new court decision. If you are facing an issue of religious liberty, the best course of action is to consult an attorney.

It is easy to assume that almost all religious life and activity hangs under a legal cloud, while in actual fact Christians are not constantly hauled before tribunals on account of their faith. Many of the issues covered in this section are resolved by local school boards, administrative offices of government agencies, city councils, labor unions, and other private and public associations.

This section of the book is divided into three major areas: public and private education, personal liberties, and religious ministries and government power. The section is meant to be a handbook of the current decisions that affect our religious liberties today. Each chapter functions as an individual entity, so you may either turn to the areas that particularly interest you or explore the entire scope of religious freedom as it exists today. A summary of the important religion cases and their decisions may be found in the appendix.

EDUCATION

9

The Battle for the Young

Children often become unwitting pawns in the struggle over values and methods. They are the victims—or beneficiaries, depending on your point of view—of reformers, bureaucrats, and every vested interest group that seeks to utilize educational power to redirect the shape of our society.

The school resides in our communities, and shapes and molds our children. Parents expect that this community institution will, as a surrogate parent, share and foster the community values. They rightfully resist forces that would use these institutions as vehicles of social engineering.

The issues fought out at the local grade school are not simply educational issues that ought to be left to "professionals," as some suggest. They are issues that frame the character of our society. Battles at the local school board involve human rights and freedom of religion as C. S. Lewis realized in *The Abolition of Man:*

> Hitherto the plans of the educationalists have achieved very little of what they attempted and indeed, when we read them—how Plato would have every infant "a bastard nursed in a bureau," and Elyot would have the boy see no man before the age of seven, and after that, no woman, and how Locke wants children to have leaky shoes and no turn to poetry—we may well thank the obstinacy of real mothers, real nurses, and (above all) real children for preserving the human race in such sanity as it still

80

possesses. But the man-moulders of the new age will be armed with the powers of an omni-competent state and an irresistible scientific technique: we shall get at last the race of condi-tioners who really can cut all posterity in what shape they please.

EDUCATION AND THE AMERICAN DREAM

Battles rage in the schools today because education is part of the American dream, the national mythology. The little red schoolhouse, *McGuffey's Reader,* and "readin', writin', and 'rithmetic" are part of our vision of how we improve ourselves. Americans were so certain education would solve human prob-lems that compulsory schooling became a national commitment. Legal constitutional scholar Philip Kurland concluded, "The United States has become one of the most schooled societies in the history of man."

But we seem to have forgotten that moral and religious values were at the core of early education. The Northwest Or-dinance of 1787 declared: "Religion, morality and knowledge being essential to good government and the happiness of mankind, schools and the means of education shall forever be encouraged."

There was a clear recognition that education, morality, and religion were inextricably linked. (It is striking that this was the same Congress that passed the First Amendment. They clearly saw no conflict between the Establishment Clause and the Northwest Ordinance's expectation that religion and morality would be a part of public education.) Even Jefferson, the much relied-upon exponent of the "wall of separation," saw the im-portance of the teaching of religion and established a chair of religion at the University of Virginia. In fact the primary pur-pose of the first universities and colleges in the United States was to train men for the ministry.

Many find it difficult to understand the Supreme Court's insistence that the framers intended to create a wall of separa-tion when those framers seem to have intended no such thing. Certainly no court saw this wall until the 1940s.

But more serious than this apparent flaw in the Court's reasoning is a feeling of betrayal. The excision of religion seems more than an exercise in neutrality. As noted Catholic commentator John Courtney Murray observed, "the sheer omission of religion from the curriculum itself is a pressure against religion. . . . The whole weight of the public school system tends to be thrown against the child's religious conscience and consciousness."

If our society increasingly insists on the centrality of education, and commits more and more of our life energies and national resources into it, how can we concurrently exclude life's fundamental commitments and the source of faith from education? It is noteworthy that the Soviet Constitution not only separates church and state, but also the school and religion; a commitment to atheism seems to require such a divorce. Atheism relegates religion to the emotive, private, and pietistic aspect of culture. Do you suppose we have achieved the same tragic result?

A DREAM AND AN ILLUSION?

Despite the infusion of vast sums of money and personnel in the last couple of decades, education's proffered dream has not materialized. Instead, the public education system has come under increasing attack from almost all quarters. Some have even called for the abolition of schools, as Ivan Ilych suggested in his volume *Deschooling Society*. Books like Silberman's *Crisis in the Classroom* have cataloged the problems in modern education: lack of discipline, departure from the basics of education, a stultifying conformity that inhibits creativity, dominance by vested interest groups and bureaucracies, and loss of local involvement. Parents could easily add such problems as the creation of a subculture of violence and drug abuse, the cultivation of antiauthoritarian patterns, and lack of accountability.

Some critics have complained of the movement to introduce into the schools "values clarification" and "life education"—components which seem to challenge traditional community and religious values. Such changes in education are rarely determined by a public process. Education has become big business at every level. The financial investment and the creation of professional teachers unions have obliterated any remaining image of the little red schoolhouse and its schoolmarm who emerged from the community. Instead we have a large and powerful industry with a host of vested interests, power structures, and tendencies toward monopoly. Sally Wertheim, professor of education at John Carroll University, writing in 1973 in *Intellect,* points to this shift of decision-making from the community to an educational elite. The result, she says, "is deference to an even narrower and less responsive circle of experts who frequently believe they alone are capable of making policy."

Consequently, parents have lost much of their sense of identity with the school. We see evidence of this in the increasing rejection of school tax levies. The schools are no longer part of "us," but of "them."

But educationalists are by no means the only creators of the tragedies of modern culture. Undoubtedly the local school becomes a misplaced target for the larger frustrations of a society that has lost its sense of direction and of families who have failed to nurture values in their own homes. Neither are the failures of education nor the problems of contemporary American life traceable to court decisions, which have struck down formalistic religious practices in public schools. In most of America, such religious exercises had either totally ceased or were mere form. Radical secularism bordering often on outright hostility to religion is not a product of the Supreme Court.

Perhaps we need to return to some more basic questions, such as "What is education? Can education be void of values, commitments, and life-shaping ideas? Are these going to emerge out of a moral vacuum or out of 'values clarification'? Can a culture really sustain a set of values without full exposure to religious values and options, which requires more than the alleged 'objective study of religion' now permitted?" Such values, philosophies, and issues lie behind many of the arguments and policies that will be reviewed in this section on religious freedom and education.

Because the problems in education are not primarily legal, the remedies are not primarily legal. The fundamental questions about the relationship of Christian life to education are much broader and the response of Christians must be more encompassing. We must become vitally involved in our public education systems and develop effective means of contributing to their improvement. Christians should begin to make major contributions to education by helping to create effective curricula, advocating school environments that involve community and parental input, and tackling urgent problems such as financing, drug abuse, and discipline. Even parents who elect to place their children in private Christian schools (where their values and religious principles may be more explicitly taught) should be interested in public education, since it will surely remain the major source of our national ethos. There is certainly no constitutional bar to the sort of human care and personal righteousness, love, and witness that Christians can bring to the larger educational context.

10

Prayer, the Bible, and Public Schools

"**A**lmighty God, we acknowledge our dependence upon Thee, and we beg Thy blessings upon us, our parents, our teachers and our Country." This twenty-two word prayer by children in New York led to the removal of prayer from the public schools of our country.

The regents of New York State had written this prayer and required that it be said in each class in the state at the beginning of the school day. The parents of ten pupils sued the state (*Engel* v. *Vitale*), insisting that the use of this official prayer in the public schools was contrary to the beliefs and religious practices of themselves and their children.

The lower state courts upheld the statute, as did the New York Court of Appeals, so long as the schools did not compel any pupil to join in the prayer. But on June 25, 1962, the United States Supreme Court overwhelmingly reversed the lower courts' decisions and held that the use of this prayer was a violation of the constitutional prohibition against the establishment of religion. Justice Hugo Black, writing for the Court, declared, ". . . we think that the constitutional prohibition against laws respecting an establishment of religion must at least mean that in this country it is no part of the business of government to compose official prayers for any group for the American people to recite as part of a religious program carried on by the government."

The Court acknowledged that our nation was founded by

85

men of prayer, and that religious faith drove many to come to this nation to find a haven for religious freedom and expression. Men of prayer, they said, led the fight for adoption of the Constitution and the Bill of Rights. But the Court argued that freedom from government-imposed prayers was precisely what these persons sought to avoid. These were men, the Court noted, who were aware that governments "had shackled men's tongues to make them speak only the religious thoughts that government wanted them to speak. . . ."

Concerned that its decision would be interpreted as hostility to religion, the Court declared, "It is neither sacrilegious nor anti-religious to say that each separate government in this country should stay out of the business of writing or sanctioning official prayers. . . ."

The outcry was immediate. The Court was pictured as anti-prayer, anti-God, ignorant of constitutional law and American history. Religious leaders as diverse as Bishop James Pike and Billy Graham attacked the *Engel* decision. But other elements of the Christian community praised the decision. *Christianity Today* called it "both defensible and commendable."

In many ways the outcry was a reflection of Christians' growing frustration with the loss of a Christian consensus and the emergence of a pluralistic, secularist predominance in national life and education. Many had not found this twenty-two word prayer or similar exercises in other locales very redemptive. The fact that so many conservative evangelical Christians objected to the decision was surprising. One would have thought that such believers would have been suspicious of government-written prayers, which were imposed by order of the state. There was certainly nothing voluntary about the practice, nor was the prayer theologically very profound.

THE PREDECESSORS OF ENGEL

The first decision concerning religion in the public schools was *McCollum* v. *Board of Education* in 1948. The Supreme Court held that a thirty-minute period of religious instruction conducted by nonschool personnel (but on school grounds and during school hours) was impermissible. The second decision, *Zorach* v. *Clausen,* in 1951 upheld a release-time program where public school students were allowed to go off the campus for religious instruction.

THE AFTERMATH OF ENGEL

Only one year after the *Engel* decision, the Supreme Court faced another religious issue: whether or not a Pennsylvania statute requiring that "at least ten verses from the Holy Bible shall be read, without comment, at the opening of each public school on each day" was constitutional. On the basis of this statute, Abington High School had adopted and implemented a program of morning, homeroom Bible reading, followed by the Lord's Prayer. Students were allowed to absent themselves if they wished.

In *Abington* v. *Schempp,* the Supreme Court noted that these devotional exercises were "prescribed as part of the curricular activities of students required by law to attend school" and were held in school buildings under school faculty supervision. The Court then enunciated a test, which became the first two prongs of the tripartite test: "What are the purpose and primary effect of the enactment? If either is the advancement or inhibition of religion, then the enactment exceeds the scope of legislative power as circumscribed by the Constitution."

Justice William Brennan, in a concurring opinion, noted the "special circumstances" of the educational setting, which required special scrutiny. Applying the test, the Court held the Pennsylvania statute invalid. The fact that students could excuse themselves on parental request furnished no defense. Nor did the notion that the exercises were protected by free exercise guarantees. The Free Exercise Clause "has never meant that a majority could use the machinery of the State to practice its beliefs," the Court said.

The Supreme Court seemed sensitive to the criticism of its *Engel* decision, and potential criticism that this decision would reflect some deprecation of the Bible or an attempt to remove it completely from the schools. The Court therefore declared:

> In addition, it might well be said that one's education is not complete without a study of comparative religion or the history of religion and its relationship to the advancement of civilization. It certainly may be said that the Bible is worthy of study for its literary and historic quality. Nothing we have said here indicates that such study of the Bible or of

religion, when presented objectively as part of a
secular program of education, may not be effected consistently with the First Amendment.

The *Schempp* and *Engel* decisions have been seen by some
as symbols of the de-Christianization of our schools and the
launching of virulent secularism. However, *Engel* only ruled
that state-written and required prayers were unconstitutional.
The decision said nothing at all about prayer times in schools,
voluntary prayer, student prayers, or meditation times. Many
defenders of the Supreme Court's decision make a strong point
of the limits of the Court's ruling to institutionally conceived
and supervised worship times.

However, the impact of the decisions has extended far
beyond those fairly narrow confines. The Supreme Court has
refused to review, and let stand, rulings of lower courts that
have consistently struck down other prayer practices in schools,
whether state-written or not. In *Johns* v. *Allen* (1964) a United
States district court struck down the unison recital of the Lord's
Prayer.

Parents in Whitestone, New York (*Stein* v. *Oshinski*), objected to a school board policy that forbade children to recite in
unison the verse/prayer, "God is great; God is good. And we
thank Him for our food." The district court upheld the parents'
objections; but the United States appeals court said that free exercise rights and free speech rights did not require the school
board to allow students to pray in unison.

In *DeSpain* v. *DeKalb Court Community School District,* a
lower court again struck down prayer, this time siding with
parent-plaintiffs, who opposed the recital of a verse in
kindergarten (which was similar to that in *Stein* but omitted any
reference to God).

More recently, widespread publicity was given to the attorney general of Tennessee who said that students on a high
school football team could not gather together before a game
and pray.

One of the major impacts of *Engel* v. *Vitale* and its successors has been the overly restrictive policies adopted by school
administrators, who have overreacted to the active role of the
American Civil Liberties Union and other groups set on
monitoring schools for religious activities. Many school ad-

ministrators are resisting even legally permissible, student-initiated activities rather than risking any legal challenges.

Recently, school officials in various districts have advised students that they could not pray as a group in their car in the school parking lot. In a Minnesota school, students who met in a hall just before class and prayed briefly by the lockers were advised that such prayers violated the Constitution. And occasionally, reports are received of students being told they may not pray over their meals in lunchrooms.

An April 1980 article in the *New York Times* entitled "Prayer: An Issue without an Amen" reported on the continuing controversy and the various attempts to blunt the current judicial posture. In many districts the ban by the Supreme Court is simply ignored. A survey in 1973 (ten years after *Engel*) revealed that 10 percent of American school districts continued to have prayer as part of their morning assemblies. Many teachers still use prayer in the classroom. As Katherine Jolley reported to the *Times,* "I know I'm not supposed to, but there are so many evil things in the schools, violence and drugs. . . . Sometimes I say just think of the Supreme Being and how much more beautiful it is to live and love."

AMENDING THE CONSTITUTION

Some persons have suggested a constitutional amendment that will clarify the free exercise rights of persons and support voluntary prayers in the schools. Attempts were made soon after the *Engel* decision by Senator Everett Dirksen and Congressman Frank Becker, and more recently through the efforts of Senator Jesse Helms. In 1982, President Ronald Reagan announced his support of a constitutional amendment. At a reception in the Rose Garden, Reagan outlined his proposal and declared, "No one will ever convince me that a moment of voluntary prayer will harm a child or threaten school or state. But I think it can strengthen our faith in a Creator who has the power to bless America."

The proposed amendment, which he sent to Congress, reads: "Nothing in this Constitution shall be construed to prohibit individual or group prayer in public schools or other public institutions. No person shall be required by the United States or by any state to participate in prayer."

However this approach has not received widespread support in the past because of the difficulty of passing constitutional amendments, the reluctance of the Congress and states to tamper with the Constitution, and the difficulty of providing effective wording for such a limited-purpose amendment.

REMOVING SUPREME COURT JURISDICTION

One approach has received widespread publicity: the attempt to utilize the provision of the United States Constitution (Article III, Secion 2), which provides that the appellate jurisdiction of the Supreme Court is under the regulation of the Congress. The clause provides that Congress may make exceptions to this appellate jurisdiction.

On this basis, bills have been introduced (and in fact passed in 1979 in the Senate), which would abolish federal court jurisdiction over cases involving school prayer. A current bill, commonly referred to as the Helms Amendment (Senate Bill 450) has attracted widespread comment, both positive and negative.

At hearings in the House of Representatives, Campus Crusade founder and president Bill Bright testified, "The Supreme Court decision puts us in a straitjacket. . . . What is happening is not far removed from what is happening in the Soviet Union, preparing our students for no God." Evangelist James Robison, though acknowledging that school prayer will not solve our ills, said present court rulings have "intimidated every person who wants to pray." On the other hand, other religious luminaries have warned of the dangers of seeking to rewrite constitutional law. Such persons warn that religious liberty would be threatened by any return to state involvement in religious exercise.

VOLUNTARY PRAYER LITIGATION

In an article in *Liberty* magazine, the author states that while *Engel* banned state-sponsored prayer, the government "may not forbid a nonstate-sponsored prayer. If a group of students on their own, without school involvement or sponsorship, spend a few moments in prayer before school starts, the state cannot prohibit them from doing so. . . ." That the students are "in a public school building at the time would not be a sufficient connection with the state to raise a constitutional problem." Indeed, one would have thought that the writer was correct. But such is not the case.

As we mentioned in chapter one, a small group of students at Guilderland High School in New York State asked the principal if they could meet in a room for prayer before school started. The case (*Brandon* v. *Guilderland School District*) was appealed to the United States Supreme Court, which refused to review the lower courts' decision that such practices would be "too dangerous to permit."

The *Brandon* case illustrates how far the *Engel* decision has been carried by lower courts and school officials. It is one thing to say that the state may not produce prayers and distribute them to teachers for official readings. But it is quite another for the state to prohibit students from meeting and praying on their own.

An even more restrictive rule was set forth by the Fifth Circuit Court of Appeals. The court invalidated a Lubbock, Texas, school policy that permitted students to meet for religious purposes on the same basis as they meet for other purposes (see further discussion in chapter 15).

LEGISLATIVE REMEDIES

Various states have attempted to provide for voluntary prayer in the schools by legislative remedies. In 1979, the state of Massachusetts enacted a statute entitled "An act offering a period of prayer in public schools." The act provided that "at the commencement of the first class of each day in all grades in all public schools the teacher in charge . . . shall announce that a period of prayer may be offered by a volunteer student. . . ." The statute provided for the excusal of any objecting student.

This might be called state-mandated voluntary prayer: each teacher and school are required to have voluntary prayer times. The Supreme Judicial Court of Massachusetts in *Kent* v. *Commissioner of Education* (1980) held that prayer always has a religious purpose; the fact that the prayers were offered by volunteers did not save the statute from unconstitutionality. The practice was not really voluntary, the court argued, when one considered the impact on impressionable youth. The prayers would inevitably reflect the religious views chiefly held in the community and place the state on the side of certain beliefs.

The state of Louisiana provided a somewhat different structure for voluntary prayer, passing a statute permitting (but not requiring) local officials to provide for a voluntary prayer time. The Jefferson school board created a program of voluntary prayer at the beginning of the school day for those students who had parental approval to participate. A United States district court upheld the constitutionality of the statute (*Karen B.* v. *Treen*), but a United States court of appeals struck down the practice.

Barring a constitutional amendment or other dramatic shift in the Supreme Court's posture, attempts by school officials or state legislatures to involve the school system in facilitating prayer, however voluntary, will apparently be held unconstitutional. Courts presently seem to bend over backwards to find elements of school sponsorship and involvement. In *Brandon,* for instance, the court held that the mere use of school property and the general supervision the school offers to all on its premises was sufficient to find state support for the prayers of students who voluntarily assemble in a room before school.

There is currently no court-approved ban on students praying on their own when the school has no role in offering a special room, announcing, or structuring the activities. While school officials may seek to resist students who informally gather in parking lots or hallways and pray, it would seem that students clearly have such rights and can challenge attempts to inhibit such exercises of free speech, assembly, and free exercise.

THE AFTEREFFECTS OF SCHEMPP

While the *Schempp* decision has not had the continuing controversy of the prayer decision, its legacy is seen in a number of decisions that invalidate the use of religious materials in public schools. Its real legacy is the beginning of the tripartite test, and specifically the "purpose" and "effect" tests.

In 1980 the Supreme Court struck down a Kentucky statute that permitted the posting of the Ten Commandments in classrooms if the funding was provided by private sources. A similar result was reached in North Dakota where a federal court struck down a statute similar to that in Kentucky.

The *Schempp* Court left open the opportunity to use the Bible and other religious literature in educational contexts, but little effort has been made to do so. This is an area parents and teachers may wish to explore, although there would be no opportunity to teach the real meaning of the Bible as God's Word.

11

Texts, Curriculum, and Parents—Clashing Values

A group of senior citizens gathered in a parking lot in 1977 for a book-burning, which included forty copies of *Values Clarification* that were used in the Warsaw, Indiana, high school. The event was the culmination of a community protest over the use of the materials in the school curriculum. Throughout the nation, parents and community groups are complaining of school materials. And school boards are reassessing curriculum, and even books in school libraries. Works by Ginsberg, Heller, Orwell, Salinger, Solzhenitsyn, and Vonnegut are among those outlawed by some schools.

It is "a surge of book censorship which seems designed to cut off independent thought at its educational roots . . . (by) intellectual terrorists laying siege to school boards," writes Stephen Arons in the *Saturday Review,* June 1981. Mel Gabler of Educational Research Analysts, a large group that reports on what they believe are inappropriate materials, says, "The basic issue is parental rights." And Jerry Falwell declares, "We will not allow the liberals and humanists to twist and pervert our children's minds and characters, . . . The seeds of decadence are being sown in the public schools."

Behind these complaints are complex legal, educational, and social issues. At work is an increasing sense by religious and conservative community groups that school-promoted programs and literature are too often in radical conflict with their values.

In the Indiana book-burning controversy, the school board banned five books, eliminated seven literature courses, and dismissed three teachers in response to complaints from community members. Two students then filed suit (*Zykan* v. *Warsaw Community School Corporation*), charging that the school violated their rights by these actions. Following the dismissal of the suit by a district court, an appeal was filed in the United States court of appeals. Briefs were filed in support of the appeal by the American Library Association, the National Education Association, and other groups complaining that the public school should be a "vibrant, free market of ideas." However the court upheld the school board's right to reject certain materials, noting the absence of any allegation that the actions were taken to establish some orthodoxy of thought.

A year before the Warsaw, Indiana, book-burning, the school board of the Island Trees Union Free School District on Long Island, New York, removed ten books (including *Soul on Ice* and *Slaughterhouse Five*) from the libraries and curriculum of the school system. The board found that the books were "anti-American, anti-Christian, anti-Semitic, and just plain filthy." An attorney for the students, Alan Levine, determined to show that the "irrationality and roughshod emotionalism of the book-banning have left teachers, students and members of the community intimidated. . . ." The United States Supreme Court agreed to review this case.

ACLU Director Ira Glasser finds all of this an "epidemic of future shock" among insecure individuals who "fear a world they no longer understand." In June of 1981, the ACLU, the Association of American Publishers, and the American Library Association sponsored a two-day colloquium to discuss political and legal strategies for the "coming book wars."

If not a war, the controversy is at least a bitter and heated debate, pitting "parents concerned about transmitting their own conservative moral, political and religious values . . ." against an amalgam of parents, students, and teachers who are angered by attempts to cut off their access to these materials. The disputes are apparently as broad as they are deep. *Publishers Weekly* in August 1981 reported the results of a survey of 1,900 public school administrators and librarians. According to the survey, 22 percent of the respondents reported challenges to books or other classroom materials, and 33 percent of this number indicated that these challenges had resulted in changes in books and materials. The survey noted most of the challenges were by individual parents; less than 20 percent came from organized groups. Thirty percent were from other staff members.

The issues these complaints raise are not primarily issues of religious liberty or of the First Amendment Establishment Clause, although these constitutional provisions are not irrelevant to the inquiry. Yet behind much of the concern is the widely expressed sense that the schools are increasingly dominated by secular humanistic perspectives, which become evident in the curricular materials. Parents are complaining of values clarification courses, sex education materials, and novels that are perceived as raw, violent, coarse—espousing values contrary to those of the majority of the community. As Dr. Onalee McGraw of the Heritage Foundation noted, these are parents "who finally had to take a stand because something was just not right in public schools."

The concern about secular humanism is widespread, though the term is often used without much definition. In general, the claim is that public education has ceased to be neutral as to religion. It is dominated by humanistic perspectives, which so influence the values and presumptions that they are in effect a religion. John Whitehead and John Conlan pointed out in the *Texas Tech Law Review* that "while secular humanism is nontheistic, it is religious because it directs itself toward religious beliefs and practices that are in active opposition to traditional theism. Humanism is a doctrine centered solely on human interests or values. . . . Both humanism and theism worship their own 'god'. . . . Secular Humanism is a religion whose doctrine worships Man as the source of all knowledge and truth. . . ."

In 1933, the *Humanist Manifesto* was published by a group that included noted educator John Dewey. The *Humanist Manifesto* was a statement of secularist faith. In 1973, an updated version, the *Humanist Manifesto II,* was published and signed by 120 public figures, including B. F. Skinner, the noted Harvard behavioralist; Dr. Alan Guttmacher, president of the Planned Parenthood Foundation of America; and Andrei Sakharov, the noted Russian physicist. The *Humanist Manifesto* declared that notions of salvation or damnation are "illusory and harmful," and that dogmatic religions "do a disservice to the human species. . . . Ethics is autonomous and situational, needing no theological or ideological sanction."

Many find this sort of secularism in the operative philosophy of modern education. The comments of Paul Blanshard, a signer of the *Humanist Manifesto,* seem to support this: "I think that the most important factor moving us toward a secular society has been the educational factor. Our schools may not teach Johnny to read properly, but the fact that Johnny is in school until he is sixteen tends to lead toward the elimination of religious superstition."[1]

A similar comment in the *American Atheist* links a secular education to the destruction of religious life: "We need only insure that our schools teach only secular knowledge. . . . If we could achieve this, god would indeed be shortly due for a funeral service."[2]

Can atheism be a religion? In a legal sense, it may be possible. The United States Supreme Court in *Torcaso* v. *Watkins* noted that not all religions are theistic. In a now-famous footnote, the Court listed a number of nontheistic religions, including ethical culture and secular humanism.

It would be difficult, however, to prove that the dominance of humanistic philosophy in public education has instituted an establishment of humanistic religion, which would be an unconstitutional establishment of religion. More would have to be shown than a mere convergence of certain ideas. It would seem essential to show an almost studied hostility to religion as well as direct links with those who attack religion.

Where attempts have been made to charge that some programs constitute an establishment of religion, courts are usually persuaded that the programs (however contrary to the religious beliefs of some, and however value laden) are authentically neutral and not religious. Thus family and sex education courses are seen as legitimate public health interests of the state.

Despite such a lack of success, efforts still persist to obtain judicial recognition of such claims. In December of 1980, parents and other taxpayers filed a suit (in *Grove* v. *Mead School District No. 354*) in Washington State, alleging that a portion of the high school curriculum that used a book entitled *The Learning Tree* was a constitutional violation of their First Amendment rights. The complaint alleged that the materials were profane and obscene, described premarital sex and lewd behavior, and contained blasphemies against Jesus Christ. The book tended to inculcate the anti-God religion of humanism.

This case is still pending a decision of the United States district court in Washington State.

In Oregon, Citizens for a Responsive and Economic Education District filed suit against a local school board (*Winston* v. *Dillard School Board*), alleging that its elementary school guidance program constituted a state promotion of a religion, which is based on a sincere belief that "the individual is of ultimate concern." This case is awaiting the decision of an Oregon circuit court.

In California in late 1981, the Women's Committee for Responsible Government filed a suit (*Women's Committee for Responsible Government* v. *Aved*), alleging that the sex education program for California public schools constituted an impermissible establishment of religion, namely secularism. The complaint alleged that the government-funded program developed by Planned Parenthood constitutes unlawful thought control, which intrudes upon family and pupil privacy and inhibits the moral and ethical viewpoints of the petitioners. The California courts denied petitions by the Women's Committee; the courts therefore indicated that the committee must begin its lawsuit at the superior court level. As you can see, curriculum lawsuits are currently in the books of several courts in the United States.

An exception to the usual court rejection of such suits was the *Yogi* v. *Malnak* case, in which a New Jersey school system offered an elective course in transcendental meditation. The plaintiffs challenged that TM was at root a religious practice and its inclusion in the schools was a violation of the Establishment Clause. The trial court granted the plaintiffs' motion for summary judgment, barring such courses. And the decision was upheld on appeal. Of course, the TM case provided ample opportunity to show direct links between the school practices and religious activities, particularly because of the use of chants and rituals.

How are courts or school boards to weigh academic freedom, community values, parental concerns, and student rights? What are the constitutional bases for decisions about curricular content? Library holdings? Must materials meet the "obscenity" test in order to be removed from the school's library? And finally, what can individuals or groups do to affect the school's practices and policies? Various alternatives are available: shaping school policies, seeking judicial protection, arguing for rights of excusal, or securing equal time for Christian perspectives.

SHAPING SCHOOL POLICIES

The events in Warsaw, Indiana—however dramatic or misguided—illustrate the potential for direct parental and community participation in school decision-making. Certainly citizen involvement in education is a major public responsibility. If carried out in a responsible manner, it may indeed assist the schools to develop effective educational programs.

Where parents have convinced school boards to change curricula or remove or place certain books on limited access, courts have been reluctant to intervene and become "super school boards," though in some cases they have found school board procedures arbitrary and improper.

In *Pico* v. *Island Trees Union Free School District,* the Tenth Circuit Court of Appeals reversed the dismissal of the students' complaint by the district court and ordered the case to trial. The appeals court said that the school board's criteria seemed excessively general and overbroad and suggested an attempt to "express an official policy with regard to God and country." A trial was warranted to "determine precisely what happened [and] why it happened." This opinion has been appealed to the Supreme Court.

However, the same court on the same day upheld a book removal by a Vermont school board because of "vulgarity and indecency of language." And in an earlier case, this court of appeals had upheld the right of a school board to ban certain books from the English curriculm, including *The Exorcist* and *Clockwork Orange.* "The Board was acting within its rights in omitting the books, even though the decision was a political one influenced by the personal views of the members," the court said.

Courts seem to give wide latitude to school boards, especially in developing curriculum. They are apparently more willing to review decisions that involve the removal of general library materials, because they fear arbitrary censorship, which has been stimulated by community pressure groups. Courts may review school board actions more carefully when there are no clear published standards and procedures for the review of literature.

Opponents of school materials ought to develop sound rationales for their concerns. At times certain groups have seemed extreme in their approach to permissible curricular materials. Concerned parents also ought to be willing to participate in other school policies and activities. School boards and schools need help as they struggle with the difficult issues that face public education today.

JUDICIAL RECOURSE

When parents or community groups have been unsuccessful in persuading school authorities about desired policies, there have been efforts to obtain judicial relief. Efforts to have courts order the elimination of opposed school materials have been almost totally unsuccessful, so much so that Professor Charles Rice of the Notre Dame Law School refers to such efforts as a "forlorn enterprise" and "utterly hopeless." As he indicated in a 1978 Brigham Young University Law Review article, "One can argue cogently in principle that the involvement of the public schools in such matters as family life and sex education entails a violation of the religious neutrality required by the Establishment Clause and incidentally invades the privacy rights of parents and pupils." But in the light of actual cases "such contentions will accomplish little in the courts today."[3]

Thus in *Cornwell* v. *State Board of Education,* a federal district court rejected the parents' claims that they had an exclusive constitutional right to teach their children about sexual matters. A similar argument claiming rights of privacy was rejected in *Medeiros* v. *Kivosaki,* where the court further held that the sex education program involved was not overly broad.

In such cases the court frequently acknowledges the tensions created, "placing the children between the Scylla of obeying their parent's religious teachings and the Charybdis of obeying the commands of their teachers and school authorities." Nevertheless when courts weigh the interests of the two parties, the balance usually tips in favor of the state.

A STUDENT'S RIGHT TO NONPARTICIPATION

Can a student be excused from participation in objectionable school activities? There are clearly some activities that may not be required if participation would impinge on the religious beliefs of the student. The prominent and leading case

(*Barnette* v. *West Virginia*) held that requiring students to daily salute the flag and say the Pledge of Allegiance could not be enforced against Jehovah's Witnesses. The court noted that the school's requirement forced the student to assert and state (by action) a belief or commitment directly contrary to conscience. Where curriculum or school activities require affirmation contrary to religious belief, the courts apparently support an accommodation to religious diversity that excuses the student from participation.

A few courts have also held that schools must exempt students from religiously objectionable activities. In an Illinois case (*Moody* v. *Cronin* in 1979), a federal court excused students from participating in a physical education class, despite a state law mandating the course and forbidding such exemptions. The students, members of the United Pentecostal Church, objected to the "immodest" attire required in the coeducational classes. But in a similar situation in Vermont, a student who sought excusal on nonreligious ground because of immodesty was denied relief.

While schools may as a matter of policy allow religious exemptions, there is not a right to such in most instances. If the state shows sufficient educational reasons for the component, the court will find a sufficiently compelling state interest. In one frequently cited case, *Davis* v. *Page*, parents were denied an exemption for their daughter from participating in music and health classes based on a religious objection to the use of audiovisual materials. A federal court found that the state had a legitimate interest in a uniform educational program, and that accommodating various religious objections on all matters would be impossible. Excusal is primarily a matter of discretion.

Several cases have sustained compulsory sex education programs without any right to excusal, and no appellate court has required excusal. The situation is such that Professor Charles Rice of Notre Dame Law School declared "an attempt to use the courts to compel excusal . . . is a waste of time."

EQUAL TIME

One of the ways in which schools may deal with controversial elements of curriculum and program is to include alternative viewpoints—an "equal time" policy. Such an approach has been pursued in the highly publicized issue of the inclusion of creation science as an alternative theory to evolution science. The legal issues in this area illustrate both the concerns and the problems of this approach.

When editorial cartoonists render the creation/evolution controversy, the old Scopes Trial of 1927 is dusted off. Monkeys appear in headlines and drawings on editorial pages. The comparison is not only inviting but instructive, because now the party excluded from the academic marketplace is creation. The generally liberal tradition that insisted that evolution be included in 1927 is now unwilling to open the portals of inquiry to alternatives such as creation science.

Support for such inclusions has been broad. *Time Magazine* reported that a poll indicated 76 percent of the people favor equal treatment of creation and evolution views. Eighteen states have or are considering statutes that provide for "balanced treatment" of the two views. State textbook commissions in at least five states have added texts that present a model of creation to the approved list of general and supplementary materials. The California Board of Education failed by only a single vote to provide equal treatment for evolution and creation models in state schools.

The debate has stirred controversy in a number of communities across the nation. In Hillsboro, Oregon, in 1980, June Ruyle's efforts finally resulted in a school board decision to teach scientific creationism in the classroom. June declared, "It isn't fair to teach one theory and not the other. I pay just as many taxes as the next person, but my children aren't getting a total education. . . . By and large people are evolutionists because that is the only thing presented in school." She complained that teachers were one-sided, and that the evolutionary perspective invaded the entire curriculum and not just the science courses. The new school policy was not without its opponents, and the near-unanimous opposition of the science teachers led to the placement of the unit outside the science department.

In Dallas, Texas, the controversy was even more heated. In 1975, the Dallas Independent School District instructed school officials "to insure that the district's curriculum offers a balanced presentation" of theories of origins. Teaching objectives included the goal that students understand the major theories and be able to indicate scientific evidences for each. In order to implement this policy, the school board in 1977 voted to purchase one set of a frequently cited and controversial creationist text *Biology: The Search for Order in Complexity* for each classroom.

The result was a storm of controversy and threatened lawsuits by some clergy and ACLU groups. The suit was avoided when an agreement was reached between various parties, providing that the presentation of viewpoints would be made in such a way "that neither the student's religious beliefs nor the intellectual honesty of the material" would be compromised. The agreement stated that use of the creationist text would not be mandatory.

Similar controversies have occurred throughout the nation, dividing not only creationists from evolutionists but parents from teachers, school boards, and faculties—and often even dividing the Christian community.

At the present time, the most significant legal debates have raged over the constitutionality of Louisiana and Arkansas statutes, both of which call for "balanced treatment" between creation science and evolution science. The Arkansas statute signed into law in March 1981 specifically prohibited any inclusion of religious instruction or reference to religious writings in the discussions of origins. The stated purpose of the statute was to protect student academic freedom, ensure neutrality toward religion, guarantee free speech, prevent the establishment of religion, and assist students in their search for truth. The Louisiana bill required that creation and evolution be taught as theories, and prohibited discrimination against any student or teacher based on their acceptance or rejection of any particular theory of origins.

From a constitutional perspective, the inclusion of material reflecting alternative viewpoints creates no problem so long as the basis for such inclusion is secular. However, as Patricia Lines, author of a handbook entitled *Religious and Moral Values in Public Schools: A Constitutional Analysis,* points out, "inclusion of material because of its religious value to a portion of the community" is constitutionally impermissible.

As Lines writes, educational policymakers may have legitimate secular reasons for including the views of dissenters. "It is the purpose or motive of the school officials that the court must examine, and not that of the dissenter." On the particular issue of creation and evolution, Lines argues that "the inclusion of creationist theory alongside evolutionary theory would clearly be secular if both were subject to critical discussion. If not, and especially if this approach followed requests from religious groups, the court would be failing in their duty if they did not find an unconstitutional intent to establish a religious view."

Naturally the persons most concerned with a more balanced approach, which includes creationist options, are those with religious commitments. Creationists tend to believe in a Creator. The very act of these groups is turned against them in a rationale such as Patricia Lines's, which seeks to determine if the underlying motives are religious in character. Advocates of creation science have tried to avoid the religious aspects by limiting public school consideration of creation to scientific evidences and avoiding terms such as "biblical creation."

Advocates are insisting that the monopoly of the evolutionary perspective is not only constitutionally impermissible, but constitutes an assault on the religious views of many creationists. At the same time the American Humanist Association is insisting on an exclusive presentation of evolution, particularly in a 1977 petition it sent to major school boards across the country. "There are no alternative theories to the principle of evolution," the Humanist Association asserted. "Moreover, the principle is so important for an understanding of the world we live in and of ourselves that the public in general, including students taking biology in school, should be made aware of it and the fact that it is firmly established in the view of the modern scientific community."

Such a dominance of the scene by evolution is perceived by many as a profound assault on ethics and theism. Noted evolutionist Julian Huxley observed that evolution itself would replace God as a "principle to coordinate man's beliefs and hopes." Carl Vogt, a disciple of Darwin, put it more bluntly when he declared that Darwin's view "turns the Creator out of doors and does not leave the smallest room for such a Being."

Jacques Monod, renowned molecular biologist, wrote in his provocative volume *Chance and Necessity* that modern science has cut the root from the values we profess. We have been too slow to recognize that our new scientific knowledge gives a profound message: "the defining of a new and unique source of truth." While many Christians would challenge the assertion that evolutionary theories eliminate God, others find the tensions between scientific evolution and Christian faith simply too great to be harmonized, and thus the struggle.

This concern about the dominance and threat of evolution as the modern orthodoxy has led to the rise of creation-science organizations (most notably the Creation Research Society) and a variety of publications and seminars on the subject. However, creation advocates have not united in a common strategy of publications, courses, and litigation. Even biblically committed scientists find themselves widely separated on issues such as the age of the earth.

Wendell Bird's article in the *Yale Law Journal* ("Freedom of Religion and Science Instruction in Public Schools") has probably become the primary legal source for advocates of equal time. Bird argues that the exclusive focus on evolutionary theory and the concurrent exclusion of creationist perspectives establishes a constitutionally impermissible burden on religious exercise. Such exclusion undermines faith, compels students to make statements against religious conscience, and interferes with parental rights.

The present situation has resulted in the establishment of religions that are evolutionary as against those that are not evolutionary, Bird contends. Both creation and evolution may be examined in the scientific context; both are tenets of major religious systems—evolution being linked to the religion of secular humanism. Bird thus challenges the concept that creation is a religious view whereas evolution is a "scientific" concept. Bird concludes that schools must either cease to teach about origins at all or allow instruction in both theories.

The courts are just beginning to face this highly charged issue. In 1968 the Supreme Court rendered its decision in *Epperson* v. *Arkansas,* which rejected as unconstitutional the exclusion of the Darwinian theory from public schools for religious reasons. But the *Epperson* decision did not deal with the "equal time" attempts of modern legislation.

More recent cases have forced lower courts to face these more complex questions. In *Daniels* v. *Waters,* the Fifth Circuit Court of Appeals struck down a Tennessee statute that required that evolution be taught only as a theory. The statute had barred textbooks that taught evolution as fact, and had required that texts give equal time to creationist theories. Disclaimers were also required, making it clear that evolution was a theory. The court noted that the statute did not require similar disclaimers for the creationist perspective and creationist texts were not required to include the evolutionary view. The court held that the clear favoring of the biblical view created an impermissible establishment.

The court did not hold that the inclusion of the creation perspective itself would be unconstitutional. In fact, a number of states require such inclusion, and opinions of the attorney general in Oregon and other states have held that creationist theories, if taught from a secular perspective, would not be unconstitutional.

However, Judge William Overton in Arkansas held an Arkansas "equal time" statute unconstitutional in January of 1982. "Darwin Wins," noted a *Time Magazine* article. The judge held that creation science was "not science because it depends upon supernatural intervention, which is not guided by natural law." He then declared that "the only real effect . . . is the advancement of religion."

The trial of the case (*McLean* v. *Arkansas*) was filled with controversy, ranging from debates about the effectiveness of witnesses to the seriousness with which the state attorney general pursued the case (especially after news broke that the attorney general had recently participated in a fund raiser for the ACLU, the opponent in the case). *Christianity Today* suggested that the appropriate biblical setting for the Arkansas case was not the Garden of Eden but the Tower of Babel.

Undoubtedly, debate will range in the courts for some years to come. Judge Overton suggested to one witness that creation science belongs in the Sunday school, not the public school. If talk of origins can only consist of one side of the conversation, whatever happened to the marketplace of ideas? The state is aligning itself with one particular position, and therefore, it is not maintaining religious neutrality.

The ongoing controversy over the addition of the creationist perspective demonstrates the difficulty Christians will have reinserting the particular concerns of the Christian community into American education. The more important those concerns are to humanists and secular educators, the greater the controversy is likely to be.

12

The Rights of
Christian Teachers

If prayer and Bible reading are impermissible in the public schools, what—if anything—can a Christian teacher say about religious values? Can a teacher answer students' questions about religious matters or be a sponsor for a student religious club or an off-campus Christian organization? What about the use of religious symbols and bulletin board displays?

The pressure to severely limit the expression of religious ideas and values is often enormous. School officials and outside groups exert pressure on teachers or administrators to avoid any assertion of religious perspectives in class materials or teacher conversations and activities. Christian teachers' lack of knowledge of their rights in this area often makes them vulnerable to challenges by others, even when they are clearly within their rights.

For example, a principal may suggest that a teacher cannot have a Bible on the classroom desk. The teacher may naively accept that as constitutional law, although it is not. An informed and sensitive community of Christian teachers seems essential in the current context.

The courts have expressly approved the study of religion and the academically oriented, neutral examination of the historic and cultural aspects of religious life. Such opportunities, however, are often limited and fraught with difficulties of defining "study" and "neutrality." Clearly, such activities may not be a ruse for proselytizing efforts.

The restrictions on a teacher's freedom of religious expression seem to be increasing. This is surprising when teachers have been given increased freedom to express themselves and to limit the extent school authorities may control their conduct. In fact, the protection of the teacher's constitutional rights has been a significant trend in the last few decades.

David Rubin's *The Rights of Teachers,* published by the American Civil Liberties Union, provides a general survey of the current scope of these protected liberties. Constitutional rights of free speech, association, and due process have been vigorously pursued by teachers, more often successfully than not.

ACADEMIC FREEDOM

In 1968, in *Epperson* v. *Arkansas,* a tenth-grade teacher complained that an Arkansas statute, which prohibited the teaching of evolution, violated her First Amendment right. The Supreme Court agreed, commenting that "it is much too late to argue that the State may impose upon the teachers in its schools any conditions it chooses, however restrictive they may be of constitutional liberties."

A year later in *Tinker* v. *Des Moines,* the Court declared that neither students nor teachers "shed their constitutional rights to freedom of speech or expression at the schoolhouse gate."

These cases illustrate an increased acceptance of the teacher's right of expression. The cases have provided an especially broad scope of academic freedom for teachers in public colleges and universities. In *Keyishian* v. *Board of Regents* and in *Sweezy* v. *State of New Hampshire,* the Supreme Court strongly affirmed the scope of academic freedom, "which does not tolerate laws that cast a pall of orthodoxy over the classroom." The Court spoke of the concept of the school as a marketplace of ideas and the values of free exchange.

Although academic freedom has primarily emerged in the university context, the considerations of this freedom are not irrelevant to elementary and secondary levels. A federal district court in New York in 1968 noted in *Albaum* v. *Carey* that an environment of free inquiry is also relevant for grade school children. "The considerations which militate in favor of academic freedom—our historical commitment to free speech for all, the peculiar importance of academic inquiry to the progress of society, the need that both teacher and student operate in an atmosphere of open inquiry, feeling always free to challenge and improve established ideas—are relevant to elementary and secondary schools as well as to institutions of higher learning."

Such academic freedom is not absolute. Courts have sustained limitations on the rights of teachers to academic freedom. The state has been held to have the power to establish the general curriculum and to require that it be followed. In *Mailloux* v. *Kiley,* 1971, a United States court of appeals noted that "free speech does not grant teachers a license to say or write in class whatever they feel like. . . ." The court noted that the propriety of limitations will take into account the age and sophistication of students, the context and manner of presentation, and the degree of relationship to valid educational objectives. Academic freedom does not provide a cloak for teachers to lead class prayers or structure time for daily religious exercises.

However, not all religious expression by a teacher is necessarily impermissible. The legality of a particular activity or expression will likely depend on the weighing of various factors to assess whether the conduct constitutes an impermissible establishment of religion. Among the critical factors are likely to be the scope of the activity: who does it involve? How much time? How much prominence is it given? The age and maturity of the students, the use of public funds, and the relevance of the activity to valid educational goals and specific curriculum will also be evaluated. The courts will be likely to assess the degree to which the activity appears to promote religious beliefs (or indoctrinate students) and the activity's effect: does it disrupt the educational process and task of the school?

In South Dakota for example, a school board dismissed a teacher who insisted on devoting a substantial portion of a biology class to the issue of creation versus evolution (*Dale* v. *Board of Education*). The board objected to the extent of attention given to this discussion in a course designed with much broader objectives. The court upheld the teacher's dismissal.

Teachers often wonder if they may respond to students' questions about religious matters. Factors that are likely to be important are the relevance of the discussion, the age of the students, and the scope of the activity. Questions about the beliefs of Christians and their impact on the Reformation or Christians' influence on Roman society in the first century would seem relevant. Likewise a teacher could answer a question regarding his or her personal beliefs about issues, values, and ideas. Where questions are unrelated to the class subject matter or highly personal or require extensive discussion, an offer to discuss the matter after class or after school may be more appropriate.

OUT-OF-SCHOOL ACTIVITIES

In earlier times, teachers were often subject to disciplinary action and removal for a wide variety of out-of-class activities, which were felt by school authorities to bring disrepute to the school or which appeared to place the teacher in political controversy. The rights of teachers have expanded so that generally they may not be disciplined for exercising constitutionally protected rights of free speech and expression, including political activities. Theoretically, such protections would also apply to a Christian teacher's participation in out-of-school religious activities.

Courts have also protected teachers' rights to engage in political activities with their colleagues at the school during their free time. In some cases faculty mailboxes may be used to promote such issues. For example, the California Supreme Court held unconstitutional a Los Angeles City Board of Education's regulation prohibiting the circulation of petitions on school premises during duty-free periods.

Of special relevance was the court's comment that freedom of speech contemplates effectiveness: the schools' premises were the most effective places for teachers to engage in conversation with other teachers. The Court further noted that the mere fact that the petition was controversial and created a certain amount of unrest was not adequate grounds for preventing the activity. More than "public inconvenience, annoyance or unrest" must be demonstrated.

In this case and a number of others involving inter-faculty communication, the substance has related to the special interests of teachers, such as pending state legislation on education or school board policies. It is unclear if the use of school communication systems might be protected when the content was unrelated to education. However, restrictions of such communication would undoubtedly be subject to careful scrutiny as content-based prohibition of speech.

LEGAL IMMUNITIES AND REMEDIES

Where teachers are engaged in constitutionally protected activities, courts have provided strong protection against disciplinary action. Teachers may not be dismissed, punitively transferred, denied promotion or tenure, or in any other way disciplined because of their engagement in constitutionally protected activities either in the school or elsewhere. Nor may teachers be indirectly punished when the alleged insubordination relates to constitutionally protected conduct.

These protections extend to teachers whether tenured or nontenured. In *Perry* v. *Sindermann,* the United States Supreme Court ruled that a school board could not refuse to rehire a nontenured teacher because the teacher insisted on exercising academic freedom over the board's objection to that exercise.

Where teachers have been subjected to—or are threatened with—sanctions for otherwise constitutionally permissible activities, a variety of remedies are available. Union contracts may provide specific forms of relief. The Civil Rights Act and other federal legislation provides a variety of remedies, including injunctive relief, reinstatement, back pay, and occasionally, damages for loss of opportunities for advancement and damages to reputations.

PROCEDURAL DUE PROCESS

A further important right that courts have established for teachers is the right to *procedural due process*—a guarantee that procedures dealing with important rights (such as teachers' jobs) must not be unreasonable, arbitrary, or oppressive. In practice, teachers must generally be afforded the right to be represented by counsel at a hearing, with the opportunity to confront witnesses and challenge evidence. Teacher contracts and school board policies or state law may provide specific procedures, which are to be followed before any sanctions may be applied. Such procedures must not be unreasonable.

While the issue of "What can a Christian teacher do?" is important in an increasingly secular system, the Christian community must not be trying to find ways to "sneak" religion into the classroom under some educational guise. Christian teachers should try to play a creative and effective role in assisting our troubled educational milieu to address the critical problems: nurturing human beings, instilling values, preparing young people for effective living in a depersonalized, technically oriented age, and assisting persons to find both self-worth and life-sustaining beliefs. Christian teachers who can contribute to these urgent tasks and reach out in love to children demonstrate wholeness of character. By their example they invite people to moral living. Such teachers are immune from constitutional challenge and are likely to be given wide freedom by supervisors, peers, and students.

13

Religious Instruction and the Public School

Is the public school doomed to be a secular wasteland? Or are there still some opportunities for schoolchildren to be introduced to religion and Judeo-Christian morals and ethics? Back in 1964 the American Association of School Administrators acknowledged the need for religion in the public school curriculum.

"A curriculum which ignored religion would itself have serious religious implications," they admitted at that time. "It would seem to proclaim that religion has not been as real in men's lives as health or politics or economics. By omission it would appear to deny that religion has been and is important in man's history—a denial of the obvious."

As a subject of objective study, religion has not been barred from the public schools. In fact, the Supreme Court in *Abington* v. *Schempp* specifically said as much when it declared, "nothing we have said here indicates that such study of the Bible or of religion, when presented objectively as part of a secular program of education, may not be effected consistent with the First Amendment."

Thus although the decision in *Abington* v. *Schempp* barred the devotional reading of Scripture, *Engel* barred religious exercises, and *McCollum* barred on-campus religious instruction, there is no bar to the objective, academic study of religion, including the study of the Bible.

As authors James Panoch and David Barr, advocates of such instruction, contend, "The school teaches religion whether

112

it teaches religion or not. . . . One way or the other it teaches something about religion.'' The authors insist that the school that excludes religion teaches by inference that religion is not an important area of concern for students. To exclude religion from study on the grounds of ''neutrality'' is, as they suggest, to ''confuse neutrality with sterility.''[1]

The Supreme Court has not removed religion from the public schools, Panoch and Barr insist. ''We did. Uninformed teachers, an unconcerned public, unconscious churchmen—all have had their hand in systematically eliminating all mention of the Bible and religion from significant areas of school life.''

While the scope of teaching religion on an objective basis is unclear, a number of organizations have sprung up to promote such teaching. Several books and articles review programs and materials such as Nicholas Pediscalzi's and William E. Collie's *Teaching about Religion in Public School* (Argus, 1977) and materials from the Public Education Religious Studies Center at Wright State University, Dayton, Ohio. Research studies suggest a substantial growth from 1967 to 1974 in the number of school districts in several states that have instituted courses in religion.

However, most religious studies are units within other subject areas: the arts, literature, or history. A study of European history might well involve some study of the Reformation—its personalities and concepts and their impact on the intellectual thought and political history of Europe. A study on literature or art or music would hardly be adequate without an examination of religious themes. Nothing in court decisions bars the direct use of the Bible in literature courses (for instance, Bible as literature courses at college and high school levels).

More educators need to realize that including materials of a religious source is essential to a complete understanding of many courses. As Raymond English, director of the Education Research Council of America's Social Science Program, argued, ''To study human behavior and societies without paying attention to religious motivations, is like studying chemistry without recognizing the presence of oxygen in the atmosphere.''

Such objective study of religion or the Bible has not been without problems, both legal and otherwise. Courts have often carefully scrutinized such programs to assure that they were not promoting religion. In Tennessee, Bible instruction programs have been carried out for a number of years, but a program in

Chattanooga and the surrounding county was held unconstitutional by a United States district court in *Wiley* v. *Franklin*. In reviewing tapes of class sessions, the court held that the classes showed an intent to "convey a religious message," and were thus impermissible.

The case illustrates that such programs must be rigidly objective and may not be a guise for advocacy. But serious questions exist as to whether religion can be taught—or ought to be taught—objectively. Could a Christian teach Islam objectively? Or a humanist teach Christianity objectively? While the· Bible might simply be read as literature, with class discussions on the meaning and ideas in the literature, the teacher might also express directly—or by inflection or questions—his or her suspicions about its validity. In such a context, many have opted not to pursue such courses, and have even discouraged their children from taking them.

RELEASE-TIME PROGRAMS

However, Christian parents and educators have failed to utilize the opportunity for children to be involved in release-time programs. Public schools may release students from school upon parental request so they can attend religious education classes of their choice. These classes are administered and taught by nonschool persons and are conducted away from the public school premises.

The legality of such programs was established in *Zorach* v. *Clauson,* which involved a New York State program that provided for a one-hour weekly instructional period. The sponsors of the release-time program kept attendance records, which were given to public school officials. Nonparticipating students remained in school.

The Supreme Court upheld the program (by a six-to-three majority), and in effect clarified its earlier decision in *McCollum.* In this case the Court had held unconstitutional a release-time program in which pupils were permitted to attend religious instruction classes on the school premises, but taught by nonschool personnel, furnished by a religious council that was representative of the major religious groups. The Court found that the use of school structures and authority aided the groups in spreading their religious faith.

However, in *Zorach,* Supreme Court Justice William O.

Douglas sustained the accommodation of religion under the First Amendment.

> When the state encourages religious instruc-
> tion or cooperates with religious authorities by
> adjusting the schedule of public events to sec-
> tarian needs, it follows the best of our tradi-
> tions. For it then respects the religious nature of
> our people and accommodates the public ser-
> vice to their spiritual needs. To hold that it may
> not would be to find in the Constitution a re-
> quirement that the government show a callous
> indifference to religious groups. That would be
> preferring those who believe in no religion over
> those who do believe.

Douglas further noted that the public school was used to promote religious instruction in *McCollum,* whereas in *Zorach* the school only accommodated such instruction.

While the precise distinguishing factors were not fully delineated, certainly the most obvious distinction is between on-campus and off-campus instruction. Subsequent state and lower federal court decisions have likewise sustained off-campus release-time programs. *Lewis* v. *Spaulding* upheld a *Zorach* type program in New York. *Dilger* v. *School District* upheld a similar Oregon program, and a release-time program in Washington State was upheld in *Perry* v. *School District,* though the court held that the distribution of registration cards in public schools or making announcements or explanations to obtain parent's consent would be impermissible. *Lanner* v. *Wimner* upheld a one-hour, daily program on the provision that no public school credit be given and all administrative responsibilities be handled by nonschool personnel. Courts in Virginia (in *Smith* v. *Smith*) and in Wisconsin (in *Holt* v. *Thompson*) have also upheld such programs.

In *Smith* v. *Smith* children in grades three through six were released one hour per week to attend religious instruction classes given by the Rockingham Weekday Religious Education Coun-cil, an affiliate of the Virginia Council of Churches. The classes were held in trailers of buildings immediately adjacent to the schools. The district court initially held that the program created "an impression of an endorsement of the program . . . and the principal effect of that cooperation upon the more impressionable elementary school children was to advance the weekly religious education program." However, the Fourth Circuit Court of Appeals held that the *Zorach* decision had not been repudiated and sustained the program.

In 1975, The United States Supreme Court denied a petition for a writ of certiorari by parties (including the ACLU of New York) who sought a review of the court of appeals decision. In the lawsuit, the petitioners unsuccessfully urged the Court to reconsider *Zorach* in the light of subsequent cases.

No court has held that a state school system must provide such release-time options, but rather that they may. Many states have statutes that allow such programs, though the number of communities where religious organizations have taken advantage of these opportunities has been minimal in recent years. Persons considering such a program should consult with local school and state officials to determine if a statute exists in your state and what conditions it contains.

Release-time programs do provide the opportunity for children to be introduced to the Bible as God's Word, a meaningful guide to everyday life. Local churches and church groups should consider establishing such programs to fill the religious vacuum that exists in current public school education.

14

Jingle Bells v.
Silent Night

Can children still sing Christmas carols in public schools? Can there be a Christmas tree in the school lobby or classroom? (The Soviets have changed Christmas trees to "New Year's trees.") Can a teacher put up a display with shepherds, read the Christmas story, or use religious art?

These questions are not as absurd as they once would have sounded. With the increased secularization of the public schools, the *Music Education Journal* asked these questions as long ago as 1976. An article in the journal reflected a growing concern about the legality of public school observances of religious holidays, especially Christmas.

Holiday observances in the public schools had been hotly debated. Even the designation of the December holiday as "Christmas break" had been changed to "winter break." The article mentioned an ACLU letter that suggested guidelines for holidays to California school superintendents in 1971. The ACLU had stated, "the observance in public schools . . . of such occasions as Christmas . . . as religious holidays is contrary to the separation principle."[1] The guidelines in the ACLU letter had created a flurry of newspaper headlines and criticisms. One citizen group challenged the constitutional views of the ACLU, and offered to defend any educator harassed or brought to court on such issues.

The *Music Education Journal* ended its article by developing a rationale for school Christmas music. Such music adds to the historical context of the season, is part of the American

117

culture, and serves legitimate instructional purposes.

A year after this article, the controversy emerged in Williamsburg, Virginia. Outraged parents protested against the school board's restrictive policy on the observance of religious holidays in the public schools. After widespread contention the Virginia attorney general finally issued an opinion that the policies did not need to be so "widesweeping." The school board did not need to "completely ban religious holiday programs, religious music, or religious symbols," he said.

In spite of such fairly widespread controversy, the issue never reached the courts in any substantial fashion until 1978 when Roger Florey and others objected to the "liberal" guidelines on religion established by their school board. The policies had initially been created by a citizens committee charged with studying the issue of church and state in relation to school functions. The Sioux Falls policy statement is an example of the kind of policy courts have found permissible:

> *Recognition of Religious Beliefs and Customs*
> It is accepted that no religious belief or non-belief should be promoted by the school district or its employees, and none should be disparaged. Instead, the school district should encourage all students and staff members to appreciate and be tolerant of each other's religious views. The school district should utilize its opportunity to foster understanding and mutual respect among students and parents, whether it involves race, culture, economic background or religious beliefs. In that spirit of tolerance, students and staff members should be excused from participating in practices which are contrary to their religious beliefs unless there are clear issues of overriding concern that would prevent it.
>
> The Sioux Falls School District recognizes that one of its educational goals is to advance the students' knowledge and appreciation of the role that our religious heritage has played in the social, cultural and historical development of civilization.

Observance of Religious Holidays

The practice of the Sioux Falls School District shall be as follows:

1. The several holidays throughout the year which have a religious and a secular basis may be observed in the public schools.
2. The historical and contemporary values and the origin of religious holidays may be explained in an unbiased and objective manner without sectarian indoctrination.
3. Music, art, literature and drama having religious themes or basis are permitted as part of the curriculum for school-sponsored activities and programs if presented in a prudent and objective manner and as a traditional part of the cultural and religious heritage of the particular holiday.
4. The use of religious symbols such as a cross, menorah, crescent, Star of David, creche, symbols of native American religions or other symbols that are a part of a religious holiday are permitted as a teaching aid or resource provided such symbols are displayed as an example of the cultural and religious heritage of the holiday and are temporary in nature. Among these holidays are included Christmas, Easter, Passover, Hannukah, St. Valentine's Day, St. Patrick's Day, Thanksgiving and Halloween.
5. The school district's calendar should be prepared so as to minimize conflicts with religious holidays of all faiths.

Religion in the Curriculum

Religious institutions and orientations are central to human experience, past and present. An education excluding such a significant aspect would be incomplete. It is essential that the teaching *about*—and not *of*—religion be conducted in a factual, objective and respectful manner.

Therefore, the practice of the Sioux Falls School District shall be as follows:

1. The District supports the inclusion of religious literature, music, drama and the arts in the curriculum and in school activities provided it is intrinsic to the learning experience in the various fields of study and is presented objectively.

2. The emphasis on religious themes in the arts, literature and history should be only as extensive as necessary for a balanced and comprehensive study of these areas. Such studies should never foster any particular religious tenets or demean any religious beliefs.

3. Student-initiated expressions to questions or assignments which reflect their beliefs or non-beliefs about a religious theme shall be accommodated. For example, students are free to express religious belief or nonbelief in compositions, art forms, music, speech and debate.

Dedications and Commencement

Traditions are a cherished part of the community life, and the Sioux Falls School District expresses an interest in maintaining those traditions which have had a significance to the community. Such ceremonies should recognize the religious pluralism of the community.

Therefore, the practice of the Sioux Falls School District shall be as follows:

1. A dedication ceremony should recognize the religious pluralism of the community and be appropriate to those who use the facility. An open invitation should be extended to all citizens to participate in the ceremony.

2. Traditions, i.e., invocation and benediction, inherent in commencement ceremonies, should be honored in the spirit of accommodation and good taste.

3. Because the baccalaureate service is tradi-

tionally religious in nature, it should be
sponsored by agencies separate from the
Sioux Falls School District.

Roger Florey filed suit in November 1978, seeking a court
order to declare certain aspects of these policies in violation of
the Establishment Clause of the Constitution. Florey was supported by the ACLU and a number of religious groups, including the United Presbyterian Church. The suit alleged that
the use of religious music in Christmas programs violated the
constitutional prohibition against aid to religion. Because of
this, the case became known as the "Silent Night" case. The
school board contended that allowing school observances only
when there was a concurrent secular purpose legitimized these
observances.

The United States district court held that although the case
presented an "extremely close question of law," the policies and
rules were constitutional. The opinion cited the Supreme Court
in *McCollum* where the Court declared, "music without sacred
music, architecture minus the cathedral . . . would be eccentric
and incomplete." Thus the district court declared, "to rule unconstitutional a policy which allows Christmas assemblies to
contain material having religious significance . . . would leave
the schools in the posture of only being permitted to present programs that are eccentric and incomplete."

The decision was appealed to the Eighth Circuit Court of
Appeals, which upheld the district court decision. The court held
that the policies did have a secular purpose in the "advancement
of the student's knowledge of society's cultural and religious
heritage" and "the provision of an opportunity for students to
perform a full range of music, poetry and drama. . . ." The
court also said that the policy did not have an impermissible effect of aiding religion. "The First Amendment does not forbid
all mention of religion in public schools. . . . Hence the *study* of
religion is not forbidden. . . . We view the term 'study' to include more than mere classroom instruction; public performance may be a legitimate part of the secular study. . . . When
the primary purpose served by a given school activity is secular,
that activity is not made unconstitutional by the inclusion of
some religious content."

In November 1980, the United States Supreme Court (by a 7

to 2 majority) declined to review the decision of the Eighth Circuit. The ACLU had argued that the Court ought to review the case since it potentially affected millions of students. If the policies of Sioux Falls were allowed to stand, they were likely to be adopted by school districts throughout the nation.

While the refusal to review the appeals court decision does not have the full effect of an affirmance, it does mean that at least for the present, schools are free to sponsor programs celebrating religious holidays where there is a concurrent secular basis. Schools may also use religious symbols and music that are part of our national and cultural heritage. Johnny may not be able to pray, but he can sing.

Following the decision, a legal memorandum prepared by the Christian Legal Society suggested guidelines for the permissible observance of religious holidays. Those guidelines included a series of "Suggestions for Ensuring Neutrality for School Programs":

> 1. The primary purpose should be to advance students' knowledge and appreciation of the traditional and cultural aspects of any holiday season. Religious origins and values of the holiday must be explained in an unbiased and objective manner without promoting or downplaying the religious aspects. The Christmas story, for example, may be told—perhaps utilizing secular encyclopedias and commonly used films and anthologies.
>
> 2. Christmas displays and symbols are permissible provided they are temporary and are included as an example of the cultural and religious heritage of a given season.
>
> 3. Clergy or formal religious representatives should not be involved in the planning or presentations or assemblies, in order to avoid risks of religious indoctrination or influence.
>
> 4. Religious music such as Christmas carols may be included in Christmas programs, provided they are used for educational and instructional purposes and not to promote any particular religious belief. The *Florey* decision

fully supports this posture. The Court declared it was "clear to us that carols have achieved a cultural significance that justifies their being sung in the public schools . . . if done in accordance with the policy and rules adopted. . . ."

5. Students should be free to defer any participation in programs that they find are contrary to their religious beliefs. But the fact that some may object to a particular curricular component on religious grounds is not a sufficient basis for prohibiting that component.

6. Essay and art assignments related to holidays may be utilized, so long as no student is compelled to participate in some component that violates his or her convictions. Students are certainly free to express their own values, beliefs, and opinions regarding a holiday season in themes, artwork, music, and other forms of creative expression.

The *Florey* decision establishes the principle that the separation of church and state does not require rigid exclusion of all religious elements of our cultural and national life from public schools. School boards and citizens committees throughout the country can consider the Sioux Falls policy statement as a guideline for their own policies. The religious connotations and traditions of our national holidays may still be presented in public school classrooms.

15

Student Rights and Religious Liberties

"**T**he evidence demands a verdict," said Josh McDowell at a meeting at the University of Nebraska, sponsored by the Baptist Student Union, Navigators, Campus Crusade, and InterVarsity. McDowell's presentation consisted of factual evidence for Christ's resurrection. No prayers or other elements of worship were part of his presentation.

But some university students filed charges with the student court, alleging that the campus ministry groups had violated the Regents Policy on religion on campus. The policy stated: "University facilities will not be available for any organized event or activity if one of its essential features is religious worship or testimony in any of its various forms."

In considering the case, the student court defined the word *testimony* to mean "an open, public declaration of a personal, religious, or spiritual revelation." On the basis of this definition, the student groups were convicted of "testimony" and placed on probation for one year. The student court declined to read a defense brief, which sought to introduce constitutional issues of religious freedom.

If Josh McDowell had been a psychological theorist or had advocated some sociological principle, his right to express his belief at the University of Nebraska would never have been questioned. Such is the dichotomy of free speech rights in many of our universities today.

Later, perhaps because of the possibility of legal action, the Board of Regents of the University reconsidered its policy and adopted a new one: "University buildings may be rented by any group or organization for occasional religious services . . . provided, that such space shall not be rented for the regular recurring religious services of any particular group or organization."

But the Board of Regents did not take any action on the probationary status of the student ministry groups.

What are students' religious rights in today's society? Do students have constitutional rights of religious expression and free exercise? May they meet together, form a club, pray, distribute literature, and exercise the rights of citizenship that would be theirs outside the school? In order to discuss a student's religious rights, we must first explore a student's general rights, such as expression and association.

STUDENT RIGHTS OF EXPRESSION

Any discussion of student rights must begin with the watershed case of *Tinker v. Des Moines Independent Community School District,* decided by the Supreme Court in 1969. Three high school students violated a school regulation that prohibited them from wearing black armbands to protest the Vietnam War. When the school suspended the students, the *Tinker* suit was filed. Despite the lack of evidence that the student conduct had created any disruption, the district court and the court of appeals dismissed the students' complaint.

However, the Supreme Court reversed the lower court rulings. The Court maintained that the wearing of armbands was a protected form of expression under the Constitution. "In the absence of a specific showing of constitutionally valid reasons to regulate their speech, students are entitled to freedom of expression of their views. . . . It can hardly be argued," the court declared, "that either students or teachers shed their constitutional rights to freedom of speech or expression at the schoolhouse gate." And in strong language, widely quoted, the Court went on:

> In our system, state operated schools may not be enclaves of totalitarianism. School officials do not possess absolute authority over their students. Students in school as well as out of school are "persons" under the Constitution. They are possessed of fundamental rights which

the state must respect. . . . In our system, students may not be regarded as closed circuit recipients of only that which the state chooses to communicate.

The Court then established an important test to determine whether the legitimate interests of the school outweigh the students' rights of expression. Student conduct must "materially and substantially" interfere with the operation of the schools or impinge on the rights of others for student rights to be abridged. A general feeling that student expression or action might be disruptive will not suffice.

In California, the *Tinker* standard has been enacted in a statute, which provides that:

Students of the public schools have the right to exercise free expression including but not limited to, the use of bulletin boards, the distribution of printed materials or petitions, and the wearing of buttons, badges and other insignia, except that expression which is obscene, libelous or slanderous according to current legal standards, or which so incites students as to create a clear and present danger of the commission of unlawful acts on school premises or the violation of lawful school regulations, or the substantial disruption of the orderly operation of the school.

Under *Tinker* students in high school possess rights of speech and expression as do college students.

RIGHTS OF ASSOCIATION

The rights of students to exercise their faith is often protected by constitutional rights of association. The existence of rights of association was first upheld in a 1948 case, *Marshall* v. *Alabama*. The Court declared that the "freedom to engage in association for the advancement of beliefs and ideas is an inseparable aspect of the 'liberty' assured by the due process clause . . . which embraces freedom of speech."

In 1972 this associational right was extended to students in

Healy v. *James,* a case involving a group of student activists (the Students for a Democratic Society) who sought recognition as a student organization at Central Connecticut State College. The students had complied with all the procedural requirements, and their petition had been approved by the appropriate committee. However, the president rejected the application on the grounds that the group's philosophy was antithetical to school policies. The consequences were outlined by the Court: "Its members were deprived of the opportunity to place announcements regarding meetings, rallies or other activities in the student newspaper . . . and most importantly—non recognition barred them from using campus facilities for holding meetings."

The Supreme Court found that there was a constitutional freedom at stake: "Among the rights protected by the First Amendment is the right of individuals to associate to further their personal beliefs. While the freedom of association is not explicitly set out . . . it has long been held to be implicit. . . . There can be no doubt that denial of official recognition, without justification, to college organizations burdens or abridges that associational right." The Court noted that the university might restrain such rights if groups "infringe reasonable campus rules, disrupt classes, or substantially interfere with the opportunity of other students to obtain an education."

A subsequent decision (*Gay Students* v. *Bonner*) by a lower federal court again upheld the rights of student association. "It is immaterial whether the beliefs sought to be advanced by associations pertain to political, economic, religious or cultural matters." Thus the University of New Hampshire could not hinder the social functions of gay students. *Healy* and *Gay Students* taken together clearly establish the rights of association for the advancement of ideas at the college level without regard to the state's approval of those ideas.

While no Supreme Court cases have dealt directly with student associational rights at high schools, the principles seem applicable. Several lower courts have applied similar principles to invalidate high school authorities' denial of recognition to unpopular groups. In a 1973 case, *Dixon* v. *Beresh,* a federal court in Michigan held as "patently unconstitutional" a high school policy denying recognition to groups advocating controversial ideas.

RIGHTS TO DISTRIBUTE LITERATURE

It would seem that the *Tinker* standard of "material disruption" would cover the distribution of literature. Several lower court decisions have upheld student rights to distribute political literature. In a 1974 case (*Cintron* v. *State Board of Education*), the court struck down the suspension of students for distributing political handbills. School regulations had prohibited the circulation of materials "including all political, religious, or commercial literature, notices or posters." And a California federal court struck down a state regulation that prohibited the distribution of any sectarian or denominational literature on school property.

In 1970, the Seventh Circuit Court of Appeals overruled the suspension of students for distributing an underground newspaper critical of school policies. The court applied the *Tinker* standard, holding that the high school had not met its burden of showing disruption. And the Ninth Circuit Court of Appeals struck down a University of Arizona regulation banning handbilling anywhere on the campus. Rights of leaflet distribution are discussed at greater length in chapter 22.

PUBLIC FORUM RIGHTS

At the college or university level

Another important aspect of constitutional law that affects student rights is the concept of the "public forum." The general principles associated with this concept were established by the Court in *Mosley* in 1972: "Once a forum is opened up to assembly or speaking by some groups, government may not prohibit others from assembling or speaking on the basis of what they intend to say."

Certain state properties are almost always public forums, but whether any particular property will be viewed as a public forum depends on the nature of its use. As the Supreme Court declared in *Grayned* v. *City of Rockford,* "The crucial question is whether the manner of expression is basically incompatible with the normal activity of a particular place at a particular time."

While the public university is different from streets or parks, it is, at least for the students, a semipublic forum, and students have rights of access to that forum. The fact that public forums are proper places for the exercise of religious expression was made quite clear when noted atheist Madalyn Murray O'Hair attempted to enjoin the secretary of the interior from allowing the use of the National Mall for a mass celebrated by Pope John Paul II in 1979. The court of appeals declared, "the government may not allocate access to a public place available for communication among citizens on the basis of the religious content of the messages."

It seems strange therefore that a number of universities and colleges have recently attempted to restrict the right of religious students at public universities to organize and use university facilities for their religious groups. In 1979 Santa Monica College initially prohibited religious students from meeting, even on the college's lawn. The University of Missouri at Saint Louis denied Christian students the right to use a campus "free speech platform."

The University of Missouri at Kansas City prevented a Christian student group, Cornerstone, from meeting there, arguing that it would be an impermissible aid to religion. The university contended that the United States Constitution and the Missouri Constitution prohibited such aid. The United States district court agreed, holding that the university must prohibit such religious use of its facilities. The court of appeals reversed this decision, and the case was appealed to the Supreme Court, which in December of 1981 handed down its decision, *Widmar* v. *Vincent.*

By an eight-to-one majority the Supreme Court affirmed the decision of the court of appeals, holding that where the university had created a public forum for student expression it could not discriminate on the basis of the content of the speech and deny public forum rights to religious students. Incidental benefits to religion through the use of the facilities was not a sufficient basis, the Court said, for the denial of access.

Nor did the Court accept the state's contention that religious worship was distinct from speech and therefore permissibly barred. Worship was, the Court declared, a protected form of speech. This decision will likely dispose of a United States district court decision in Washington State, which had upheld regulations of Western Washington University that restricted religious students from using university facilities for their meetings. The case had been appealed to the court of appeals, which apparently withheld judgment, pending the Supreme Court's decision in *Vincent.*

The *Vincent* decision would appear to settle the right of students at public universities to organize, meet in university facilities, and speak with the same rights that other students possess. The decision was based not primarily on free exercise grounds, but on the impermissible content-based restriction on free speech in a public forum. Now a student ministry group should not be placed on probation for sponsoring a speech by Josh McDowell or any other Christian leader.

At the high school level

In certain contexts it is clear that the public high school has some of the character of a public forum. In *Tinker* the Court declared, "[a school] is a public place, and its dedication to specific uses does not imply that the constitutional rights of persons entitled to be there are to be gauged as if the premises were purely private property. . . .

"A student's rights, therefore, do not embrace merely the classroom hours," the Court declared. "When he is in the cafeteria, or on the playing field, or on the campus during authorized hours, he may express his opinions."

In 1976, a federal district court in Wisconsin (in *Lawrence University Bicentennial Commission* v. *City of Appleton*) held that a school board guideline prohibiting the use of the public high school for religious or political purposes was an impermissible regulation of speech on the basis of content. A New Hampshire federal court (in *Vail* v. *Board of Education*) held that if a high school provides a forum, "it must do so in a manner consistent with constitutional principles. Access to the podium must be permitted without discrimination. It is not for the school to control the influence of a public forum by censoring the ideas, the proponents or the audience."

In 1976, an Oregon court overturned a board action that banned all political speakers from the high school campus (*Wilson* v. *Chancellor*). The court noted that the purpose was to bar a Communist speaker from a political science class, but speakers of other political persuasions had been allowed to participate in the program.

Despite these rulings, the broad language of *Tinker,* and the recent decision of the Supreme Court in *Vincent,* lower courts have sustained substantial restrictions on the rights of religious students to form student associations and use high school facilities. Such cases have not generally involved the issues of state control and sponsorship, which led to the invalidation of school-sponsored prayer and Bible reading. However, the courts have tended to find some form of sponsorship by the mere geographic location, the use of school facilities, or the generalized supervision and protection of the property inherent in any use of facilities.

While substantial arguments may be made on the basis of free exercise, equal protection, rights of association, and public forum, the rights of Christian high school students to form religiously oriented clubs and meet before school or during activity times have most often been denied. The one exception is a 1965 federal district court decision (*Reed* v. *Van Hoven*), which upheld voluntary, on-campus religious activities subject to several guidelines to insure that the meetings were not perceived as state sponsored.

Other decisions have denied such rights to students. A federal court in West Virginia (in *Hunt* v. *Board of Education*) denied students the right to hold group prayer meetings on high school premises prior to the commencement of the school day; the court upheld school board regulations and state law that prohibited the use of school buildings for religious purposes.

Similarly in *Johnson* v. *Huntington Beach Union High School District,* the California Court of Appeal ruled two-to-one that allowing a student Bible club to meet in a high school classroom during the lunch hour would violate the constitutional requirement of separation of church and state. Permitting the group to organize would provide direct state aid in the form of rent-free space and supervision of a paid faculty sponsor, the court said, and would tend to put the state's approval on the activity. The court rejected the student claims of rights of free speech and free exercise, arguing that there was no infringement since students were free to believe and express their beliefs on an individual basis and free to meet as a group off-campus.

Justice McDaniel disagreed with the opinion of the two other judges. He stated:

> What is the value of these communication
> rights? It might be argued that to deny these

students the privilege of studying the Bible during lunch hour does not completely destroy their right to communicate. It only eliminates one subject matter, leaving communication perfectly open on all other subjects. . . . A not dissimilar argument was made in *Thomas* v. *Collins,* wherein a national labor union officer was held in contempt of an ex parte restraining order enjoining him from soliciting union members without first registering with the state. It was argued that it was a small thing to ask him to register. The court replied, "[t]he restraint is not small when it is considered what was restrained" and held that in weighing the value of First Amendment freedoms against the right of a state to exercise the police power, "it is the character of the right, not of the limitation" which is placed upon the scales of justice.

To conclude this portion of my dissent, I can do no better than to defer to the comments of counsel for the plaintiffs who observe, "[t]he practical realities are that if students are to communicate with students on any subject they must do so where students come together: at school! On one side of the scale is an empty school room. Being empty, it would hardly move the scale even if it were being balanced against nothing, especially since there is no governmental purpose other than to be fair, grant equality and give an opportunity for student intercommunication. On the students' side of the scale there is to be weighed almost every one of the freedoms that are most valued by our nation's fundamental laws.

Finally Justice McDaniel used this occasion to express his concern about current court interpretations of the First Amendment:

It remains to give vent to what has increasingly troubled me about the trend of the decisions

purporting to construe and apply the Establishment Clause. I have long been awaiting this
chance to express a deep concern which
hopefully will fall upon interested ears and then
be equally shared. . . . I see the necessity for a
re-evaluation of the cases construing the
Establishment Clause. With due respect for the
sincerity of those who have authored the cases
relied upon by the majority, it seems to me that
their sweeping interpretations of the simple
phrase that "Congress shall make no law
respecting an establishment of religion, or prohibiting the free exercise thereof . . ." (U.S.
Const., Amend. I) have distorted out of
rational proportion both what the framers of
the Constitution intended and what is fundamental to the survival of an ethical society.

Judge McDaniel added the following footnote to the end of
his opinion: "Lest this tract be construed by anyone to be an art-
fully disguised effort to promote and advance the teachings of
the Bible, let it be known that I am an ardent and practicing
Buddhist and a member of the Nichiren Shoshu Soka Gakkai."

The *Huntington Beach* case was appealed to the Supreme
Court, which refused to hear the case because of a procedural
problem. Christian students at Huntington Beach High School
are still not allowed to organize and meet in a classroom before
school.

The same rationale as in *Huntington Beach* was employed
by the New York State Appellate Court in *Trietley* v. *Board of
Education of Buffalo* in upholding the denial of six students' request to use a classroom for Bible study purposes. The court
held that this would "go beyond mere accommodating" and
that no denial of student rights occurred since there was no
"state coercion."

Most recently, the Supreme Court declined to review the
decision (*Brandon* v. *Guilderland School District*) of a court of
appeals that refused to allow students organized as "Students
for Voluntary Prayer" the right to use a classroom for group
prayer before school. The court of appeals had held that there
was no constitutionally cognizable limitation placed on the

students' rights of free expression and exercise. The students, the court noted, are free to worship before and after school and on weekends.

Even if student rights were infringed, the court said it was justified, because of the separation of church and state, which would be violated by any "authorization of student initiated voluntary prayer."

In a statement that seems contrary to recent student rights decisions and seems hostile to religion, the court declared, "To an impressionable student, even the mere appearance of secular involvement in religious activities might indicate the state has put its imprimatur on a particular religious creed. This symbolic inference is too dangerous to permit. . . ." Finally, the court of appeals rejected the student arguments of rights of expression, holding that the high school was not a public forum where religious views may be freely aired.

What, then, is the impact of the expansion of student rights on religious liberty? Court decisions in student rights cases have created the legal framework for a substantial recognition of student rights. These rights include not only the rights of speech and expression, but of procedural due process as well.

The impact on religious rights is still unclear, although at the collegiate level, the recent *Vincent* decision should have a substantial impact in preserving students' rights of religious expression, including evangelistic activities, rights to organize, to use campus facilities, and to distribute literature.

However, student rights cases at the high school level do not seem to have extended to religious expression. The courts apparently are reluctant to grant the same freedom to religious expression as that given to political expression.

It would seem that Karl Marx may be discussed but not God. Communist speakers may present their views but not ministers or religiously motivated lay persons. Rights of free speech, association, equal protection, and other constitutional liberties are encumbered by the courts' insistence on an hermetic separation of church and state and the concept, rejected at the college level, that the mere use of facilities constitutes real or apparent sponsorship. The idea persists that high school students are unable to distinguish a school-sponsored event from a student-sponsored event, and that students will be intimidated into participation in a prayer group.

We need to remember that in these major high school cases, students were seeking court orders to require the school boards to adopt a more neutral approach. The students were suing the school board. In another case (*Reed*), opponents of a school board policy that allowed religious groups to use school facilities were unable to overturn this policy.

In a few cases now in lower courts, this pattern is again being tested. In an Orange County, California, case (*Anderson* v. *Saddleback Valley Unified School District Board*), a high school adopted a policy that encouraged student groups to organize and meet to discuss issues and interests as part of a commitment to assist students in making choices and decisions. The policy (which committed the school to such exchanges without regard to political, sexual, racial, or religious discrimination) distinguished between school groups that were related to the school's official program (sponsored clubs) and those that were student initiated. The latter were not school sponsored but only school recognized, and did not receive school financial support. Nonsponsored clubs had to obtain their own volunteer supervisors from parents or faculty. The case was not pursued when a new school board rejected these policies.

In a case (*Lubbock Civil Liberties Union* v. *Lubbock Independent School District,* 1982), which may well reach the Supreme Court and establish the law in this area, a federal court of appeals has invalidated policies of the Lubbock, Texas, school district. Early in 1979 the school board adopted written policies regarding religion and prayer in the school district, and the next year adopted new policies prohibiting the daily recital of prayer and Bible passages over the public address system. But the board did permit students to meet for religious purposes on the same basis as other student organizations.

The Lubbock Civil Liberties Union brought suit challenging the policy. The trial court upheld the policy as a proper balancing of the prohibition of government establishing religion and the protection of free exercise rights. The trial court noted the policy was neutral, permitting student groups of all types to gather.

The court of appeals reversed, holding the policy was primarily aimed at facilitating religious groups. Allowing the meetings "at a time closely associated with the beginning or end of the school day implies recognition of religious activities and meetings as an integral part of the [school] . . . and carried with it an implicit approval. . . ." The decision is now being appealed.

It remains to be seen whether or not courts will overturn these neutral policies. The hostility to religious expression in schools may take its toll even in such structures. When the original decisions dealing with school prayer were handed down, there was much talk about how the court had not prohibited student-initiated prayer, only official state-sponsored prayer. It is now clear that even student-initiated prayers have been eliminated. If high school students want to debate or promote political ideas, social ideas, or philosophical ideas, all the resources of student rights, equal protection, public forum, and free speech and association are available. If faith, God, or Scripture is the topic, forming any group is forbidden.

However, nothing any court has presently said prohibits student conversation, religious witness, or even religious literature distribution at the high school, so long as it is not disruptive. Neither is there a prohibition to students informally assembling wherever students gather—halls, parking lots, cafeterias—and talking about religion or praying. To restrict such activity would seem difficult under present constitutional law.

THE RIGHTS OF NONSTUDENTS

To what extent may ministries such as Young Life and Youth for Christ have access to students on high school campuses? May religious workers or those with religious commitments meet with students at high schools to establish friendships, counsel with interested persons, or speak to clubs or classes? These questions have become increasingly urgent in a number of school districts across the United States. Many districts have had to review or establish policies, because of the complaints of some parents, students, or outside groups.

One of the most unusual incidents involved the "Glen Ellyn Nine" of suburban Chicago. The "Nine" complained because the Glenbard West football team was praying before games and because Young Life team members were talking to high school students about Christ on the school's grounds. Believe it or not, the Glen Ellyn Nine were clergymen. They demanded that the school district develop specific policy statements regarding religious activities, including access to the students of Glenbard West. Even Jay Miller of the Chicago branch of the ACLU said such a policy statement was "rare. It's without precedent."

The policy adopted by the school board read as follows:

> In the interest of maintaining an orderly and efficient education process, all persons desiring to visit the school campus must have a valid educational or business reason for such visit as determined by the building principal or his designee. . . . No person may visit a student on campus (including lunch and unscheduled time) except upon the principal's determination that the purpose of such visit cannot be accomplished off the school campus and is necessary to the immediate personal or educational welfare of the student, i.e., child abuse, family emergency, etc.

Though the policy does not mention religion, it was clearly intended to prohibit workers of groups such as Young Life from visiting the campus.

The policy split students, community leaders, and the city clergy council, which by a sixteen-to-six vote disassociated itself from the nine. Some clergy charged the complaints were motivated more by professional jealousy than anything else, and one suggested it was a "complete sell-out to secularism." Public and student opinion strongly favored continuing to allow representatives of religious groups to visit with interested students during the free time at the open campus. Legal advocates sparred over whether the issue was one of free speech and student rights or separation of church and state. Still the school board refused to modify the policy.

The rights of outsiders to visit schools involve the rights of students to receive information, their right to be exposed to speakers, and the nonstudents' rights of access to a public forum.

Nonstudents at the University Level

At the college level, courts have increasingly protected the rights of nonstudents to exercise First Amendment rights on public campuses, especially when they have been invited by students or faculty. In *Stacy* v. *Williams* (1969), students successfully challenged University of Mississippi restrictions on off-campus speakers. The Court declared that this constituted impermissible censorship. The Court set forth its own model regulations for off-campus speakers, which seem to prohibit outside speakers only when it appears that the speaker would incite violence.

The Court in *Stacy* also held that the University may not give the administration power to invite speakers without the opportunity for students to make similar invitations. And the Court invalidated a regulation that buildings and facilities could not be made available to off-campus groups for public religious meetings or gatherings, since it might prohibit student religious groups from inviting speakers on religious topics.

Where the issue involves the rights of uninvited students to have access to public campuses, the courts have given varied decisions. A federal district court upheld a Tennessee regulation restricting its campus to students, faculty, staff, and invited guests (*Smith* v. *Ellington,* 1971). And a California court upheld a state law authorizing the administration of a campus to ban persons upon a reasonable belief such persons would willfully disrupt the orderly operation of the campus.

But another court declared a college could not constitutionally distinguish between the First Amendment rights of sponsored or charitable organizations and uninvited organizations. "Advocates of ideas not popular enough to obtain invitation from an established organization . . . are those who most need the First Amendment rights . . ." (*Brubaker* v. *Moelchert,* 1975).

Nonstudents at the High School Level

The rights of nonstudents at high schools are more complex, but student rights of association and expression should prevail, according to the Supreme Court's *Tinker* and *Healy* decisions, unless that expression "materially and substantially interferes" with the proper functioning of the school. As *Tinker* declared, officials cannot regard students as "closed circuit recipients of only that which the state chooses to communicate." As the Court declared in *Healy,* students have rights of association and rights to meet as a group. These student rights extend to the distribution of literature, promotion of concepts, and the right to hear divergent viewpoints in the high school so long as the exercise of such rights does not materially interfere with the discipline and function of the school. Teachers also have constitutional rights and rights of academic freedom, which may impact the use of nonstudent speakers who address religious issues in an educational context.

In the light of these student and teacher rights, the question may now be framed more effectively: may a school prohibit students (without a showing of substantial disruption of the school program or discipline) from inviting nonstudents to visit with them during their free times or to meet with one or more of them to discuss issues?

If the school permits persons to visit the campus either to meet privately with persons or with groups of students and to address classes on issues of interest, then a school's attempt to bar one class of nonstudent based on the potential content of that person's speech or their religious identity would seem to be an impermissible prior restraint, a denial of equal protection and students' rights to hear, and a content-based abridgment of free speech in a public forum.

No court case has addressed this specific issue. But in addition to legal issues the following questions would be raised:

- Who initiated the presence or activity?
- Is it sponsored, financed, promoted by the state or school?
- Have others been allowed to express themselves in a similar manner?
- If the speech is in the classroom, is it relevant to the topic at hand? Is there an educational purpose? Is the matter being discussed in an educational, objective manner?
- Does the activity disrupt the normal educational process of the school?
- Has the school singled out one category of person (religious) or speech content (religious) and totally prohibited that?
- Have there been incidents or patterns of abuse so there is legitimate concern about the rights of others?

In a Glen Ellyn type of situation, the courts will most likely be reluctant to force a school board to adopt a particular policy, but the courts will probably approve an already established one. As long as those policies do not step beyond the bounds of constitutional law, the courts will probably defer to the judgments of school officials. School board members, administrators, and other policymakers must be convinced that a free exchange of ideas and maximum student rights are constitutionally permissible (within the limits of the *Tinker* case) and are in the public's and the students' best interests.

Concerned citizens can make a difference in the current uncertain legal environment. The ACLU is often jealously guarding the wall of separation between church and state. If Christians would as carefully monitor and advocate student religious rights, our public school systems might, indeed, be a free marketplace of ideas.

16

Private Education v. Government Regulation

Levi Whisner is the pastor of a modest brick church in Darke County, Ohio. In 1973 he and his parishioners decided to found a Christian school, which would provide an alternative to the academic and moral deterioration in the public schools. Whisner and his parishioners felt that children "were being exposed to un-Christian philosophy during an impressionable period of their lives."

The Tabernacle Christian School, its twenty-three students, and the members of the church's congregation would not seem to be a threat to the local community or the state of Ohio. Yet in 1974 Pastor Whisner and thirteen parents of children who attended the school were charged with criminal violations of Ohio's truancy laws. Their crime? Sending their children to an unaccredited private school.

In the next year Whisner and the parents were tried in the Darke County common pleas court and convicted of violating section 3321.38 of the Ohio Revised Code. Unless the Tabernacle Church and School met the state's "Minimum Standards for Ohio Elementary Schools," Whisner and the thirteen parents would be fined or imprisoned.

But submitting to state curriculum requirements left an inadequate time for Bible study and spiritual training, Whisner argued, one of the primary reasons for founding the school. The state's curriculum requirements, he felt, gave the state a "blank

141

check to control the operations of the school.''

Pastor Whisner and the thirteen parents could have yielded to court pressure. They could have agreed to go along with state requirements, and the state would have been willing to lead them through the maze of the chartering process. Instead they appealed their case to the district court, and finally the Ohio supreme court. In July of 1976, the supreme court reversed their conviction. Ohio's minimum standards were ''so pervasive and all-encompassing,'' the court said, ''that total compliance with each and every standard by a nonpublic school would effectively eradicate the distinction between public and nonpublic education.''

The experience of Levi Whisner and the Tabernacle Christian School is not unique. Many Christian educators are determined to insure their schools' freedom to be wholly Christian. And the number of private religious schools is growing at rates some claim to exceed one new school every six hours. This explosive growth may constitute an educational revolution. Historically private religious schools have been chiefly Catholic institutions, with a smaller number of Lutheran and Reform schools. Now conservative groups, dissatisfied with the character of public education, have established schools— dramatically differing in their level of sophistication, size, and willingness to cooperate with government authorities.

The fight to guarantee the existence of private schools and to establish parents' rights to send children to these schools began in 1922 when the state of Oregon passed a law that required every child between the ages of eight and sixteen to attend a public school. This bill seemed deliberately targeted at Catholic parochial schools. The sisters of the Holy Names and Hill Military Academy filed suit (*Pierce* v. *Society of Sisters*), seeking to enjoin the governor from enforcing the law. They argued that the statute violated parental rights ''to choose schools wherein their children will receive appropriate mental and religious training.''

The state of Oregon countered that public education itself would be threatened if the statute were struck down. One common melting pot, one great ethos was the state's cry. If private schools persisted, the claims of ''the religion to which they belonged'' might be seen as ''superior to the claims of the United States.''

But in a landmark decision in 1925, the Supreme Court declared that a child "is not a mere creature of the state." Those who nurture the child should also prepare the children for "additional obligations," the court contended.

Leo Pfeffer, a premier separationist attorney, called the decision the "Magna Charta of the American parochial system." The unanimous decision is still widely quoted, and the Supreme Court itself called *Pierce* "a charter of the rights of parents to direct the religious upbringing of their children."

But while the Court has clearly established that the state does not have a monopoly on education, it frequently asserts the state's interest in education and its right to establish reasonable regulations for private schools. The Court summarized these principles in *Board of Education* v. *Allen* in 1968:

> [A] substantial body of case law has confirmed
> the power of the states to insist that attendance
> at private schools, if it is to satisfy the state
> compulsory-attendance laws, be at institutions
> which provide minimum hours of instruction,
> employ teachers of specified training, and cover
> prescribed subjects of instruction. . . ."

How extensive are these state powers? And how shall the free exercise rights and sincerely held religious convictions of parents and school administrators be weighed against these state interests? As the author of an article in an Ohio law journal put it: "To what degree may the state regulate and control the religious school?"

The Whisner case is one answer: the extensive requirements of Ohio's Minimum Standards yield to the sincerely held religious convictions of the parents. The Court rejected the Ohio attorney general's argument that the state's interest in providing minimum standards outweighed what he called a "minimum infringement on the parents' religious freedom." Clearly the infringement was not seen as "minimal."

Other states have also struck down overly broad and burdensome regulations. The Kentucky supreme court rejected state claims that it had the power to certify teachers in private schools and also to approve the textbooks being used (*Kentucky State Board for Elementary and Secondary Education* v. *Rudasill*).

These private schools did not oppose state health, fire, and safety regulations, but argued successfully that the state's intrusion into other areas was an impermissible burden on their free exercise of religion. The Court observed that these private schools were established because of parents' objections to the content of public school texts. To require such schools to use these texts would contravene the "very heart" of their objections to public education.

In Vermont the state supreme court (in *State* v. *LaBarge*) reviewed the case of parents who had been arrested for sending their children to a religiously affiliated school, which had been denied "approval." The Vermont court took a different route from Ohio and Kentucky. It held that a Vermont statutory provision that permitted "equivalent education" provided an alternative to state "approval." The Court noted that the state's interest was in education, not the type of schools a child attended.

A highly publicized 1981 case (*Nebraska ex rel. Douglas* v. *Faith Baptist Church*) seems to contradict these earlier cases. The Faith Baptist School refused to comply with state statutes, which provided that all teachers have state certification, that schools submit reports indicating student attendance, and that private schools file annual reports. A lower court held that these requirements were neither arbitrary nor unreasonable. The Nebraska supreme court upheld this decision, indicating that the Nebraska regulations were not as sweeping as in Ohio and did not interfere with the religious mission of the school. When the church's pastor, Everett Sileven, ignored the court's orders, district judge Raymond Case had the church padlocked from Mondays through Fridays, so the Christian school could not function.

In February of 1982 the judge sentenced Reverend Sileven to four months in the Cass County Jail for operating the school in contempt of a court order. As Sileven sat in jail, the Nebraska legislature began to consider Bill 652, which would allow private schools to obtain waivers from state education regulations.

But the legislature's decision will affect many more persons than this one Christian pastor. There are at least forty-two Christian schools in Nebraska, and half of them are operating without state accreditation. At least six of these schools have already been sued by Nebraska's department of education. If the legislature does not pass Bill 652, it is possible that over twenty

Christian schools will be sued by the state.

These are not isolated cases. Of the thirty-one states that regulate private schools, twelve have filed suits that have raised the issue of free exercise of religion, according to a survey by C. Scott Romans for Kent State University. In many states, legislation is being introduced to clarify this issue, such as the statute in North Carolina that exempts religious schools from state regulations other than health and safety standards.

HIGHER EDUCATION NOT IMMUNE

Issues of government regulation are not limited to primary and secondary schools, but include religiously affiliated institutions of higher education. Theodore Hesburgh, president of Notre Dame University, declared, "We are by now painfully aware of the dramatic increase in legal problems which have risen to confront colleges and universities in the past decade or so. . . ." Church related institutions have been increasingly subjected to government regulation. The Center for Constitutional Studies at Notre Dame University was established to respond to such growing issues by providing basic legal research and engaging in advocacy on behalf of independent and religiously affiliated institutions.

The issues facing such colleges and universities generally seem to relate to federal rather than state regulations. Should these institutions and their students be eligible for financial aid from public sources? Are federal labor, civil rights, and similar regulations applicable to their operations? The plight of Presbyterian Grove City College was highlighted in *Reader's Digest:*

> In April 1977, one of Washington's largest bureaucracies, the U.S. Department of Health, Education and Welfare (140,000 employees, $162-billion budget), mailed a routine form to one of the nation's smaller schools of higher learning, western Pennsylvania's Grove City College (2200 students, $7-million budget.) The letter advised that all colleges receiving federal aid would have to execute an "assurance of compliance" with a 1972 law forbidding colleges to discriminate against women. Otherwise, they would lose federal funding.

Discrimination was no problem at Grove City. In its 101 years, the college had never discriminated against women, blacks or anybody else. As for receiving government aid—federal or otherwise—Grove City had always turned its back on such help, convinced that the hand that gives inevitably becomes the hand that controls. So when HEW's compliance form arrived, the college refused to sign.

With this simple act, Grove City College started a chain of events that reveals much about big government, the arbitrary dictates of bureaucracy run wild, and the doughty spirit of a small American college. . . .

HEW had no way to force the college to comply—there was no government largess to withhold. So HEW decided to punish the college's students. On their own initiative, some 700 of Grove City's 2200 students were getting federal loans or grants. . . .

Like other government agencies, which can make laws by administrative fiat, HEW has its own administrative law courts to rule on disputed matters. Joseph Califano, then HEW Secretary, summoned Grove City before such a court in Philadelphia, where the college was ordered to show why the student grants and loans should not be ended.

Before Judge Albert Feldman, Grove City repeated its argument that it was not a recipient of federal assistance. Loans and grants worked out between students and the government, the college insisted, did not constitute federal aid to the school. On behalf of its students, Grove City also argued that HEW's threat to cut off these student-assistance programs exceeded both the authority and intent of the law.

Grove City lost on both counts. In the fall of 1978, Judge Feldman ruled that since the students paid these funds to the college for tuition, Grove City was a recipient of federal funds. He authorized HEW to cut off the funds.*

Grove City now filed suit in Pittsburgh's federal court, requesting that Secretary Califano and HEW be forbidden both to punish the students and to further harass the college. The school also claimed that the bureau's regulations were illegal and unconstitutional, because they exceeded the scope of the law and violated several constitutional rights, including a student's right to due process of law.

In November 1979, after both sides had filed lengthy briefs, Judge Paul Simmons heard oral arguments. He shot questions at Mark Rutzick, the lawyer defending HEW and its new Secretary, Patricia Harris. Why, he asked, doesn't HEW simply pursue violators of women's rights instead of hounding colleges that actually support such rights? "Why do you want them to fill in blanks on forms if it is not in any way to prevent discrimination?"

Rutzick replied that the purpose of the Philadelphia hearing was not to look for discrimination but to establish that the college refused to sign the form.

"Don't you think," the judge fired back, "that there has to be a limit to bureaucratic pressures and meddling with the rights of people? In this day and age, when most institutions have their hands out trying to get money from the government, an institution is saying, 'We don't want the government to give us anything.' The government is discouraging what some might believe a laudable position."

---

*In fact, however, HEW did not actually end the aid programs for Grove City students. To do so, it would first have had to give Congress 30 days' notice. Since Grove City's case was already drawing support in Congress and in the press, this would only have stirred up more trouble for HEW.

In March of 1980, Judge Simmons handed down his decision. It was almost a clean sweep for Grove City:

•The college does not have to sign HEW's discrimination compliance form.

•HEW has no power to cut off Guaranteed Student Loans because the law creating them specifically exempts them from such action.

•Though the Basic Educational Opportunity Grants must be considered financial aid to the college, HEW cannot cut off any student's grant *unless* it first proves that the college is guilty of sexual discrimination and not until it also provides hearings for each student.

"Because the college failed to file a form as a matter of conscience," Judge Simons wrote, "both male and female students—although totally innocent of any wrongdoing—[would be] irreparably harmed by losing their financial aid, and in a case where there is absolutely no evidence of sex discrimination. Certainly, Congress never intended such an absurd result."

Amen![1]

The events at Grove City College have implications for other Christian universities. Suppose a college had a rule that the president must be a male. HEW might consider this a discriminatory practice, whereas the university would consider this rule an outgrowth of their religious beliefs about male authority. Decisions for—or against—schools such as Grove City College do make a difference.

Southwestern Baptist Theological Seminary has also been engaged in court struggles to protect its right to include religious factors in its hiring practices. Questions are also emerging about the rights of religious institutions to exercise their religious commitments in student discipline and student admissions. An analysis of these issues is beyond the intent of this volume, but it must be recognized that such institutions encounter problems at least as vexing and legally challenging as do the elementary and secondary schools.

Four related questions form the basic issues concerning private schools and the scope of government regulation: what basic legal arguments and principles are employed to weigh the competing constitutional claims? What are the parental and family rights? How committed is the public to pluralism in education? And what is a biblically and socially sound jurisprudence on the government's role as it relates to the church and its institutions?

JUDICIAL BALANCING OF INTERESTS

While the debates concerning parental rights, pluralism, and jurisprudence are the foundation for almost all the disputes in this arena, the courts rarely speak directly to such abstract questions. The courts are usually weighing the clashing rights of the state against those of parents and religious liberty: have the schools or parents raised a valid claim of free exercise of religion? And if the state's claim seems greater, is there a compelling state interest in the disputed form of regulation—an interest which overwhelms the religious rights, and has this interest been pursued with the least disruption of these fundamental rights? This places a considerable burden of proof upon the state. As Cynthia West, writing in the *Duke University Law Journal* in 1980 observed:

> It is not enough, however, for a state to show that its interests in an educated citizenry override religious groups' general opposition to state regulatory authority over sectarian schools. . . . The state must justify the means by which it has chosen to regulate sectarian schools, as well as justifying its general power to regulate.

Assuming the opponents of regulation raise a valid free exercise claim, the task of the would-be regulator is to show that there is a legitimate and overpowering state interest in regulating the schools. Those advocating broad state regulatory powers cite a number of alleged compelling state concerns; one frequently mentioned is the state's interest in the quality of education. Illinois state commissioner William Sanders argued: "It is contrary to the public interest that any youth be poorly educated by unfit persons. . . . Freedom of parents to choose a school other than a public . . . is not threatened by the insistence that teachers be qualified personally and academically, that schools have adequate libraries and laboratories, that they be financially responsible, and that the educational programs offered be what they purport to be."[2]

Others have seen powerful state interests in education's socializing, equalizing role. Kevin Phillips, writing in *Harpers,* asserted that if society is moving toward diversity and the loss of cultural integration, there will be an increasing need for regulation of private education in the area of democratic principles and socialization.[3] This view that public education is the "great equalizer," to use Horace Mann's phrase, is widespread.

Compelling state interests are also alleged in the duty of the state to protect children—an interest that is perhaps self-evident in areas of health and safety, but has often gone beyond these functions to broader social and educational visions.

Opponents of regulation must establish either that the state does not have a compelling interest sufficient to counter the parental or free exercise interest, or that the state has used means that are too broad and coercive.

A threshold question often arises: do the contemplated regulations infringe a sincerely held religious belief and is this belief central?

Proponents of state regulation would answer no! They are frequently unconvinced that the disputed regulations constitute an infringement of religious liberty. As Carl Esbeck, professor of constitutional law at the University of Missouri, noted, "The most difficult hurdle for the church or para-church ministry is demonstrating that the religious conduct is central to the faith. . . ."[4] This is particularly the case when the regulations do not directly challenge a religious practice, but only indirectly infringe or threaten to infringe religious rights.

It is in this context that private schools have often successfully raised the claim that the regulations violate the other religion clause: the Establishment Clause. (The proposed state regulations constitute an impermissible entanglement with the religious schools, an entanglement prohibited by the tripartite test reviewed in chapter 7.) William Ball, a noted constitutional attorney, effectively used the entanglement argument in several religious school cases. Writing in *Theology, News and Notes,* Ball expressed the concerns of entanglement:

> . . .government may not become excessively "entangled" with religious schools . . . it may not monitor instruction therein, make determinations as to what is "secular" and what is "religious," create administrative involvements with religious entities.[5]

What the state wishes to regulate may be perceived by the state as merely "secular," but the religious schools may see it as integrally related to their religious life. However, if the subject matter of the regulation is defined as "secular," the state may avoid the burden of showing a compelling state interest and the use of the least restrictive means.

Only a summary reading of the cases involving school regulation is necessary to recognize that the issues are legally complex. Hiding behind the legal terminology of compelling state interest and least restrictive means are often fundamental differences in the whole concept of education, religion, and the roles of parents, churches, and the government.

PARENTAL RIGHTS

The Supreme Court's language illustrates the interplay that exists in many cases between constitutional rights of religious liberty and parental rights. The Court has frequently declared that a high degree of protection must be afforded parental rights and family life. In *Smith* v. *Organization of Foster Families* in 1977 the Court spoke of a "private realm of family life which the state cannot enter." This realm includes broad powers not only to "conceive and raise one's children" but to prepare those children "for obligations the state can neither supply nor hinder." Government is precluded from "standardizing its children and its adults."

The authors of *Society, State and Schools* note that this concern for the rights of families is worldwide, and that the constitutions of a number of nations provide specific protections for the family unit and its role in decisions regarding the education of children. The Irish Constitution, for example, notes: "The State recognizes the Family as a natural primary and fundamental unit group of Society, and as a moral institution possessing inalienable and imprescriptible rights, antecedent and superior to all positive law.''

And the Dutch Constitution speaks specifically of educational freedom: ''In these regulations the freedom of private education concerning the choice of means of instruction and appointment of teachers shall particularly be respected.''

The United Nations Declaration of Human Rights declares, ''Parents have a prior right to choose the kind of education that shall be given to their children.''

If one read only the language of decisions such as *Pierce, Yoder,* and *Smith,* one might conclude that although our Constitution has no clear provision regarding family and educational rights, they are strongly secured by Court decisions. The issue is, however, considerably more complex. Courts have frequently found ''compelling state interests,'' which outweigh parental rights, and thus have limited parental and traditional family powers.

When one reviews all the decisions granting and limiting family autonomy, constitutional authority Laurence Tribe notes that ''one cannot avoid the conclusion that the stereotypical 'family unit' that is so much a part of our constitutional rhetoric is becoming decreasingly central to our constitutional reality.'' The shifting perspective of the law, Tribe insists, raises a sharp issue: ''Once the State, whether acting through its courts or otherwise, has 'liberated' the child—and the adult—from the shackles of such intermediate groups as family, what is to defend the individual against the combined tyranny of the state and her own alienation?'' It is precisely such tyranny that concerns many who note the scope of government regulatory activity.

Tribe's concern has been part of the reason a number of commentators (such as Peter L. Berger and Richard J. Neuhaus) have called for a reform in our public policy to recognize the important role of what they call ''mediating structures'' in public life. Our policy has focused too exclusively on individuals on the one hand and government on the other. We have ignored the structures that are essential for a viable sense of public life: smaller communities and associations, which are larger than individuals but smaller than the largely unresponsive, feared, and distrusted ''megastructures.'' They note in particular four primary ''mediating structures,'' which need the support of law and public policy: family, neighborhood, church, and voluntary association.[6] The private Christian school seems to fit precisely within such categories.

THE SCOPE OF PLURALISM IN EDUCATION

As noted on a number of occasions in this volume, a critical emerging issue in American society and constitutional law is the extent of our willingness to tolerate pluralism. This may appear striking since in so many ways, the pluralism in our society has been loud and growing. Yet there are areas where the political and social pressures for uniformity are great. This is seen in the increasing use of the concept of "public policy" in government regulation and in the increased application of extensive "standards" to both public and private education.

There seems to be a body of well-meaning people intent on saving us from ourselves. These people invariably know better than we what is good for ourselves and our children. Perhaps most striking of all, these controllers call themselves "liberals"! William Ball observes this tendency to control and guide:

> As we watch the machinery of the future being assembled, we see the immense pressure to move all control of life out of the hands of individuals and to establish that control totally in the State. Those mountains of totalitarianism rising on East and West bring to mind too vividly Spengler's terrible prediction of the sure recurrence of the Age of Dictators. . . .
>
> But the largest and most significant assemblage of machinery that has been set up is the one that controls all the others. The other assemblages depend on how people act, what they believe, and whether they can reason. The family, sex, communications, politics, government, the workings of science and technology, law, violence, decency, peace, wars—all of these depend on what will be in the minds and spirits of the millions of our children as a result of their educational process.

John E. Coons and Stephen D. Sugarman (authors of

Education by Choice) have called for an end to monolithic, state-dominated education and the development of what they call "education by choice." We must end, they insist, the focus on "melting pot" education whose goals are really assimilation.

Openness to pluralism in education and in the values such education inculcates may depend upon the willingness of government and the courts to forego the dangerous myth of the public school as the "symbol of our secular unity" and endorse precisely what others have criticized: the "balkanization" of education, which encourages deliberate and healthy choice and variety.

A PROPER VIEW OF GOVERNMENT AND THE CHURCH

As one reviews the response of the religious community to government regulation, there are certainly heros like Levi Whisner. It is not at all clear, however, that all schools have resisted government regulation on such firm political or biblical grounds.

The biblical duty of parents to educate their children seems clear. To allow the state to dictate the standards and procedures of such Christian education is, according to those at Bob Jones University, "the subjugation of Christian homes and churches to secular domination" and must be regarded as "vicious" and "incompatible with the aims of spiritual ministry."[7]

Many Christians share these sentiments. As public education has become increasingly dominated by secularist and humanist perspectives, the tension between Christian values and the values implicit in state standards has become sharper. There has been a legitimate concern that the "trojan horse" (as Alan Grover, executive director of Christian schools in Ohio described it) of government regulation not undermine and destroy the very character of the Christian educational commitment.

There is, however, no apparent consensus on precisely what constitutes an impermissible government regulation. Some Christian schools have taken the posture that their freedom of religion exempts them from virtually all regulations—even traditional health and safety laws. Others are willing to concede limited state powers in such fire, health, and safety areas. Still others accept the state's legitimate concern for the education of citizens and have no difficulty with state regulations concerning compulsory school attendance, minimum number of days for schools to provide education, and requirements that certain basic subjects be included in the curriculum.

The objections become stronger and more universal when state regulations expand into areas of teacher certification, school accreditation, state testing, and other matters that infringe on the school's right to select its staff and shape its life according to religious commitments. While neutral agencies of accreditation and certification might at first blush seem unobjectionable, values inexorably are part of such processes. The law school of Oral Roberts University gained accreditation only after filing a lawsuit that challenged the American Bar Association's powers and its denial of the university's religious freedom to admit only Christian students and hire only Christian faculty members.

To believe that secularist and perhaps even anti-Christian values will not affect accreditation and licensing processes seems naive at best. Yet relatively few Christians would argue that any group of persons may create a school with no requirements to assure that indeed a school exists.

The Christian school movement needs a more carefully articulated perspective on the legitimate role of government and the areas where regulation begins to interfere with religious mission. The more extreme viewpoint that freedom of religion precludes any government role seems not only contrary to law but to a biblical view of government. Nor does such a position seem to be logically convincing. The mere fact that regulation of a religious organization occurs seems insufficient as a basis for a free exercise claim. The experience of private school associations seems to confirm that legislatures and courts are sensitive to an effectively presented case for broad freedom for such schools.

As the private school movement grows confrontations between state and educational authorities on the one hand and parents and private school administrators are likely to increase. The private school is, after all, in some sense a direct philosophic challenge to the power of the state and the common ethos. It is a threat to the little red schoolhouse as a symbol of our commonality. And in certain circumstances it poses an economic threat to those institutions and persons who have an investment in public education.

However, private education is clearly within the very best

traditions of our nation. Education in this country began as private education, and private institutions continue to rank among the very best of our colleges and universities. Private education is a powerful affirmation of freedom and the plurality of traditions, which make up the American culture. As public education has become more uniform and less subject to local community control, private education would seem a healthy antidote to conformity and lethargy.

William Ball, who has successfully represented many of the parents and schools in private education cases, has noted that "we are being overrun by a lava of governmental regulation." In *Litigation in Education: In Defense of Freedom,* he warned that we are seeing the increasing use of the criminal law to enforce the "institutionalizing of every child in the public education system . . . whose interests may run counter to those of the child, his parents and taxpayers." The task, Ball insists, is to challenge the "large mass of patently unconstitutional regulation" so as to achieve "breakthroughs for educational freedom." Whisner, Ball suggests, is an appropriate illustration:

> I salute Pastor Whisner. . . . I believe they could have made, in the long run, some sort of dishonest peace with the state. (But) Pastor Whisner refused to make a corrupt bargain.
> . . . He was perceptive enough to realize (the Minimum Standards) impinged upon the religious, educational, parental and economic liberties of his people. He did not, therefore, quail at being presented with the State's "standard brand" of regulation. He did not knuckle under, sighing, "Well, it's the law." And so he successfully resisted.

17

Public Aid
to Private Schools

"**I** would like to think that we are offering help to the inner-city child who faces a world of drugs and crime, the child with special needs, and to families who still believe the Lord's Prayer will do them less harm in the schoolroom than good."

President Ronald Reagan made this statement in April of 1982 when he proposed a tax credit of $500.00 for each child attending a private school whose parents' annual income was $50,000 or less. A few of his words were lost amid the clapping of nuns, priests, and teachers who attended the National Catholic Educators Association meeting, at which he chose to propose this tax relief.

Tuition tax credits for elementary and secondary students, Reagan said, would be phased in over a three-year period: $100.00 or half the tuition (whichever is less) in 1983, $300.00 in 1984, and the full $500.00 by 1985. Approximately 11 percent of the nation's 48 million students attend private schools; two-thirds of these students are in Catholic schools.

Only hours later Albert Shanker, president of the American Federation of Teachers, said his union would fight "tooth and nail" against "this nasty tonic." Congressional leaders like Dan Rostenkowski, chairman of the House Ways and Means Committee, predicted that Reagan's plan would not be passed by Congress because of the "soaring deficits" in the president's current budget. And Senator Harrison P. Schmitt said, "There's one big fly in the ointment. . . . The proposal won't survive a constitutional test."

The issue of aid to private education has been the classic context for controversy between government and private education, even though public aid went to a wide variety of schools in early America. Not until the nineteenth century was there a legal attempt to draw a line between public and private schools to limit aid to the private sector. Horace Mann, the vigorous advocate of public education, championed the cause of public education in Massachusetts, and it became the first state to establish government funding exclusively for public schools. New York soon followed suit. A report of their Law Committee concluded that aid ought to go to the public schools, and that "if religion be taught in a school, it strips it of one of the characteristics of a common school. . . ." This conclusion would have been unthinkable a century earlier, for it is built on an assumption that religion is irrelevant to the common good. Finally the Morrill Act of 1862 provided federal support for land grant colleges, and thus gave further impetus to the shifting of financial support to public schools.

But even so, cases raising constitutional questions did not reach the Supreme Court until the late 1940s, the same period as the prayer and Bible reading cases. Since then some of the most significant cases on church/state relations have been aid-to-education cases. The concept of "separation" and much of the oft-quoted language of the Court on the Religion Clauses come from these "parochiaid" (parochial school aid) cases. In the three years from 1968 to 1971, the Supreme Court decided four major cases that established both the language and the basic posture of subsequent litigation on aid cases.

The issue became sharp in this period not simply because of growing separationist pressures in legal and political thought, but because of the soaring costs of private education. The Roman Catholic parochial stystem was particulary hard hit because of the decline of members in teaching orders, who had substantially reduced the costs of operating such schools. During this period, Frank Sorauf noted in his *Wall of Separation* that the debate over public support for private education was "in fact a debate over aid to Catholic schools." With the increased involvement of many other religious groups today, Sorauf's point would no longer hold true.

The parochiaid cases came to the Court in a period Sorauf describes as "ambiguously unfriendly." Knowing this, a number of institutions of higher education sought to minimize their religious orientation in order to qualify. Conservative William Buckley accused one Catholic university of divesting itself of its very Catholicity. *"Radix omnium malorum cupiditas est"* ("The root of all evil is greed"), declared Buckley. Washington attorney Edward Bennet Williams, counsel for four colleges in the Tilton case, had reportedly put them through a process of "secularization," including the removal of crucifixes from classroom walls.

In spite of increasing Supreme Court reluctance to countenance aid (especially to elementary and secondary parochial schools), prominent political leadership and vigorous lobbying efforts have advocated such aid, in recognition of the financial plight of private education and its vital role in contributing to the educational mix in American society. Presidents Johnson and Nixon advocated this aid before Ronald Reagan's speech to the Catholic educators.

The National Defense Education Act of 1958, passed in the shadow of Sputnik, provided long-term loans to nonpublic schools for equipment for science, mathematics, and foreign languages. And in 1965 Congress passed the Elementary and Secondary Education Act, which provided for public funds to both public and private schools, especially those that served low—and middle—income constituencies. This aid was tailored to the permissible aid limits established by the Supreme Court in *Everson* v. *Board of Education.*

Everson was the first time the Court reviewed aid to parochial schools under the Establishment Clause. The Court upheld (five-to-four) a New Jersey statute that provided aid for the transportation of students to and from parochial schools. "The State contributes no money to the schools. It does not support them," wrote Justice Hugo Black for the majority. The provision of transportation is, the Court declared, part of a program of general benefits, like police protection. These benefits may be extended to all citizens without regard to their religious belief.

The *Everson* decision was a landmark—not so much for the sustaining of the New Jersey payments as for its application of the Establishment Clause to the states through the Fourteenth Amendment. Perhaps even more far-reaching was its strong separationist language, which called for a "high and impregnable" wall of separation that cannot tolerate the "slightest breach." The contrast between this language and the Court's action of approving the aid was so sharp that Justice Jackson said it reminded him of Byron's Julia who "whispering 'I will ne'er consent'—consented."

In 1968, the Court (in *Board of Education* v. *Allen*) sustained a limited form of aid to parochial schools: "The benefit is to parents and children, not to schools," Justice Byron White declared. Again the Court noted that the law simply makes general benefits available to all children. This "child-benefit" basis has been a frequent argument, but the Court seems to have given it limited applicability.

One would think that *Everson* and *Allen,* coupled with the expanding aid of 1965 congressional action, would have opened the doors for further government assistance. However, on June 28, 1971, the Supreme Court handed down three opinions on aid to religious schools—two of which focused on aid to elementary and secondary private schools. They set the tone for Court decisions in this complex arena.

PUBLIC AID TO ELEMENTARY/SECONDARY SCHOOLS

In *Lemon* v. *Kurtzman* from Pennsylvania and *DiCenso* v. *Robinson* from Rhode Island, the Court struck down programs of aid to parochial schools. Pennsylvania had proposed to purchase secular educational services for nonpublic schools. Rhode Island was going to pay salary supplements for teachers of secular subjects in schools targeted toward low income families. In both cases the Court found a violation of the Establishment Clause.

In *Lemon,* Justice Burger added the third element to the tripartite test: the excessive entanglement test. While certain statutes might not be violative of the purpose and effect tests, they create an administrative relationship between church and state, the very relationship that the Constitution sought to avoid.

Burger saw a "grave potential for excessive entanglement," given the religious character and mission of the Catholic schools. Further the "comprehensive, discriminating and continuing state surveillance" required to insure that state-funded teachers were not impermissibly utilized would create an "enduring entanglement," as did the state's necessary inspection of school records. He also pointed to another type of entanglement: political entanglement. Such aid would become a significant political issue, he felt, forcing candidates to declare their position and creating a "divisive political potential."

The *Lemon* case seemed to set the tone for Court analyses of parochiaid cases, with the Court rejecting all but a few limited forms of state assistance. Two years later three more decisions were handed down. *Committee for Public Education v. Nyquist* (six-to-three decision) struck down amendments to New York's education and tax laws, which offered aid for facilities maintenance, equipment purchases, and tuition reimbursement. An eight-to-one decision (in *Levitt v. Committee for Public Education*) struck down another New York program, which provided funds for educational testing and other school functions required by the state. And in *Sloan v. Lemon,* the majority held unconstitutional a Pennsylvania statute providing for partial reimbursement of tuition costs.

In 1975 the Court went even further, holding that legislation to provide public funds for auxiliary services such as remedial educational programs, counseling, and testing was unconstitutional—even when such services were provided by public school personnel (*Meek v. Pittenger*). Only the textbook loan aspects of the Pennsylvania statute survived.

Justice Burger seemed particularly upset. In a vigorous dissent, he said:

> If the consequence of the Court's holding operated only to penalize *institutions* with religious affiliation, the result would be grievous enough; . . . But this holding does more; it penalizes *children*. . . . This penalty strikes them not because of any act of theirs but because of their parents' choice of religious exercise. . . .
>
> [This opinion] literally turns the Religion Clause on its head. . . .
>
> One can only hope that at some future date, the Court will come to a more enlightened and tolerant view of the First Amendment's guarantee of free exercise of religion. . . .

In 1977 the Supreme Court again faced the issue of aid for specific programs in private schools. An Ohio statute provided for a number of services: the loan of textbooks and "book substitutes"; standardized testing and scoring for private school students by public officials; diagnostic health services, guidance counseling, therapeutic services, and remedial counseling; loans of instructional equipment; and funds for field trips. Suit was brought by various Ohio taxpayers, and a district court upheld the provisions. The Supreme Court (in *Wolman* v. *Walter*) also sustained the provisions with the exception of the funds for field trips and the loan of instructional equipment. The Court seemed to indicate more flexibility in *Wolman* than it had in *Meek*.

The concurring opinion of Justice Lewis Powell suggested the Establishment Clause must be applied without "blind absolutism" even "if this endeavor means a loss of some analytical tidiness. . . ." Blackmun's plurality opinion, in fact, acknowledged that the "wall" once "high and impregnable" was in recent cases a "blurred, indistinct, and variable barrier. . . ." Whether *Wolman* represents simply an illustration of a loss of "analytical tidiness" or a weakening of the "wall" is unclear.

What is the current status, then, of permissible and impermissible public aid? *Society, State and Schools* graphically summarized the issue:

> *Permissible aid:*
>   1. Loans of secular, approved textbooks
>   2. Bus transportation
>   3. Administration of standardized tests
>   4. Administration of diagnostic tests for those with learning problems
>   5. Therapeutic services to those with learning problems
>   6. Direct payment for state-mandated record keeping and testing
>
> *Impermissible aid:*
>   1. Salaries of teachers who teach secular subjects
>   2. Maintainence of school buildings
>   3. Salary supplements for those teaching

secular subjects
4. Development and administration of tests
5. Reimbursement of tuition to low-income parents
6. State income allowances for tuition
7. Professional services of counseling, testing, and remedial education
8. Instructional materials (maps, projectors, etc.)
9. Loan of instructional materials, except secular textbooks
10. Field trips to secular sites

The authors of this summary concluded that "the divisions within the Court on these matters reveal an unstable Court, a Court divided increasingly against itself on the application of the dividing line between the secular and the religious."

HIGHER EDUCATION AND STATE AID

If the Court has seen a relatively impregnable wall barring aid to elementary and secondary schools, then the wall has appeared somewhat less formidable on the issue of aid to religiously affiliated colleges and universities.

On the same eventful day in June of 1971 that the Supreme Court handed down the two decisions against aid to elementary and secondary schools, it rendered its opinion in *Tilton* v. *Richardson,* which upheld the Higher Education Facilities Act (an act providing construction grants for secular buildings at religious colleges and universities). The Court observed that the elementary and secondary schools were thoroughly committed to religious education and indoctrination whereas the religious influence, control, and character of the colleges and universities were less marked. The Court did invalidate a statutory provision in the act, which allowed the federal government to recover its funds during a twenty-year period if the buildings were used for religious purposes. Instead the Court held that the buildings could never be used for such purposes. However, the court left open the possibility that some institutions of higher education might be so thoroughly religious as to preclude such aid.

The Court faced precisely that issue in 1976 in *Roemer* v. *Maryland.* The Court (again by a slim five-to-four majority) sustained a Maryland program of grants to independent institutions of higher education, based on the number of full-time students. The grants were direct and noncategorical, though a proviso prohibited their use for sectarian purposes.

Justice Harry Blackmun, writing for a plurality, observed that the mere fact that aid benefited a religious institution was not dispositive since "hermetic separation" was neither possible nor required, only "scrupulous neutrality." The recipient institutions must not be "pervasively sectarian," but perform "essentially secular functions." Dissenters continued to voice concerns about the impossibility of really separating the religious from the secular.

Justice William Brennan voiced concern about the creation of an "inter-dependence" between religion and state: "It is not only the non-believer who fears the injection of sectarian doctrines and controversies into the civil polity, but in as high degree it is the devout believer who fears the secularization of a creed which becomes too deeply involved with and dependent upon the government." And Justice Paul Stevens warned, perhaps prophetically, of a "pernicious tendency of a state subsidy to tempt religious schools to compromise their religious mission without wholly abandoning it."

The *Roemer* case established the framework for judging whether or not an institution of higher education was "pervasively religious." Elements that might indicate such a character were religious restrictions on faculty and student admissions, enforced obedience to religious dogma, required attendance at religious services, the study of particular religious doctrines, identification as the religious mission of a sponsoring church, religious indoctrination as part of its substantial purpose, and the imposition of religious restrictions on how and what the faculty could teach. If a university fit this composite profile, it would be considered pervasively religious and ineligible for public aid.

NEW MODELS OF AID

The increased number of persons choosing private education and the shift from a primarily Catholic enterprise to a broader more heterogeneous movement have expanded the search for constitutionally and politically feasible aid to private education.

Most options involve varieties of tax policy: tax deductions or tax credits or the more revolutionary approach of a voucher system. Advocates of such plans hope that a nondiscriminatory statute, which provides the same benefits to public and private education, would be constitutional. But they recognize that this is a larger issue of public policy, and they understand the ever-present need for political support for such measures.

Many have argued that public support for private education is required to fulfill our country's commitment to distributive justice. Parents of those who attend private schools should not have to pay for the public system, and then pay again for a private system. As attorney William Ball queries: "Is it really fair that those who help maintain private schools, in which a child can obtain an education that satisfies reasonable requirements of the state, should then have to pay taxes to support an additional school system—the public school system?"

"I believe that such double payment is totally wrong," Ball answers.

Proponents also point to the increasing ethical and religious resistance to supporting public schools that more and more reflect the secular bias of society. As these schools broaden the scope of their involvement—sex education, counseling, life education, etc.—parents increasingly object on conscience grounds to supporting institutions in which they have no ideological voice.

Others argue for nondiscriminatory aid, primarily as a means of promoting educational pluralism and diversity. Many who believe the public schools have adopted a religious viewpoint, secular humanism, argue that it is only equitable to provide aid to a wide variety of educational options, not simply one value system. As the authors of *Society, State and Schools* insist, the distinction between secular and religious schools is no longer tenable or constitutionally meaningful when the public education system indoctrinates just as thoroughly as any parochial school. Courts ought to recognize that "either tax money cannot go to public schools, or admit that the present formulation of the secular-religious distinction is faulty and therefore tax money can go to all accredited schools. . . . In either case they must break longstanding precedent. . . ."[1]

It should not be surprising that such a shift is as frightening to some as it is exciting to others. It would mean abandoning many cherished notions, including Frankfurter's dream of the little red schoolhouse as the "symbol of our secular unity." It would further mean, as Rockne McCarthy and the other authors of *Society, State and Schools* point out, the abandonment of the notion that "any single 'stretch sock' school could ever honestly and impartially reflect our religious and ideological multiformity, and the notion that America's future strength lies in a single melting pot school with the state acting as central school board. . . ."

All these concerns have led to various proposals to provide one of three types of aid to parents: tax credits, tax deductions, or voucher plans. Each of these would in one way or another provide aid to educational pluralism, including private schools. They seek to avoid constitutional problems by focusing the aid on the parent and the child rather than the school.

TAX CREDITS

Tax credits, such as those proposed by President Reagan, represent one form of the use of tax policy to assist parents who have children in private schools. Since tax credits are direct subtractions from taxes due, they amount to a 100 percent credit up to the limit provided.

In the early seventies, New York and Pennsylvania enacted tax credit statutes. But the Supreme Court struck down both plans in 1973, holding that they failed to pass the Establishment Clause test.

Congress has kept the issue alive by introducing various bills, the best known of which is the Packwood-Moynihan Bill. This bill was cosponsored by fifty senators in 1977 "to amend the Internal Revenue Code of 1954 to permit a taxpayer to claim a credit for amounts paid as tuition to provide education for himself, his spouse or his dependents, and to provide that such credit is refundable." Failure of a House-Senate committee to resolve differences between their various versions of the bill (especially whether elementary and secondary education would be included) resulted in no action.

TAX DEDUCTIONS

In 1976 the state of New Jersey sought to provide relief for parents by a statute providing for a deduction of up to $1,000 on state taxes. Since this was a tax deduction and not tax credit, it is subtracted from income rather than the tax due, which makes it substantially less of a saving. In fact, for a family earning $20,000 a year, the saving would be only $20. In spite of the limited "aid," a federal district court struck down the statute in 1978 as impermissibly aiding religion, since most parents were paying tuition to religiously oriented schools. A court of appeals affirmed, and the Supreme Court denied a writ of certiorari.

In 1955 Minnesota had enacted a similar statute except that the legislation provided the deduction of fees and other expenses of both public and private schools. In 1978 the Minnesota Civil Liberties Union challenged the statute, but the district court held that since the deduction was available both for public and private school expense it did not violate the First Amendment (*Minnesota Civil Liberties Union v. Roemer*).

VOUCHER PLANS

This approach provides a voucher, which parents may spend for any one of a number of educational programs. Such plans have been the most praised and most criticized, because they represent a substantial shift in the way education is financed and the government's role. Some see these plans as the demise of public education with the poor and minorities paying the social price. But Rockne McCarthy, political science professor at Calvin College, represents an increasingly large segment of the public when he declares that "the voucher concept is an idea whose time has come. . . ." Support for the concept goes beyond the religious community. Milton Friedman, the noted Chicago free enterprise advocate, has called for precisely such a plan to introduce consumer choice and free enterprise into education. Others have argued that vouchers create a less discriminatory system. This argument, advanced for example by Christopher Jencks, a noted sociologist, challenges the more common assertion that public schools are vital institutions to break down discrimination. They say that if funding is left up to the political process, which usually works in a prejudicial way, blacks would not receive equal aid. But if the economic power is given directly to the parents, minorities would win as well as others.

Perhaps the most noted advocates for the voucher plans have been John E. Coons and Stephen D. Sugarman, authors of *Education by Choice: The Case for Family Control*. Coons and

Sugarman, professors of law at the University of California in Berkeley, call for a return of educational power to parents, instead of the "professional garrison," which is the "family's primary competitor for power" over the child's educational experiences. Parents alone possess, they suggest, the only reliable token known to the vocation of child-rearing: "the readiness to sacrifice." We must "subsidize a much wider range of private choice than is now the case."

Many advocates of religious liberty have also endorsed the voucher concept, seeing it as giving parents the responsibility of the education of their children. Support from the religious community has come from Catholic, Reformed, Lutheran, and other communities. Rockne McCarthy and his colleagues from the Reformed tradition make a strong argument for vouchers and seek to develop a constitutional defense for such a framework.

It is striking, however, that other elements of the religious community (even those in the private school movement) have serious reservations about vouchers. The concern arises from the inevitable state involvement in certifying schools that are legitimate for purposes of "spending" the vouchers. McCarthy acknowledges such a requirement would be necessary and suggests that regulations regarding health and safety, compulsory attendance, school days per year, and the use of certified or licensed teachers are legitimate requirements. To combat the heated controversy over the last requirement, McCarthy asserts that it could be accomplished "without the state infringing on either academic or religious freedom." To be sure this is possible, one would want to know who would be determining teacher certification, under what structures, and on what bases.

Of course, secularist groups and vested public education interests have lobbied heavily against such aid. Their concerns range from objections to aiding sectarian interests, to economic arguments about potential massive federal and state outlays, to fears for the "balkanization" of education, especially along "dangerous religious lines." They also fear that the poor will be ill equipped to exercise effective choice, therefore further racial and economic segregation will take place.

Secular interests have been joined by many religious groups, creating a powerful coalition resisting not only fundamental changes such as vouchers, but any form of aid. Fre-

quently these religious groups are ones that have little investment in private education, perhaps because they sense less tension with the values and philosophy of public education. Also
opposing aid are groups that have strong separationist perspectives and fear the government controls that inevitably go with
aid. It is the sort of concern noted earlier by Justice Stevens: a
wholesome religious commitment might be destroyed by the
temptation toward neutrality, which might be necessary for aid.
While William Ball is a firm advocate of private education, he
lauds the reluctance of religious schools to get in line for federal
dollars. "It is well that administrators of fundamentalist Christian schools take a firm stand against public funding of their
schools and call upon their people to sacrifice for Christian
education." Ball notes that this very sacrifice is a form of
witness, which helps Christians to be a "people apart."
However, perhaps even groups who would not participate in
voucher programs because of government controls, ought to
welcome an advent of freedom, parental responsibility, and
pluralism to education.

18
Home Instruction

The classroom is a family living room. The Nobel children—Charity, Hope, Naomi, Priscilla, Eve, Abigail, and Luke—are being taught English, history, government, science, and Bible by their mother, who is a graduate of Calvin College in education. She and their father, Peter, structure the children's course work around a home-study curriculum provided by an Illinois-based academy. Psychological tests reveal the children are doing quite well. As *Liberty* magazine observed, they are being taught by a teacher they love and respect . . . "free of foul language, drugs and overcrowding."[1]

Not many parents will make such a commitment to their children's education. Yet in February of 1979 the Nobels were arrested for contributing to truancy. Under Michigan law at the time, home-based schooling was only permitted if the teacher was certified. Although Ruth was qualified for certification, she declined to take the test on religious grounds.

The case was taken to the district court by the state of Michigan where the judge ruled, "The interest of the state in requiring certification . . . in this particular case must give way to the free exercise of religious belief." The court noted that freedom of religion is a fundamental right, which occupies a "preferred position" in our constitutional framework. The Nobels, the court declared, have met the purpose of the statute to educate their children and "no court should interfere with the free exercise of a religious belief on the facts of this case."

The judge dismissed the charges against Peter and Ruth Nobel.

The Nobels and perhaps as many as 20,000 others in the

170

United States have taken their children out of formal schools and are teaching them at home. Leslie and Dixie Rice were also arrested for taking their daughter, Leslie Sue, out of school. Tom and Martha Lippitt were disillusioned with the permissive environment and hostility to family values of schools in South Euclid, Ohio, and withdrew their children from school. Martha, a certified secondary school teacher, set up a home school. The Lippitts were arraigned, and the court held Martha was not qualified because she had not taken a refresher course. The judge ordered the children returned to state schools. Martha left the state with the children, and Tom was jailed.

Compare these practices with the words of the Supreme Court in a seminal decision in 1925 regarding the right of parents to educate their children:

> The fundamental theory of liberty upon which all government in this Union reposes excludes any general power of the State to standardize its children by forcing them to accept instruction from public teachers only. The child is not a mere creature of the State; those who nurture him and direct his destiny have the right, coupled with the high duty, to recognize and prepare him for additional obligations.
>
> *Pierce* v. *Society of Sisters*

For a wide variety of reasons, parents are increasingly sensing those "additional obligations" and looking for alternatives to public education.

Some parents object to the increasing mechanization of education or the collapsing value systems or discipline problems or falling education standards. Others object to public education on religious grounds. Some simply wish to be more directly involved with their children in the creation of an effective family unit. The opposition to formalized education seems to be growing and attracting a wide, diverse, and reputable following. Some parents are choosing private education. Others are assuming more personal responsibility for the education of their children.

But as Alice Beshoner has observed in an article in the *University of Missouri-Kansas City Law Review,* schooling at home is not as radical a departure from tradition as one might think. It is a "closing of a circle," a return to a philosophy that prevailed in an earlier America. In colonial periods, the government may have passed laws regarding the education of children, but the state assumed that it was the task of parents to provide that education. Some "free" schools were established to assist parents with part of that task. The state merely aided the parent, which has had the effect over a period of years of eroding the parent's common law right over a child's education.

Early court decisions honored this parental right. An 1887 Illinois court declared, "The policy of our law has ever been to recognize . . . that the [parent's] natural affections and superior opportunities of knowing the physical and mental capabilities and future prospects of his child will assure the adoption of that course which will most effectively promote the child's welfare."[2]

The industrial revolution with its concentrated populations and waves of immigrants needing to be "assimilated" sped a process toward mass public education. As Beshoner suggests, "Efficiency, uniformity, conformity and standardization, the anathema of modern day critics, became the virtues. . . ."[3] Today all fifty states have statutes regulating the quality and quantity of education.

What happens when parents challenge the accepted norm and the combined machinery of the educational structure and state compulsory attendance laws? Do parents still have the right to educate their children at home? What can the state require of parents who wish to teach their own children?

PARENTAL RIGHTS IN EDUCATION

The Supreme Court has never ruled directly on home education itself, although decisions have dealt with the role of parental rights in selecting the school a child is sent to. The first major, and still important, decision was handed down in 1925 in *Pierce* v. *Society of Sisters*. The Court struck down attempts by the Oregon legislature to require parents to send their children to public schools. The decision established the language we have already quoted, which remains as a ringing declaration of parental rights: "The child is not a mere creature of the state." This decision has been the basis for assuring parental rights to nongovernmental schooling. Yet as positive as *Pierce* was, it did not contemplate the issue of home schooling, and in fact noted that regulation of education by the state was within constitutional bounds.

The Supreme Court had just two years earlier struck down an attempt in Nebraska to ban the teaching of any language but English, which reflected the anti-German feeling in the nation at that time. The Court reversed a criminal conviction of the parents, basing its decision on a fundamental liberty under the Constitution to direct the education of one's children: "That the state may do much, go very far, indeed, in order to improve the quality of its citizens, physically, mentally and morally, is clear; but the individual has certain fundamental rights which must be respected . . . not merely freedom from bodily restraint, but also the right of the individual . . . to marry, establish a home and bring up children. . . ."

The Court specifically addressed the issue of religious convictions and parents' rights in education in a relatively recent case, *Wisconsin* v. *Yoder*. The decision involved members of the old Amish religion and conservative Amish Mennonite Church, who were convicted of violating Wisconsin's compulsory attendance law, which required a child's attendance until the age of sixteen. The parents claimed that the application of the statute to them violated their constitutional rights.

The trial court agreed that the statute interfered with the religious beliefs of the parents, but held that the government regulations were a legitimate exercise of governmental interest in education. The Wisconsin Supreme Court reversed, and the United States Supreme Court affirmed the reversal, holding that the state had failed to show a compelling interest in keeping these children in school. The Court noted two rights threatened by the application of the statute to the Amish: parental rights and religious rights. The court declared:

> This case involves the fundamental interest of parents, as contrasted with that of the state, to guide the religious future and education of their children. The history and culture of western civilization reflect a strong tradition of parental concern for the nurture and upbringing of their children. This primary role of the parents . . . is now established beyond debate as an enduring American tradition.

The Court indicated that parental rights as they relate to the education of their children are fundamental rights entitled to careful protection by the courts. The "state's interest in education, however high we rank it, is not totally free from [a] balancing process when it impinges on fundamental rights and interests . . . of parents."

The Court noted that limits are appropriate whenever parental decisions would jeopardize the health or safety of the child or have a potential for significant social burdens. Decisions, such as *Pierce* v. *Society of Sisters,* did not lend support to the notion that parents might replace state requirements with "their own idiosyncratic views," the Court warned.

Pierce, Meyer, Wisconsin, and other court declarations establish that there is a strong parental right to select the educational context for their children. The state may not have a monopoly on education, nor, as other cases have clearly held, so regulate alternative schooling as to deny effective substitutes for public schooling.

STATUTORY AND LEGISLATIVE STATUS OF HOME EDUCATION

The right of parents to educate their children at home, however, is not primarily a matter of federal constitutional law, but of state statute. Every state has adopted statutes relating to educational requirements (including truancy laws, which in effect are compulsory school attendance statutes). These statutes create penalties if children are not in school during the years covered by the statute.

These statutes are grounded on the legal doctrine of the state as *parens patriae*—the power of the state to assume parental responsibilities over children whose parents fail to exercise their fundamental duties. This doctrine establishes the state's interests and rights in interposing itself into parental decisions about education. The Supreme Court, in a decision involving religious interests of parents (*Prince* v. *Massachusetts*), declared "neither rights of religion nor rights of parenthood are beyond limitation. Acting to guard the general interest in youth's well-being, the state as *parens patriae* may restrict the parents'control by requiring school attendance. . . ."

The scope of parents' rights to educate children at home is primarily a function of the state statute and the court's interpretation and application of that statute. The parental right to send children to private schools is clearly established. However, their right to educate them at home has not yet been declared a constitutional right. If there is no such right in the statutes of the state in which a family resides, parents are often unsuccessful in persuading courts to allow them to teach their children at home. An attempt to argue for such a constitutional right was made in *Scoma* v. *Board of Education,* but a United States district court rejected the argument.

However, some state statutes do specifically provide for home education. Statutes in Missouri, for example, specifically say that home education fulfills the state's requirements, provided that the course of instruction is "substantially equivalent" to that given in public schools.

Some states will permit home instruction under specifically identified provisions, frequently the prior approval by the proper authorities. Such approval may be based on the educational curriculum being planned and the qualifications of the teacher. In the Nobel case, Michigan provided for home education if the parent was a certified teacher.

In 1982 a number of states adopted statutes providing for some forms of home education. Many states have statutes that do not specifically mention home education, but allow parents to send their children to private schools or to cause them to be otherwise "equivalently instructed." New York, New Jersey, and Ohio have such statutes.

In states with these "equivalency" statutes, the issue of whether home education will meet the "equivalency" test will often be administratively or judicially determined. As Robert P. Baker says in *Legal Aspects of Compulsory Schooling,* this determination may depend on the concept of education applied. For example, if the compulsory education requirement is primarily academic in nature, evidence of the academic competence of the home education will usually suffice to establish equivalency. In such cases, courts may simply hold that the home education is, for purposes of the requirement, a "school." Such was the case in *People* v. *Levison,* a 1950 Illinois case involving parents who withdrew their daughter from school, complaining of the lack of biblical teaching and the "pugnacity" the school was instilling in her. The Illinois Supreme Court held that "the object [of compulsory education laws] is that all children shall be educated, not that they shall be educated in any particular manner or place. . . . The law was not made to punish those who provide their children with instruction equal or superior to that obtainable in the public schools. It is made for the parent who fails or refuses to properly educate his child."

In other cases, courts have held that although the home schooling was not a "school" it met the "equivalency requirement." A typical case is *State* v. *Massa,* in which some New Jersey parents were charged with failure to send their children to a public or private school. The court noted that if the legislature had intended for only a "school" to qualify, the statute would not have provided for alternatives in the "equivalency" option; the court therefore sustained the right of the parents to provide an equivalent home-based education. Where allegations have been made that the home instruction is not equivalent, the parents have been victorious when the state fails to prove that the home education is inferior.

Unfortunately some courts have held that home instruction, by its very character, could not be equivalent. Such courts tend to view the character of education and the "equivalency" not in academic terms but in terms of socialization. In *Stephens* v. *Bongart* (1937), a New Jersey court declared that since a primary objective of education is the development of good character and citizenship, "it is almost impossible for a child to be taught in the home." When the defendant father protested that he was not interested in method but in results, the judge replied, "that theory is archaic, mechanical and destructive. . . ."

Many states have what Robert Baker referred to as a "cookie cutter" statute—a provision that requires an educational pattern essentially identical to that of the public school and does not provide for an equivalency. When encountering such statutes, courts have had a more difficult time accommodating home education. In a few instances they have found that home instruction is a "school." But often, especially from a sociological perspective, they have held just the opposite. In a 1950 New Jersey case (*Knox* v. *O'Brien*), it was proven that the mother held a state teacher's certificate, and that the children were studying state-approved subjects with state-approved texts during the usual public school hours. Nevertheless the court rejected the home instruction. The court declared, "Free association with other children . . . which is afforded them at public school, leads . . . to the conclusion that they are not receiving education equivalent to that provided by the public schools.''

In a recent Minnesota case (*Minnesota* v. *Lundsten*), a court found another basis for permitting home instruction even where statutory requirements were not met. A state court overturned a jury verdict against Chester and Anvina Lundsten for violating a compulsory attendance statute, even though the Lundstens did not have the required teaching certificate. The court held that the statute as applied to them violated their constitutional rights of free exercise and privacy. Since there was evidence that they were providing quality education for their children, the state did not have a sufficiently compelling interest to overcome their free exercise rights.

WHAT DOES ALL THIS MEAN?

•There is no clear, constitutionally based right to home education, although the basis for such claims does exist.

•State laws may make specific provision for home education, including certain requirements for teachers, materials, and hours.

•State laws that are framed as equivalency statutes may provide the opportunity to demonstrate that the home education is academically equivalent. Many courts, but not all, will look sympathetically on such proof.

•State laws with no equivalency provisions pose the most difficult cases. Some judicial remedy is available by judicial determination that quality home instruction is a school.

•Courts are often sympathetic, even in the absence of specific statutory authorization, especially where religious rights are involved.

PERSONAL
LIBERTIES

19

Rights of Conscience

The protection of rights of conscience is basic to any free society and to the concept of religious freedom. The "dictates of conscience" must be given great weight in any freedom-loving society. The ability of people to live with integrity and moral consistency may, at times, overcome the governmental interest in mere conformity to the law.

While the language of the Constitution does not refer to conscience rights as such, the Free Exercise Clause and other provisions do embody and imply such rights. Many state constitutions specifically provide for such conscience-based rights. The Minnesota Constitution (Article I, Section 16) provides that "the right of every man to worship God according to the dictates of his own conscience shall never be infringed. . . ."

Thomas Jefferson, in his famous letter to the Danbury Baptists, referred to "this expression of the supreme will of the nation" as being "in behalf of the rights of conscience." The protection of rights of conscience was a central intent of the Religion Clauses of the Constitution, one which commended itself to a nation settled by people who had experienced considerable government interference with the dictates of conscience. Much suffering for the sake of conscience had also occurred within the colonies themselves.

Baptists had endured personal punishment, fines, and confiscation of properties in the Anglican-dominated southern colonies. Quakers, Catholics, and Methodists were also subjected to harassment and discrimination. One Anglican clergyman in Virginia, frustrated with the Methodist preachers' refusal to take the loyalty oaths required by individual states, declared that

179

if he were running things, he would "make their nasty stinking carcasses pay for their pretended scruples of conscience."[1]

Rights of conscience have perhaps always been resisted by people like that Anglican clergyman. Often the views of the majority are already expresssed in law, but the special sensitivities of minorities are rarely sanctioned or protected. The safeguarding of conscience claims is vital to any society that wishes religious liberty to extend beyond the popular religion.

John Adams, writing to his wife in 1775, declared, "Statesmen may plan and speculate for liberty, but it is religion and morality alone which can establish the principles upon which freedom can securely stand." And the celebrated European observer of early American society, Alexis de Tocqueville, declared that belief was essential to a democratic people. He then advised his reader, "When therefore any religion has struck its roots deep into a democracy, beware that you do not disturb it. . . ."

With the increasing secularism and religious diversity of American society, the protection of rights of conscience becomes urgent. The questions that courts and legislatures must face are not simple. They will test our resolve as a nation to recognize religious liberty and conscience against the prevailing secularist and humanist culture, and they will also test the dominant religious community's willingness to honor the conscience rights of others.

The range of issues where conscience-based exemptions from law arise is vast. To a large extent, many are legally unsettled. Among the myriad of issues are these:

- To what extent may a parent raise a religious/conscience objection to mandatory psychological testing in schools (or any other curricular component, e.g., sex education)?
- When a statute prohibits discrimination on the basis of marital status or sex, may a property owner (on conscience grounds) refuse to rent an apartment to an unmarried heterosexual couple or a homosexual couple?
- May persons object (on conscience grounds) to the payment of "war tax"—the portion of our taxes used to support the military?
- Can some religious sects (on religious grounds) be permitted, against state law, to handle poisonous snakes or take drugs in their worship services?

Courts or legislatures seem to accommodate conscience-based exemptions when they pose relatively little threat to the public goals of these mandatory actions. Thus, conscience claims by sincere, small groups are often honored.

Recently in Indiana several religious groups (including some Amish and the Pentecostal House of Prayer of Terre Haute) objected to an Indiana statute that required a photograph on driver's licenses. These groups objected on the basis of the prohibition in Exodus to "graven images" or "likenesses." This religious conviction was so strong that they would not drive if licenses with pictures were required of them. It was clear that this conviction was fundamental to their faith.

After hearing testimony, the trial court ordered that they be exempt from the photograph requirements. The state appealed, arguing that driving is a privilege subject to reasonable rules and regulations. But in 1978 the Indiana Supreme Court rejected the state's contentions, noting that the state had not shown a compelling interest for having photographs on licenses.

In other instances, conscience exemptions have come from legislatures, especially when it is evident that legislation will pose widespread conflicts with conscience. In 1973 Congress enacted a "conscience clause" to protect federally funded hospitals (most hospitals receive some federal funds) from being forced to perform abortions and to keep them from discriminating in employment or promotion of health care personnel because they refused to participate in abortions. Subsequent legislation extended these protections to health care training programs.

Two issues have produced considerable public debate or litigation: the right to conscientious objection to military service and the right of employees to act upon their religious beliefs. These issues illustrate the major concerns of all conscience claims: the role of legislation, the Supreme Court's attempt to apply constitutional principles, and the problems of seeking to accommodate religious belief under the Free Exercise Clause without creating an impermissible establishment of religion. Chapters twenty and twenty-one will examine these issues.

20

Conscientious Objection to Military Service

" ... No! We won't go" was a cry that shook our nation in the 1960s. The popular poster What If They Gave a War and Nobody Came? expressed one view of war and national policy. Youth resistance to the Vietnam War produced one of the most serious debates in American history about military service and moral/conscientious objection to war.

While the cries of the sixties have faded, the fundamental issues continue to surface. Reinstatement of draft registration in 1980 led to the suspicion that the draft was not far behind. The *New York Times* in June of 1980 declared, "People have under their belt the history of a bad war and the realization that they can say no to a bad war—that that's legitimate." There seems to be an increased sensitivity in many portions of the Christian community to the moral issues raised by war, especially the specter of nuclear conflict.

What are the rights of conscientious objectors? Is there a constitutional right to exemption? Must one belong to a religious group that believes in pacifism? What if you simply object to war on moral grounds? On political grounds? These are the questions that have shaped the rights to conscientious objector status.

HISTORY AND SOURCE OF EXEMPTION
The right to be a conscientious objector is a statutory right, and not a constitutional right. Its statutory origins go back over

one hundred years. The Draft Acts of 1864 and 1917 provided for such exemptions, the latter providing exemptions for those affiliated with a "well-recognized religious sect or organization . . . whose existing creed or principles forbade its members to participate in war in any form."

In 1940, Congress eliminated the requirement that an objector be a member of an organized church, but did require that the opposition must be based on "religious training and belief"—a phrase which has been the basis for significant judicial interpretation.

In 1948, Congress added an "individual belief in a relation to a Supreme Being" and a clause excluding those objections that were "essentially political, sociological or philosophic views, or a merely personal moral code." Thus, as of 1948, the statutory right required a belief in a supreme being and rejected personal, moral, philosophic, or political views; it also required that the objection be against "war in any form."

Three major court cases broadened these bases for obtaining CO status. In 1965, a suit was brought by three young men (*U.S.* v. *Seeger*) alleging that the requirement that one believe in a supreme being violated the Establishment and Free Exercise Clauses of the Constitution. The young men claimed that the refusal to exempt nonreligious COs and the discrimination between different forms of religious belief (theistic and nontheistic) created an impermissible establishment of religion. The Supreme Court declined to deal with this constitutional challenge, and instead focused on the interpretation of the statutory requirement of belief in a supreme being.

As the Court itself put the issue, "does the term 'Supreme Being' as used . . . mean the orthodox God or the broader concept of a power or being, or a faith, 'to which all else is subordinate or upon which all else is ultimately dependent'?" The Court then accepted the broader definition, and concluded that the requirement of belief in a supreme being was met by the following criterion: "A sincere and meaningful belief which occupies in the life of its possessor a place parallel to that filled by the God of those admittedly qualifying for the exemption. . . ."

Under this test, the three young men qualified, since each had expressed some such faith. One indicated he believed in "Godness," which was the "ultimate cause for the fact of being in the universe." Another held a "religious faith in a purely ethical creed." Based on this decision, the government dropped its requirement of a belief in a supreme being in 1967.

In 1970, the Supreme Court was faced with another conscientious objector case, one that pressed the issue of religious belief even harder than *Seeger*. Eliot A. Welsh specifically denied that his beliefs were religious, having in fact crossed out the word *religious* on his application. Welsh claimed that the requirements violated the Religion Clauses of the Constitution by favoring religious objections. Over the dissent of Justice Harlan, the Court refused to deal with these claims.

Instead it focused as it had in *Seeger* on reinterpreting the language of the statute. The Court declined to put "undue emphasis on the registrant's interpretation of his own beliefs" as not religious, and held that he qualified, within the "broad scope of the word religious." The Court held that the requirement of a religious basis for exemption was simply to exclude those "whose beliefs are not deeply held and those whose objection to war does not rest on moral, ethical or religious principle but instead rests solely upon considerations of policy, pragmatism or expedience." The Court then established the test for entitlement to CO status: "This section exempts from military service all those whose conscience, spurred by deeply held moral, ethical or religious beliefs, would give no rest or peace if they allowed themselves to become part of an instrument of war."

The final case, *Gillette* v. *U.S.* (decided with *Negre* v. *Larsen*) raised the issue of selective objection to war. Both defendants objected not to war in any form, but specifically to the Vietnam War. They alleged that the "war in any form" limitation impermissibly discriminated against certain religious beliefs, such as those historic beliefs of the Catholic church, which distinguish between just and unjust wars.

Such beliefs, they argued, were as worthy of protection as other religious beliefs; to deny them such protection violated their constitutional rights. The Supreme Court in 1971 again rejected these Religion Clause challenges to the statutes, and held that the statute was neutral on its face. The provisions did not, the Court found, violate the Establishment Clause since there was a "governmental interest of a kind and weight sufficient to justify under the Free Exercise Clause the impact of the conscription laws on those who object to particular wars."

One can note, therefore, the substantial broadening of the basis for CO status by court decisions, from a specific belief in God to a more general sort of ultimate commitment. But the Court has been unwilling to either invalidate the religious basis of the exemption on constitutional grounds or to strike down its provisions as discriminating between religions. The Court has also been unwilling to find a free exercise right to such exemption or to open the door to selective objection, even though the moral character and religious origins of such claims are well established. The Supreme Court's method of dealing with this issue reflects its reluctance to engage in constitutional adjudication when the matter may be resolved by statutory interpretation.

21

Religious Beliefs in the Work Force

Adell Sherbert, a Seventh Day Adventist, was fired from her job as a textile-mill operator because her religious beliefs would not allow her to work on Saturday. After two years of working for the company, her work week was suddenly increased from five to six days. Adell refused to work on Saturdays and was fired. In the next weeks she was unable to find employment that did not require her to work on Saturdays at the three other mills in the Spartanburg, South Carolina area.

But when she filed a claim for unemployment benefits, they were denied on the grounds that she had refused to make herself available for suitable work when it was offered to her. In filing her unemployment claim, she had expressed a willingness to accept employment at other mills, or even in another industry, so long as Saturday work was not required. Adell challenged the denial of benefits. This first major court test of employee rights of conscience (*Sherbert* v. *Verner,* 1963) has become a major policy statement on accommodation to religious beliefs.

In this case the Supreme Court was forced to decide whether or not Adell Sherbert's refusal to accept Saturday employment, which would have forced her to act against her conscience, was a sufficient basis for denying her claim for unemployment benefits. Or must her genuine religious beliefs be taken into account and accommodated by the state?

In what many constitutional commentators have seen as a major shift, the Supreme Court declared that only "the gravest abuses, endangering paramount interests'' could give occasion for the limitation of free exercise rights. The ruling held that the state had failed to show a compelling state interest critical enough to overcome Adell Sherbert's religious rights of free exercise.

The Court, in language widely quoted in subsequent arguments and cases, declared:

> Here not only is it apparent that appellant's declared ineligibility for benefits derived solely from the practice of her religion, but the pressure upon her to forego that practice is unmistakable. The ruling [of the lower court] forces her to choose between following precepts of her religion and forfeiting benefits, on the one hand, and abandoning one of the precepts of her religion to accept work, on the other hand. Government imposition of such a choice puts the same kind of burden upon the free exercise of religion as would a fine imposed against the appellant for her Saturday worship.

The *Sherbert* decision, whose impact extends far beyond the employment context, shows that it is not enough for the state to be merely neutral. The state should provide accommodating exemptions for religion if at all possible. The test is whether the state has used the least restrictive means to achieve a legitimate purpose. Courts have held that the state's interest in efficiency is not necessarily a compelling interest.

The principles of *Sherbert* were reaffirmed in an April 1981 decision of the Supreme Court, *Thomas* v. *Review Board*. Eddie C. Thomas is a Jehovah's Witness who believes that he should not participate in war or the production of war weapons. The foundry in which he worked closed a year after he was employed, so the company transferred Thomas to another department that made turrets for tanks. Thomas's religious beliefs would not permit such employment, so he sought another transfer. But all available jobs similarly involved making armaments.

When the company refused to lay him off, he quit and sought unemployment benefits. The hearing officer for the state determined that Thomas had quit for religious reasons, but the termination was not for "good cause" as required by state law. Hence Thomas was denied benefits.

The Indiana Court of Appeals reversed, but the Supreme Court of Indiana denied him benefits, holding that he quit for personal and philosophic reasons, not religious ones. Even if his reasons were religious he did not quit for good cause, the court declared. If the court gave benefits to Thomas, it would disrupt the integrity of the unemployment insurance plan and violate the Establishment Clause.

The United States Supreme Court by eight-to-one reversed. While noting the difficult and delicate task of determining sincere religious beliefs, the court affirmed that such a determination must be made independent of the Court's view of the logic, consistency, or acceptability of those views. "Courts," Justice Burger declared for the majority, "are not arbiters of scriptural interpretation." Thus the fact that some Jehovah's Witnesses would not agree with Thomas (other fellow believers continued to work for the company) was not evidence that Thomas's views were only personal.

STATUTORY PROTECTIONS

Today the Civil Rights Act of 1964 is the basis for considerable freedom for religious accommodation. Title VII of the Act attempts to root out religious discrimination in the private sector of employment. The Civil Rights Act of 1964 makes it unlawful for an employer to refuse to hire, discharge, or discriminate against a person on the basis of a variety of factors, including religion. Congress also declared it was an unlawful employment practice for a labor organization (union) to discriminate against an individual because of his religion or to cause an employer to discriminate for this reason.

In 1967, the U. S. Equal Employment Opportunity Commission (EEOC) adopted guidelines on discrimination on the basis of religion. These guidelines contained the employer's specific obligation to accommodate the religious practices of his employees so long as they do not impose an undue hardship. In 1972 Congress adopted an amendment to Title VII clarifying the scope of accommodation. The amendment gives broad scope to religious practices. It states that "the term 'religion' includes all aspects of religious observance and practice, as well as belief, unless an employer demonstrates that he is unable to reasonably accommodate an employee's or prospective employee's religious observance or practice without undue hardship on the conduct of the employer's business.''

Discrimination does not require "ill will" or necessarily "unequal treatment," but is directed at the "consequences or effects" of an employment practice or system. Consequences, not motives, are the test (*Griggs* v. *Duke Power Co., 1971*).

To establish a case under the Civil Rights Act of 1964 and its subsequent amendments, the complaining party must show three elements: first, the existence of a bona fide, sincerely held religious belief that is affected by the employment-related action. Secondly, notice of the conflict must be given to the employer. Finally, it must be proven that a discharge or other adverse action was taken against the employee.

Once these facts have been established, the employer or union must demonstrate that good faith efforts were made to accommodate the religious beliefs of the employee, and that these efforts were unsuccessful because the accommodation was not possible without undue hardship. The courts have not provided clear guidance on what constitutes *undue hardship*. The Court in *Trans World Airlines* v. *Hardison* seemed to suggest that accommodation that would require more than a small expenditure constituted undue hardship.

In 1981, the EEOC fashioned a new "Guideline on Discrimination Because of Religion." These guidelines are intended to clarify the scope of required accommodation in the light of some confusion after *Trans World Airlines*. The guidelines provide the following:

> *Reasonable Accommodation*
> (1) After an employee or prospective employee notifies the employer or labor organization of his or her need for a religious accommodation, the employer or labor organization has an obligation to reasonably accommodate the individual's religious practices. A refusal to accommodate is justified only when an employer or labor organization can demonstrate that an undue hardship would in fact result from each available alternative

method of accommodation. A mere assumption that many more people, with the same religious practices as the person being accommodated, may also need accommodation is not evidence of undue hardship.

(2) When there is more than one method of accommodation available which would not cause undue hardship, the Commission will determine whether the accommodation offered is reasonable by examining:

(i) The alternatives for accommodation considered by the employer or labor organization; and

(ii) The alternatives for accommodation, if any, actually offered to the individual requiring accommodation.

Alternatives for Accommodating Religious Practices

(1) Employees and prospective employees most frequently request an accommodation because their religious practices conflict with their work schedules. The following subsections are some means of accommodating the conflict between work schedules and religious practices which the Commission believes that employers and labor organizations should consider as part of the obligation to accommodate and which the Commission will consider in investigating a charge. These are not intended to be all-inclusive.

(i) Voluntary Substitutes and "Swaps".

Reasonable accommodation without undue hardship is generally possible where a voluntary substitute with substantially similar qualifications is available. One means of substitution is the voluntary swap. In a number of cases, the securing of a substitute has been left entirely up to the individual seeking the accommodation. The Commission believes that the obligation to accommodate requires that employers and labor organizations facilitate the securing of a voluntary substitute with substantially similar qualifications. Some means of doing this which employers and labor organizations should consider are: to publicize policies regarding accommodation and voluntary substitution; to promote an atmosphere in which such substitutions are favorably regarded; to provide a central file, bulletin board or other means for matching voluntary substitutes with positions from which substitutes are needed.

(ii) Flexible Scheduling.

One means of providing reasonable accommodation for the religious practices of employees or prospective employees which employers and labor organizations should consider is the creation of a flexible work schedule for individuals requesting accommodation.

The following list is an example of areas in which flexibility might be introduced: flexible arrival and departure times; floating or optional holidays; flexible work breaks; use of lunch time in exchange for early departure; staggered work hours; and permitting an employee to make up time lost due to the observance of religious practices.

(iii) Lateral Transfer and Change of Job Assignments

When an employee cannot be accommodated either as to his or her entire job or an assignment within the job, employers and labor organizations should consider whether or not it is possible to change the job assignment or give the employee a lateral transfer.

Payment of Dues to a Labor Organization

Some collective bargaining agreements include a provision that each employee must join the labor organization or pay the labor organization a sum equivalent to dues. When an employee's religious practices do not permit compliance with such a provision, the labor organization should accommodate the employee by not requiring the employee to join the organization and by permitting him or her to donate a sum equivalent to dues to a charitable organization.

Undue Hardship
(1) Cost.

An employer may assert undue hardship to justify a refusal to accommodate an employee's need to be absent from his or her scheduled duty hours if the employer can demonstrate that the accommodation would require "more than a *de minimis* cost". The Commission will determine what constitutes "more than a *de minimis* cost" with due regard given to the identifiable cost in relation to the size and operating cost of the employer, and the number of individuals who will in fact need a particular accommodation. The Commission interprets this phrase as it was used in the *Hardison* decision to mean that costs similar to the regular payment of premium wages of substitutes, which was at issue in *Hardison,* would constitute undue hardship. However, the Commission will presume that the infrequent payment of premium wages for a substitute or the payment of premium wages while a more permanent accommodation is being sought are costs which an employer can be required to bear as a means of providing a reasonable accommodation. The Commission will presume that generally administrative costs necessary for providing the accommodation will not constitute more than a *de minimis* cost. Administrative costs, for example, include those costs involved in rearranging schedules and recording substitutions for payroll purposes.

(2) Seniority Rights. Undue hardship would also be shown where a variance from a bona

fide seniority system is necessary in order to accommodate an employee's religious practices
when doing so would deny another employee
his or her job or shift preference guaranteed by
that system.

Selection practices
   (1) The duty to accommodate pertains to prospective employees as well as current
employees. Consequently, an employer may
not permit an applicant's need for a religious
accommodation to affect in any way its decision whether to hire the applicant unless it can
demonstrate that it cannot reasonably accommodate the applicant's religious practices
without undue hardship. . . .
   (2) The Commission will infer that the need
for an accommodation discriminatorily influenced a decision to reject an applicant when:
(i) prior to an offer of employment the
employer makes an inquiry into an applicant's
availability without having a business necessity
justification; and (ii) after the employer has
determined the applicant's need for an accommodation, the employer rejects a qualified applicant. The burden is then on the employer to
demonstrate that factors other than the need
for an accommodation were the reason for rejecting the qualified applicant, or that a
reasonable accommodation without undue
hardship was not possible.

LABOR UNION MEMBERSHIP

Recent cases and an amendment to the National Labor
Relations Act have provided clear rights for religiously based exemptions from membership in labor unions. In December 1980,
President Carter signed into law H. R. 4774, commonly referred
to as the "Conscience Clause." The act amends the National
Labor Relations Act and provides that any employee who is a
member of a religion or sect historically holding conscientious
objections to joining or financially supporting a labor organiza-

tion shall not be required to do so. But such an employee "may be required in a contract between [the] employer and a labor organization in lieu of periodic dues and initiation fees to pay sums equal to such dues and initiation fees to a nonreligious, nonlabor organization charitable fund exempt from taxation."

The stipulation is also made that if the employee "requests the labor organization to use the grievance-arbitration procedure on [his] behalf, the labor organization is authorized to charge the employee for the reasonable cost of using such procedure."

While this provision assures substantial protection for persons who belong to groups with historic objections to union membership, it provides no protection for individuals who do not belong to such a group. The fact that the statute is so narrowly drawn has raised questions regarding its constitutionality. Does the statute's favoritism to traditional religious groups without similar protection to other sincere views constitute the impermissible establishment of some religious views to the exclusion of others? Does this, then, deny equal protection and due process rights?

Several cases in recent years have also provided protection for individuals who do not belong to traditional religious groups. Bob Gervais, a young employee of International Harvester in New Hampshire, objected to taking an oath of allegiance to the Teamsters Union as a condition to keeping his job. While Bob did not have formal religious beliefs against oath-taking, he resisted the requirements and the wording of the oath. The Teamsters asked International Harvester to fire Bob.

Charges were filed against the Teamsters on Bob's behalf, based in part on the Supreme Court's ruling in *National Labor Relations Board* v. *General Motors* (1963). The Court had held that while membership in a union may be required for employment, such membership may consist only of paying the requisite dues. Membership, as a condition of employment, was "whittled down to its financial core."

The Teamsters withdrew their request that Bob be fired, and posted a notice that formal membership was not a requirement of employment. Gervais's case represents a well-established principle that formal membership is not required if the employee is willing to forward the requisite payments.

But what if you object to the way union monies are used?

The Court faced this issue in *Abood* v. *Detroit Board of Education* (1977). Anne Parks had been an employee of the Detroit school system for forty-three years. In 1969 the Detroit Federation of Teachers was named the bargaining agent for the teachers, and according to the contract that was negotiated, all teachers were required to join the union or pay an equivalent fee.

When Anne Parks refused to pay more than her share of the cost of negotiating and administering the contract, she was advised that she would be terminated. A suit was filed on her behalf. She argued that she should not be forced to pay costs that contributed to union activities she strongly objected to—including political activities and candidates supported by the union. The Supreme Court agreed. While Dr. Parks's beliefs were not religious, the principles are applicable to those whose convictions emerge from religious commitments.

It is clear that the courts and the Congress have been sensitive to religious beliefs in the context of employment and have allowed, by statute and case law, provisions for exemptions from objectionable requirements. They have also given strong impetus to the concept of the duty of government and employers to accommodate the religious beliefs of employees by affirmative action. In an increasingly pluralistic society, such accommodation may be difficult at times, but it is even more critical as an index of our country's commitment to religious liberty.

22
Free Speech
and Evangelism

Willie Harmon was active in Youth for New Life, a Christian ministry that focused on evangelistic witness in the streets of Chicago. Willie frequently distributed tracts near a local bar, The Watering Hole. Apparently this irritated the owner who insisted that Willie leave. When he refused, the proprietor called a policeman, who ordered Willie to, "Move along." Willie again refused. He was arrested for refusing to obey a police officer and for littering and obstructing a public thoroughfare.

Jane Thiesen was the leader of a church youth group in a mid-Atlantic state. Jane encouraged the youth to express their faith openly by verbal witness, literature distribution, and a music and drama group, which was informally organized.

One Saturday afternoon Jane accompanied the youngsters to a local shopping center where the drama group performed brief contemporary versions of biblical parables as the others distributed tracts to interested bystanders. Soon an official from the mall management office insisted that the group cease their performance and distribution of literature. He threatened to charge them with trespassing.

In order to reach kids in new communities, another Christian group, Little People for Jesus, drove a sound truck through neighborhoods announcing Bible club meetings at nearby public parks. They occasionally parked the truck across from a local grade school, and announced the Bible studies to children in the playground. Police received complaints from residents who objected to the noise, from some who objected to the Bible clubs in the public park, and from school officials who objected to the intrusion on the school recess and play time.

These incidents, slightly fictionalized from real cases, illustrate some of the legal issues that relate to evangelism and the public ministry and witness of believers.

Evangelism is not simply central to Christian faith—in many ways it is the Christian faith. Christianity is good news, a proclamation. Most religious faith is declaratory, prophetic, and public. Thus the Christian faith is always inviting, urging, seeking to persuade and convince. From the time of the apostles, this "witness" has created both converts and antagonism. Some walked away. Others argued. A few became involved in personal or governmental attempts to silence the witness of believers. When government sought to silence Peter's witness, he defiantly declared, "We must obey God rather than men."

The right to evangelize is a crucial freedom. Religious freedom has always included both the private right to believe and the right to communicate. By contrast, the Soviet Constitution provides for the protection of religious beliefs in theory, but reserves the right to evangelize to atheism.

All totalitarian regimes and systems hostile to religious faith seek to constrict evangelistic activity. They know they can cut the core out of faith and its future by allowing persons to believe, but prohibiting the propagation of those beliefs.

There are trends in our public life that make it necessary to ensure that our evangelistic freedom is not diminished. The secularism of our day looks with suspicion on religious belief and conversion. Secular humanists are likely to seek to confine religion geographically or to limit any religious witness to the young or to persons in the care of the state (psychiatric patients, hospital patients, prisoners, child care programs, etc.).

The emergence of aggressive new religious movements, which proselytize vigorously, has created a widespread resistance to all the evangelistic efforts of religious people. If the public's reaction to the Hare Krishnas or the Unification Church is any key, one can see how easily religious proselytizing would be restricted if the ideas seem strange or if youth are challenged to reject the values of the dominant social group. Policies we would all deplore if applied by the Soviet Union against Christians are hailed at times as legitimate. Mere offensiveness and uniqueness—or even blatant error—are never sufficient to warrant restrictions on religious liberty. After all, Christians are a peculiar people. Our values are likely to increasingly be seen as odd and out of step with that of our culture.

FREE SPEECH GUARANTEES

Religious freedoms often entail other constitutional liberties beside the Religion Clauses we have reviewed at length. The primary source of the right of evangelism and proclamation is found in the free speech protection of the First Amendment. Other constitutional protections are due process, equal protection, rights of assembly, and privacy rights. Particularly in education, the Equal Protection Clause guarantees and free speech guarantees are, in some specific contexts, more powerful bases for religious liberty rights than is the Free Exercise Clause.

The Free Speech Clause of the First Amendment is part of a general clause, which contains important protections on rights of communication and expression. Specifically the clause provides that: "Congress shall make no law . . . abridging freedom of speech, or of the press, or the right of people peacefully to assemble. . . ."

Laurence Tribe, the Harvard professor of law, has written that the Free Speech Clause is the "most majestic guarantee" of our constitutional structure. It is a cornerstone of all liberty. Justice Harlan declared in 1971 that the constitutional right of expression is based on "putting the decision as to what views shall be voiced largely into the hands of each of us . . . in the belief that no other approach would comport with the premise of individual dignity and choice upon which our political system rests."

The concept arises as well from the conviction that truth is best served by free expression, that as Justice Oliver Wendell Holmes declared in 1919, ". . .the ultimate good desired is better reached by free trade in ideas—that the best test of truth is the power of the thought to get itself accepted in the competition of the market. . . ."

So important is this right of free speech that it holds (with other First Amendment rights) what is often called a "preferred position"—a right that requires most careful scrutiny whenever attempts are made to constrict its scope.

THE RIGHT TO WITNESS OR EVANGELIZE

The Free Speech Clause clearly protects the right to communicate one's faith, to invite persons to believe, and to publicly attempt to proselytize and convert. This protection involves activity on government property—streets, parks, airports—or activity that competes with restrictive laws related to traffic, noise, public assembly, or littering. Speech protections do not normally apply to expression on private property.

This right of free speech extends beyond formal speech to include other forms of expression as well. First, it includes the right not to speak or communicate. Thus courts have upheld conscientious objection to "forced" communications. In New Hampshire, a motorist challenged a state requirement that he display a license plate bearing the motto Live Free or Die. The Supreme Court in *Wooley* v. *Maynard* (1977) held that the state could not force the motorist to display this "speech."

Second, the right to speech and association includes the right not to associate. One cannot be forced to associate with an organization or support the promotion of its ideologies through fees. Hence, the Supreme Court held that a union cannot use a member's compulsory union dues to support political candidates or views the member disagrees with that are unrelated to collective bargaining.

Thirdly, the right to speak applies to both the source and recipient—the right to hear is a corollary of the right to speak.

The right to speak also includes the protection of conduct that is incidental to speech. The distribution of membership application forms, the setting up facilities for a meeting, etc., are actions that are also entitled to free speech protection.

Fifth, the free speech protections include certain actions, which have been held to be symbolic speech. The First Amendment does not, however, protect all symbolic speech simply because it is related to the attempt to communicate an idea. The Supreme Court has upheld the prohibition of draft-card burning, noting that the prohibition was not simply to suppress communication but to assist in the orderly functioning of the draft system. On the other hand, the Supreme Court overturned an attempt to prohibit high school students from wearing black armbands to protest the Vietnam War. The Court held that the conduct was "akin to free speech," and that the state had not shown that such conduct caused any substantial interference with the functioning of the school (*Tinker* v. *Des Moines*).

FREE SPEECH NOT ABSOLUTE

Though free speech rights occupy a preferred position, the right is not absolute, as the popular expression "You can't holler 'fire' in a crowded theater" acknowledges.

Free speech rights may be limited when the content of the speech creates a "clear and present danger" to society. This is the test frequently applied in the context of political and revolutionary speech. Obscenity is also not protected by the Free Speech Clause, though problems of definitional clarity have often made limiting speech on this basis difficult.

The states may reasonably regulate the use of public places (such as streets and parks) to protect the rights of the community at large. These regulations include keeping the streets open for traffic, preserving peace and order, and limiting the amount of noise and inconvenience caused to others.

The state may regulate the time, place, and manner of the speech, provided the regulations serve some significant governmental interest. For example, the state could adopt an ordinance limiting public speaking in the parks to daylight hours. But the limitations must be the least restrictive means to achieve the state's legitimate purpose. A city could not totally ban a Nazi parade on the grounds it would incite violence if other alternatives for controlling violence exist, which are less intrusive upon the important free speech liberty. The regulations must not be so broad as to effectively deny the opportunity for communication. Adequate alternatives must be made available.

Regulations and limits on free speech that seek to limit the content of speech in advance are scrutinized most carefully by the courts. In general, the government cannot constitutionally regulate in advance what expressions may be uttered or published—even if such utterances would be defamations or obscenities. This is *prior restraint*—an act of government, which in advance of any judicial determination that the speech is unprotected restrains its expression. Any statute involving a form of prior restraint bears a heavy presumption against its constitutionality.

Finally, any regulations or restraints on free speech will be held invalid if they are "overbroad" or "vague." For instance, the scope of a regulation may be overbroad (such as prohibiting all membership in certain groups) or the language may be vague or imprecise. Such "standardless" statutes are dangerous because they permit law enforcement agencies to be selective and discriminatory. Courts strike down such impediments on the grounds that they have the effect of broadly "chilling" the exercise of free speech.

For example, the Supreme Court struck down a Cincinnati, Ohio, ordinance that made it a crime for three or more persons to assemble on the sidewalks "and there conduct themselves in a manner annoying to persons passing by." The Court held the statute was vague, violated rights of assembly, and invited discriminatory and arbitrary enforcement.

FREE SPEECH AND PUBLIC PLACES

The accessibility of public property for speech purposes is controlled by the concept of the public forum (property owned or used by the government that is suitable for the exercise of free speech). Not all public property is a public forum (see chapter 15). For example, the White House, though publicly owned, is not suitable for the exercise of free speech, nor is the war room of the Pentagon.

Streets, sidewalks, and public parks are perhaps the oldest public forums. They have been long recognized as proper places for assembly, speech, and discussion. The broadest rights of free speech are allowed in these forums. One is free to give speeches, distribute literature, carry placards, and form a parade within legitimate time, manner, and place limitations.

Recent decisions of some courts have also held that airports are public forums. However, due to their primary purpose of handling heavy traffic flow, airport authorities are permitted to restrict free speech activities to certain locations. Other mass transportation terminals that are publicly owned have also been held to be public forums, such as bus and mass transport terminals.

Public education campuses are also public forums. In *Keegan* v. *University of Delaware,* the Delaware Supreme Court held that the university was a public forum, and university officials could not prohibit religious meetings from occurring in the dormitory commons. High school campuses are a more limited form of public forum; courts have permitted serious restrictions on religious communications in high schools.

In December of 1981, the Supreme Court handed down its decision in a crucial case, *Widmar* v. *Vincent,* which involved the free speech rights of Christian students at public universities. The University of Missouri-Kansas City attempted to prohibit Cornerstone, a student organization, from using university facilities for religious worship and meetings. To allow religious groups access to facilities would constitute an impermissible aid to religion, the university said. Religious worship was not protected speech.

The Supreme Court rejected the university's argument, and held that whenever a university opens its facilities and creates a public forum, it can not discriminate on the basis of the content of the speech. The university could not constitutionally allow student political and social groups to meet, and refuse the same access to religious students.

The Court declared that religious worship is a protected form of speech. This inclusion of worship as protected speech represents a vital protection for religious persons and the expression of their faith.

PERMITS AND REGISTRATIONS

May the state require you to obtain a permit or registration before you can exercise free speech rights in a public forum? Yes, if it is essential for order. Permit requirements that are designed to prevent scheduled events in a public park from overlapping are permissible. But if the permit system is an attempt to control the content of speech or if it leaves broad discretion to the government official as to whether to grant the permit, it is probably unconstitutional. Such permits allow the system to operate as a censor over the content of speech.

Similarly, registration before the exercise of free speech rights in an airport is probably constitutional, providing such registration is intended to give notice to airport officials that a person or group is present in the facility. However, the registration system must not function so as to burden free speech rights.

The Seventh Circuit Court of Appeals ruled that a daily, thirty-minute registration period at Chicago airports acted as a total prohibition on those who were not able to appear during the designated half hour. Therefore, it was unconstitutional. Likewise, in a case involving Jews for Jesus, a Portland, Oregon, statute was declared unconstitutional because it required advance notice of one business day to exercise free speech rights at the Oregon airport and the disclosure of the names, addresses, and phone numbers of the persons involved. The statute was seen as a prior restraint and an unjustified burden on free speech rights.

SOUND AMPLIFICATION AND LEAFLET DISTRIBUTION

While a total ban on the use of loudspeakers has been held unconstitutional, governmental entities may regulate the time, place, and volume of sound amplification, in order to preserve community tranquility and traffic safety. Loudspeakers might constitutionally be banned near schools and hospitals, and limits placed on the decibel level and the hours of use in residential neighborhoods.

Leaflet distribution has long been recognized as part of the exercise of free speech and is allowed in almost every public forum. Persons may not be barred from knocking on doors to distribute literature, nor may leaflet distribution be banned merely because it creates litter (*Martin* v. *City of Struthers,* 1943). The person cannot be lawfully arrested for littering and does not have a legal duty to pick up leaflets others have dropped (though most groups attempt to do so). Municipalities may, however, prohibit the distribution of literature.

In 1981, the Supreme Court decided an important case having potential effects on religious proselytizing and leaflet distribution. In *Heffron* v. *ISKCON,* the Supreme Court upheld a Minnesota State Fair rule that limited all distribution of literature and solicitation of funds to those with booths provided by the fairgrounds. The Hare Krishnas had challenged such requirements as a violation of rights of free speech. But the Court held that while the Krishna members were free to mingle with the crowd and discuss their viewpoints, they were not free to solicit contributions or distribute literature. The state's interest in the orderly movement and control of the crowds justified limiting the distribution of literature to the booths, which were available for rent on a nondiscriminatory basis. The fair was, the Court said, "a limited public forum."

While the decision does not necessarily invalidate literature distribution at all state fairs, it does seem to provide the opportunity for other fairs to adopt similar rules. Whether the *Hef-*

fron rationale will be limited to large fairs with limited space or extend to other public forums that are congested by large crowds will be important to watch.

EVANGELISM, FREE SPEECH, AND PRIVATE PROPERTY

The First Amendment does not generally provide free speech rights on private property, nor does the free exercise right extend to private property and relationships except where special interests have created statutory rights.

An exception to this is private property that has been held (because of its use and history) to be like a public forum. In 1946, the Supreme Court heard an appeal from a Jehovah's Witness who had been arrested for violating a state trespassing ordinance. The person had been distributing religious literature on the streets of a company-owned town in Alabama.

Though the town's streets were privately owned, the Supreme Court (*Marsh* v. *Alabama*) ruled that they were in effect a public place, and that neither the state nor a private owner could totally ban freedom of expression in such places. Nor can state trespassing laws be used to enforce any attempted ban by the owners. Justice Black observed, "the more an owner for his own advantage opens up his property for use by the public in general, the more do his rights become circumscribed by the statutory and constitutional rights of those who use it."

PRIVATELY OWNED SHOPPING CENTERS

When the Supreme Court initially dealt with the exercise of free speech rights in shopping centers, it held that a shopping center was analogous to a company town as in *Marsh*. But later cases have seen a retreat from this view. Courts have held that privately owned shopping centers are not proper forums for the exercise of free speech. Only those First Amendment exercises that are related to the function of the shopping center are allowed. Thus union picketing against business practices in the shopping center would be permitted. But antiwar leaflet distribution was rejected in *Lloyd Corp.* v. *Tanner*. The rejection of a pubic forum notion for shopping centers was solidified in *Hudgens* v. *NLRB* (1976).

But what if you're in California? In a 1980 decision, *Pruneyard* v. *Robins,* the Supreme Court held that California may, on the basis of its state constitution, grant free speech access to a privately owned shopping center without violating the owner's federal property or free speech rights. Thus, in California, most shopping centers can be forums for broader exercise of First Amendment rights than those in other states with less permissive constitutions.

PRIVATE COLLEGES

The Supreme Court dismissed an appeal of a decision of a lower court (*New Jersey* v. *Schmid*) that a trespassing conviction of a person for distributing political literature on the Princeton campus violated New Jersey's constitutional speech and assembly rights. The New Jersey court based its decision on the state constitution and not on the First Amendment. When a university opens itself to the public and encourages their presence, it may not seek to constrict that right by preventing the very exchange of information and ideas it sought to establish. Whether this position will be adopted by other states is unclear. But the decision is highly significant for the exercise of First Amendment rights and evangelistic activities.

EVANGELISM AND THE
WORK ENVIRONMENT

To what extent do free speech rights extend to your working place? Can a worker be dismissed or disciplined for the content of speech during work time?

These questions have an immediate relevance for many persons who seek to witness on the job. But the answers are not totally clear.

All speech, including any religious speech, may certainly be subject to reasonable rules concerning permitted activities during work hours. If, for example, talking is not permitted in certain areas or at certain times, that restriction—if valid—would apply to religious conversation as well.

However, if general conversation is allowed throughout the day, it is unclear whether or not an employer could ban certain categories of speech. If the employer could show that religious discussions (or a particular person's religious conversations) produced disruption and interfered with work, then such restrictions would seem valid. Often the restrictions are only applied when employees have complained of being harassed or bothered by persistent religious witnessing. But an employer would seem to have little justification for regulating the speech of employees in nonwork times such as breaks and lunch hours.

While the free speech protections do not normally apply to private property, there are several legal bases for such rights in the work place. If the employer is a government entity or has sufficient involvement with the government through contracts or funding, the employee might claim the actions of the employer are "state actions" (actions of the government), and thus subject to the constitutional guarantees of free speech, free exercise, and other relevant provisions.

Employees may also argue that any discipline or dismissal because of evangelistic witness was religious discrimination, which is prohibited under Title VII of the Civil Rights Act of 1964. The Act prohibits discrimination based on religion, and covers employers having at least fifteen employees. Many states have similar statutes, and those may extend to employers with less than fifteen employees. Union contracts or other employer-employee contracts may also bar religious discrimination.

PUBLIC EMPLOYEES

In 1977 a supervisor, who was in charge of evaluating employee efficiency, was suspended for three days for discussing religious matters with subordinates during work hours. The workers had complained to the supervisor's department head that they felt intimidated by the discussions and pressured to accept the supervisor's religious beliefs. The department head ordered the supervisor to cease religious discussion, except during coffee breaks or lunch hours. When the supervisor violated this order, he was suspended for three days, which he said violated his rights of freedom of speech and religion.

The Washington State Supreme Court did not directly address the speech claims, but the court upheld the suspension because the supervisor was an employee of the state of Washington, which had a compelling interest in remaining neutral in matters of religion (*Kallas* v. *Department of Motor Vehicles*). The court noted that the employee was a supervisor, and that the religious discussions occurred during work hours.

This decision reflects the various factors that are likely to be weighed: the potential for pressure or intimidation by supervisory personnel and the time of the discussions, whether during work hours or the employee's free time.

In a Virginia case now in the courts, an employee is challenging the disciplinary action of a government-funded private employer. The employee refused to sign a policy statement that prohibited religious discussion (among other things) with current or former clients or volunteers of the agency, including off-the-job letters on private stationery.

As you can see, most problems related to evangelism on the job are issues of style and appropriateness and not law. Activities that tend to produce complaints from fellow employees might well be scrutinized for their effectiveness.

23

Clergy Malpractice: Who Writes the Definitions?

The year is 1990. Times are tough. You lost your job five months ago and have been unable to find work. With each passing day your depression deepens. Finally you go to your pastor for counseling. On the door of his office you read this sign:

> ATTENTION COUNSELEE
>
> Due to potential lawsuits for spiritual malpractice, we are no longer available to deal with anything other than clearly superficial problems. We suggest the use of prayer and Scripture, but you do so at your own risk.
>
> If government-sponsored counseling services are unavailable, due to a lack of mental health funds, and you cannot afford private psychiatric care, a list of possible churches that may be insured is available upon request at the front office after signing A Release from Referral Liability. If your problem is urgent and really serious, please be assured our prayers are with you. We wish you "God speed" and hope you will visit when you are better.

This notice might seem a little exaggerated. Yet if spiritual-counseling malpractice lawsuits are permitted, one possible consequence might be the posting of disclaimer signs, warning the "consumer" of the subjective nature of the cure.

The possibility of clergy malpractice suits began in the fall of 1979, when a story circulated through the insurance and religious media that a clergyman had been sued and held liable in a "clergy malpractice" case. The story was initiated by the insurance industry, apparently to generate interest in a new product known as "clergy malpractice insurance." The story was false. But the seed was planted.

In March of 1980, the seed bore fruit in a much-publicized suit in California (*Nally* v. *Grace Community Church of the Valley*), brought by the parents of a twenty-four-year-old seminary student who had committed suicide in 1979. The Nallys sued the largest Protestant congregation in Los Angeles County and its staff, alleging clergy malpractice, negligence, and outrageous conduct. This was the first case of its kind.

The complaint alleged that the church and its staff had counseled the student to read the Bible, pray, listen to taped sermons, and counsel with church counselors rather than consulting a professional psychiatrist or psychologist. Further, the church had been negligent in the training, selection, and hiring of its lay spiritual counselors who were unavailable to counsel the young man upon his request.

Finally, the suit alleged that the church had ridiculed the parents' religion, faith, and belief. This, they said, deepened their son's preexisting feelings of guilt, anxiety, and depression.

A year and a half later, the church succeeded in having the case summarily dismissed. The court found that there was no substance to the allegations, and ordered the Nallys to reimburse the church for the costs incurred in defending this suit.

Counseling by pastors, priests, rabbis, and other spiritual counselors is not new. For nearly 2,000 years, the clergy and others have provided the balm for those suffering from depression, guilt, and anxiety. Only in relatively recent times have psychiatrists and psychologists begun to offer theories and remedies.

Should ministers be subjected to malpractice suits? Or is spiritual counseling different from medical and legal consultation?

The religious community should not expect special treatment when the conduct in question has little or nothing to do with its religious or spiritual mission. The liability arising out of traditional theories of personal injury, battery, assault, or property ownership should not differ simply because the defendant happens to be a religious organization or a clergyman. But when the conduct flows directly from a religious and spiritual mission, it does not seem proper for the state to judge the clergy's counsel.

Serious problems will emerge if the courts choose to accept clergy malpractice suits. The first issue is one of definition. Before the law will consider anyone liable for conduct that may have caused harm, there must be a breach of a legally recognizable duty—or obligation—which requires the spiritual counselor to conform to a certain standard of conduct. The difficulty of defining a clergyman's duty is amplified by the uncertainty of what is "spiritual" counseling as opposed to "psychological" or "psychiatric" counseling.

What is the nature of the problem plaguing the counselee? Is it poor mental health, thus requiring a mental health professional? Or is the problem poor moral health, requiring a clergyman? How shall a court determine whether a counselee's problem is "sin related" or its psychological equivalent?

It is impossible to separate the "cure of minds" from the "cure of souls." Attempts to delineate the functions of clergy counseling from that of psychiatrists or psychologists have been rebutted by such leading professionals as Sigmund Freud and Carl Jung. Freud held that psychoanalysis was a branch of religion and not a specialized branch of medicine. In fact, he described the analyst as a "secular pastoral worker". "We do not seek to bring [the patient] relief by receiving him into the Catholic, Protestant, or Socialist community. We seek rather to enrich him from his own internal sources. . . . Such activity as this is pastoral work in the best sense of the words."

And Carl Jung, the coarchitect of modern psychiatry, was even more emphatic:

> In most cases the sufferer consults the doctor
> in the first place, because he supposes himself
> to be physically ill. . . . That is why patients
> force the psychotherapist into the role of a
> priest, and expect and demand of him that he
> shall free them from their distress. That is why
> we psychotherapists must occupy ourselves

with problems which, strictly speaking, belong
to the theologian.

Renowned psychiatrist Karl Menninger, founder of the
Menninger Clinic, believes that mental health and moral health
are identical, and that the recognition of the reality of sin offers
real hope to the suffering, anxious world.

The difficulty of separating psychiatry and psychology
from the religious and spiritual realms is further reflected in
Psychology As Religion: The Cult of Self-Worship by Paul C.
Vitz, an associate professor of psychology at New York University. The thesis of the book is that psychology exists as religion
throughout the United States, and that this "religion" is hostile
to most other religions. In fact, "psychology as religion is deeply
anti-Christian," according to Vitz.

Thus, the issue facing the courts in spiritual-counseling
malpractice cases may become one of choosing between competing religious dogmas.

A second problem will be how the courts identify the scope
and nature of church-related counseling. As a matter of law,
what constitutes spiritual guidance and counseling? Does it include the one-time, five-minute emergency telephone call that
pastors and counselors receive in the course of their day from
distressed individuals—members as well as nonmembers of their
congregations? Does it include confessions? Or is "spiritual
counseling" limited to formal office visits, in which a pastor or
other counselor counsels, notebook in hand, on a regular basis
over a long period of time? In the California case, the complainants alleged that the church staff failed to make themselves
available to the counselee when he requested their guidance. The
courts will thus be called upon to determine the scope of a
church's duty to be available to counselees.

A third area is whether or not the duty owed to a counselee
would depend upon the nature of the counselor's ecclesiastical
office. All religions identify various positions, offices, or titles
that reflect a person's authority and service. For example, the
Roman Catholic Church has nuns, mother superiors, brothers,
priests, bishops, cardinals, and the Pope. Protestants differentiate persons as evangelists, pastors, elders, deacons,
deaconesses, youth ministers, and Sunday school teachers.
Other religions have their apostles, prophets, rabbis, vicars,

divine masters, seers, and even presidents.

The relationship a counselee has with a counselor may depend upon the nature and function of counselor's office. Obviously, the various offices of a given faith are not to be treated legally alike in counseling cases, any more than a nurse, surgeon, orderly, anesthesiologist, or laboratory technician has the same medical responsibility.

Fourth, as in other "professional" malpractice, the courts must review the training and competence of individual counselors. This will present the court with a host of new problems. Shall the review be limited to the training received in secular institutions on secular subjects: psychology, psychiatry, and mental health counseling? Would a degree in clinical psychology from an accredited university provide the desired training? A 1976 article by two psychiatrists in the *American Journal of Psychiatry* said, "To date psychiatry has not clearly defined the skills, knowledge, and attitudes that the psychiatrists in training must demonstrate in order to be certified as competent. It is our belief that the profession can no longer avoid beginning the difficult, often emotional task of specifying of what a psychiatrist should know and be able to do."[1]

If the professional jury is still out on what secular professionals should know, what standards can the court use to determine the competence and training of church counselors? Shall a counselor's library be reviewed to see which books are used? If the Bible is the primary source, shall the court determine the depth of the counselor's training in Scriptures?

Aside from secular training, a Christian counselor's competence may depend upon many spiritual qualifications, such as the counselor's spiritual gifts and his or her spiritual maturity. The Bible indicates that spiritual counseling is the work of the Holy Spirit, and that effective counseling cannot be done apart from him. There is no doubt that all religions consider spiritual maturity a significant factor in evaluating a counselor's competence. A secular court, however, may decide to apply purely secular criteria and dismiss the religious standard as irrelevant and inapplicable.

A fifth area facing the court relates to the content of the counsel given by the clergyman or church counselor. For example, the California case alleged that the counselors told the seminary student to read the Bible, pray, listen to taped sermons, and church counselors while discouraging him from seeking professional psychiatric or psychological help. Wholly apart from the constitutional prohibitions, the courts are not equipped to evaluate counsel in light of the church's doctrinal stance.

It is inevitable that two inherently inconsistent world views will clash. The secular humanist will echo the views set forth, for example, in the *Humanist Manifesto*: "Traditional theism, especially in the prayer-hearing God, assumed to love and care for persons, to hear and understand their prayers, and to be able to do something about them, is an unproved and outmoded faith."

The opposite world view is the Christian belief in a personal God, who cares and answers prayer and has spoken through his Word—the Holy Bible. The counsel given to a distressed person by those who hold such diametrically opposed views will probably be just as disparate.

WHAT ABOUT THE CLERGYMAN/ PENITENT PRIVILEGE?

The mind-boggling implications raised by the idea of spiritual-counseling malpractice are not limited to definitions. Historically, the law has recognized certain types of communications as being privileged from disclosure, including communications between a clergyman and a penitent. This privilege recognizes the individual's need to confess and share matters with a clergyman, free of fear that the matter will be disclosed to others.

A clergyman should not be placed in a position where he would be punished for refusing to violate the confidentiality of the penitent's communication. If the courts adopt the theory of spiritual-counseling malpractice, clergymen will feel pressured to disclose to the family, or others, the content of discussions with a counselee. Often a counselee desires to protect his own reputation, as well as that of his family and others, in discussing a problem with his clergyman. If the courts impose disclosure on the clergy, a counselee might not be as candid. As a practical matter, effective counseling would be seriously hampered.

WHAT ABOUT MALPRACTICE INSURANCE?

Some might assert that churches can always buy counseling malpractice insurance if they want to fulfill their mission to be

Good Samaritans. However, counseling malpractice insurance may be unfeasible. The insured has a duty to cooperate with the insurer to defend a lawsuit. Without such cooperation, the insurer is severely handicapped and may in some instances be absolutely precluded from advancing any defense. If the penitent/counselee is not available to testify, the defense may hinge on a clergyman, who would have to disclose confidential communications. If the clergyman refuses, he might be held to have violated his duty to cooperate with the insurer, which would release the insurer from an obligation to defend the suit. Malpractice insurance may not offer church counselors effective protection.

IS THERE A DUTY TO REFER?

The theory of spiritual-counseling malpractice also raises the question of the clergyman's duty to refer the most difficult problems to professional specialists: psychiatrists, psychologists, and other mental health workers. In the medical field, there is a duty on the part of a general practitioner to refer his patient to a specialist or recommend the assistance of a specialist. However, the nature of pastoral counseling may bar such action.

In the Christian religion, a pastor's role is often described as that of a shepherd, caring for his troubled flock. The pastor is under a mandate to protect those in his care from counsel that might undermine their faith. There may not be a professional psychiatrist, psychologist, or other mental health worker available who is supportive of the doctrinal stance of the church. It would seem untenable that a legal duty would be created, forcing such churches and their clergy to refer their troubled members to professionals who may, in fact, be hostile to the members' faith.

If clergy must refer certain mental health cases to mental health professionals, should psychiatrists and psychologists refer all spiritual cases—the simple as well as the serious—to clergymen? Should mental health professionals be liable for failing to refer their patients to the "proper" clergyman in the event of a suicide?

ARE THE CLERGY
EXEMPT FROM LICENSING?

The practical ramifications of developing criteria to judge

the qualifications, competence, and content of counseling by a clergyman are far-reaching. States such as California have chosen not to establish statutory criteria to evelute spiritual counselors. In fact, several California statutes expressly exempt such counselors from licensing requirements. These statutes specifically state that they shall not be construed to "regulate, prohibit, or apply to any kind of treatment of prayer, nor interfere in any way with the practice of religion."

Similar language is found in the law governing licensing of psychiatrists and psychiatric technicians, which provides that the act "does not prohibit the provisions of services regulated herein, with or without compensation or personal profit, when done by the tenets of any well recognized church or denomination. . . ." Another example of the exemption of these counselors from state defined criteria is found in the licensing of marriage, family, child, and domestic counselors, which provides that the act "shall not apply to any priest, rabbi, or minister of the gospel of any religious denomination when performing counseling services as part of his pastoral or professional duties." However, the law does not define what "counseling services" entail.

Exemption provisions, such as those in California, indicate that legislatures recognize that clergymen face the same counseling situations as licensed and regulated professionals. However, the legislature has recognized that the secular state is not equipped to ascertain the competence of counseling when performed by those affiliated with religious organizations.

THE FIRST AMENDMENT AND COUNSELING

Finally, judicial review of counseling by clergymen will inevitably draw the courts into the dangerous ground of evaluating the truth or error of the counseling given. The courts are not equipped as a practical matter to deal with the issues in this arena, and it is questionable whether they are constitutionally permitted to render this kind of decision.

The most significant case heard by the United States Supreme Court on this issue is *United States* v. *Ballard,* which involved the "I Am" movement, founded by Guy and Edna Ballard and their son, Donald. The Ballards were indicted and convicted in federal district court for using, and conspiring to use, the mails to defraud. The Ballards said that by virtue of their supernatural powers they could cure persons of diseases normally classified as curable, as well as heal those with incurable diseases. In fact, they claimed they had cured hundreds of persons afflicted with these diseases and ailments.

The trial court had instructed the jury that they were not permitted to decide whether any of the religious claims made by the Ballards were actually true. The central question was whether the Ballards honestly and in good faith believed their own claims to be true.

Writing for the majority, which reversed the Ballards' original conviction, Justice Douglas stated that the First Amendment forbids the courts from examining the truth or verity of religious representations:

> Men may believe what they cannot prove. They may not be put to the proof of their religious doctrines or beliefs. Religious experiences which are as real as life to some may be incomprehensible to others. Yet the fact that they may be beyond the ken of mortals does not mean that they can be made suspect before the law. . . . Man's relation to his God was made no concern of the state. He was granted the right to worship as he pleased and to answer to no man for the verity of his religious views. The religious views espoused by respondents might seem incredible, if not preposterous, to most people. But if those doctrines are subject to trial before a jury charged with finding their truth or falsity, then the same can be done with the religious beliefs of any sect. When the triers of fact undertake that task, they enter a forbidden domain. The First Amendment does not select any one group or any one type of religion for preferred treatment. It puts them all in that position.

This analysis by Justice Douglas would apply with equal force to clergy malpractice cases. The First Amendment protects the communication of beliefs that cannot be proven and "might seem incredible, if not preposterous, to most people." Thus, under *Ballard,* the only issue for the secular courts would be a determination of whether the asserted religious belief was sincerely held.

The courts are often the battleground for social theory. Each new theory raises far more questions than answers, and the theory of spiritual-counseling malpractice is no exception. Since such cases inevitably deal with doctrinal, ecclesiastical, and spiritual issues, judicial review will force the courts into dangerous territory. It seems clear that the First Amendment will bar the introduction of spiritual-counseling malpractice into the legal arena.

24

Cults and Deprogramming

When new religions are introduced into any society, reactions are sure to follow. During the 1970s the United States was faced with a wave of new religions from the Far East and elsewhere, many of which were referred to as cults. The groups receiving the most notoriety were the Unification Church (the "Moonies," led by the Reverend Moon of South Korea), the Children of God, the International Society for Krishna Consciousness, Inc. (known as the Hare Krishnas), and The Way International. Often at the heart of the debate concerning these groups was the alleged use of mind control and coercive persuasion of new converts. Concerned family, clergy, and legislators proposed legislation that would permit "deprogramming" of new converts of religious groups who purportedly utilized deceptive methods and tactics in recruiting.

Deprogramming is the term used to describe the abduction of the new convert from the cult, and the use of systematic methods of persuasion ("reverse brainwashing") to restore prior values. Often the techniques involved in deprogramming are more severe than those applied by the cults. Charges of kidnapping have often resulted from the conduct of deprogrammers.

A case that involved the Unification Church is typical. In March of 1977, parents who were concerned about their children's involvement in this church obtained a court order from Judge S. Lee Vavuris, granting them custody of their adult children. The judge refused to bar the parents' deprogramming efforts. He declared, "The child is the child even though the parent may be ninety and the child sixty."

However, on appeal, the California Court of Appeal for-

218

bade the parents from deprogramming, and in April the Court released the young adults from their parents' custody, holding that the California conservatorship statute that allowed such custody was unconstitutionally vague. The court noted that "there may be severe inroads on the individual's freedom to practice his religion and to associate with whom he pleases because of the threat of proceedings such as this" (*Katz* v. *Superior Court*).

The court went on to warn that unless a real emergency requires custody, there is a danger that such procedures "license kidnapping for the purpose of thought control." Finally the court noted the danger to religious freedoms: "In the absence of such action [as would] render the adult believer gravely disabled as defined in the law of this state, the process of this state cannot be used to deprive the believer of his freedom of action and to subject him to involuntary treatment."

The *Katz* decision shows the courts' reluctance to interfere with religious freedom just because parents are unhappy with their adult children's religious beliefs and practices. In fact, a number of other cases have upheld the child's right to bring suit against parents and others for violation of the young adult's civil rights, for assault and battery, and for false imprisonment.

The California supreme court has recently refused to review the case of Ted Patrick who was convicted of kidnapping and conspiracy to kidnap. Patrick, a professional deprogrammer, was hired by Roberta McElfish's family to deprogram her from a religious cult called the Thomas family.

And in another case, a United States district court granted a permanent injunction, which prohibited Ted Patrick from interfering with all present and future members of The Way International. Patrick was restrained from "conspiring to kidnap or abduct, . . . invading the privacy of, or intentionally inflicting emotional distress on or attempting in any way to change the religious beliefs of the members."

A very few cases have upheld "deprogramming." In Minnesota, the state supreme court upheld a lower court's denial of the right of a twenty-one-year-old woman to sue her parents for false imprisonment. A majority of the court held that the woman's cooperation with the deprogrammer after an initial three days of resistance constituted "assent"; therefore she had consented to the "kidnapping."

"When parents . . . acting under the conviction that the judgmental capacity of an adult child is impaired, seek to extricate that child from what they reasonably believe to be a . . . cult and the child at same juncture, assents, . . . limitation on the child's mobility does not constitute meaningful deprivation of personal liberty. . . ." One vigorous dissent warned that the majority was establishing a "dangerous precedent," and another declared that the result was totally at odds with the basic right of a person to "think unorthodox thoughts, to join unorthodox groups, and to proclaim unorthodox views."

Although many Christians applauded efforts to halt the progress of "new religions," others soon realized that important issues of religious liberty were at stake, and that the shield of protection offered by deprogramming could easily be turned into a sword aimed directly at Christians' own freedom to evangelize.

DEPROGRAMMING STATUTES

In 1981 more than a dozen states introduced legislation seeking "deprogramming" or "anticonversion" statutes. By definition, *conversion* means change in the life of the convert. Often, these changes are not simply surface issues, but affect the convert's values, life-style, and relationship with family and friends. The new convert may leave his family in order to involve himself full time in his newfound religion.

The legal basis for deprogramming statutes is highly questionable. In a case decided by the United States Supreme Court involving a new religion, *United States* v. *Ballard,* the Ballards were indicted and convicted for using the mails to defraud. The Ballards had founded the "I Am" Movement and made broad representations about their supernatural powers to cure persons of diseases and ailments. In reversing the conviction of the lower court, Justice Douglas made it clear that the First Amendment prohibited the courts from examining the truth or falsity of religious beliefs. "Men may believe what they cannot prove. They may not be put to the proof of their religious doctrines or beliefs."

Some courts have adopted the rationale of *United States* v. *Ballard* and viewed the suspect religion's proselytizing and the new convert's decision as protected religious activities. In one case, the court refused to appoint a conservator for the purposes of deprogramming. In order to do so, the court said it would have to consider whether the conversion was the result of "brainwashing," which would drag the court into the forbidden arena of determining the validity of a religion and religious beliefs.

The proposed legislation introduced in more than twelve legislatures in 1981 would legalize deprogramming of those persons who have been found to be victims of mind control evangelism.

The New York legislation, which passed its assembly by one vote but was vetoed by Governor Carey, authorized state courts to appoint temporary guardians for any adult who experienced "psychological deterioration" in exposure to the mind-control techniques of a group. Proof of "psychological deterioration" could be shown by evidence of any of the following:

- Abrupt and drastic alteration of basic values and life-styles;
- Blunted emotional responses;
- Regression to childlike levels of behavior;
- Presence of certain psychotic symptoms, including disassociation, obsessional ruminations, delusional thinking, and hallucinations.

Other proposed statutes have included loss of weight and changed friendships.

As can be seen, these characteristics are wholly subjective, overly vague, and in many cases undefinable. Much of the legislation could easily apply to a conversion to Christianity. Such statutes seem dangerous and intrude into areas of conscience, privacy, and religious liberty. They smack of the sort of "corrective" techniques repressive societies apply to their dissidents. Surely such statutes could have been used against first-century Christians, or against Christians in communist countries.

The battle and the controversy between Christianity and the cults is a spiritual one. To use the strong arm of the law to bring converts out of the cults is a misapplication of the legal and judicial processes. The power of the gospel cannot rest with the magistrate.

RELIGIOUS MINISTRIES AND GOVERNMENT POWER

25

Church Political Activity

Throughout American history, church groups have sought to influence public policy, sometimes quite successfully. Their general right to do so is respected by the courts, but indirect challenges persist. The participation of church groups in political issues, especially if such activities prove effective, is always viewed with alarm by those whose interests are adversely affected.

Complaints are heard that such involvement by churches is unfair, undemocratic, and even unconstitutional. The churches are told that they should stick to their spiritual mission, respect the principle of "separation of church and state," and not impose their values on secular, temporal, and political affairs. Clergymen are told that they are meddling in secular affairs in which they have no expertise. Yet actors, athletes, television personalities, and other superstars speak out on political and social issues without criticism of their "expertise" or right to be involved.

The political issues on which churches take action have often been moral and spiritual issues long before they ever surfaced in the political arena. Abortion, birth control, and homosexuality were issues within the church long before they took on high visibility in politics. When the political realm chooses to meddle in affairs long considered to be religious, one might ask why the churches should cease their activity. The real question is: who is meddling in whose business?

Some fundamentalist churches in California received letters from the Franchise Tax Board in 1978, threatening revocation of their tax exempt for speaking out against "gay rights." Alarm-

223

ed, pastors charged that the state was trying to shackle the pulpit. In New York, the tax commissioner was unsuccessful in his efforts to revoke the property tax exemption of the Unification Church on the grounds that its theology was too interwoven with political, economic, and social issues. Still another suit seeks to revoke the exempt status of the Roman Catholic Church on the grounds that the church's opposition to abortion is an improper meddling in governmental and political affairs.

Scripture makes it clear that God's people have an obligation to pursue justice. The obligation is more than simply showing loving-kindness to one's fellow human beings, important as that may be. The people of Israel were told by the prophets Isaiah, Amos, and Micah that God was not as concerned with their sacrifices and ceremonies as he was with how they treated one another.

When Christ announced the beginning of his ministry in the synagogue, he read from Isaiah: "The Spirit of the Lord is upon me, because he has anointed me to preach good news to the poor. He has sent me to proclaim release to the captives and recovering of sight to the blind, to set at liberty those who are oppressed, to proclaim the acceptable year of the Lord" (Luke 4:18, 19).

Christ had strong words to those who neglected the call to do justice. He rebuked the Pharisees for tithing "mint and dill and cummin," and neglecting the "weightier matters of the law, justice and mercy and faith" (Matt. 23:23).

The responsibility of Christians in a democracy such as ours is great. There is no valid biblical or theological basis for excusing Christians from the call to "do justice," to "set at liberty those who are oppressed," and to "proclaim release to the captives."

The retort by some that political action by churches has not been the norm in American history simply fails to square with facts. Ever since our nation's birth, churches have taken an active role in political and social issues. The "Black Regiment" of colonial clergy played a major role in precipitating the American Revolution. Sermons from the pulpits of New England, the meeting houses of the middle colonies, and the parishes of the South resounded with the call for independence.

Churches' efforts in the early nineteenth century to eliminate dueling in the United States are one of the clearest examples of their nationwide activity to change laws. The action was led almost entirely by clergymen acting through the churches rather than by citizen groups in which church members participated.

Another political struggle in which clergymen played a central role was the antilottery campaign during the nineteenth century. Prior to the Revolution, lotteries were widely used to raise money for colleges, churches, and other causes. At the turn of the nineteenth century, clergymen began to question the lottery as a means of fund raising. They established a Society for the Suppression of Lotteries in 1834. After decades of unusual persistence, federal law banned lotteries from the mails in 1890. Then an extraordinary mail campaign, using religious newspaper subscription rolls, church registers, and other lists, urged thousands to contact their congressmen. This led to the passage of the Lottery Act in 1895.

Churches were also some of the first groups to seriously attempt to free the slaves. On both sides of the issue, churches zealously declared views of what God and the Bible required. When petitions proved ineffective, many churches openly advocated the colonization of Liberia so that American blacks could be relocated there. Some churches suggested civil disobedience, and finally the violence of a civil war.

In the twentieth century, the success of zealous church efforts to pass national prohibition is well known. Critics point to this as an example of the tragic results of church participation in the political arena. But the methods used by millions of church people to back this effort were legal, constitutional, and consistent with other movements for reformation in our history.

Today, many of those who criticize churches involved in the prolife and profamily movements are the same persons who criticized evangelicals for not becoming more involved in the civil rights and peace movements of the 1960s and early 1970s.

Neither Scripture nor American history support the position that churches should refrain from active involvement in secular and political affairs. Yet one hears the charge that the constitutional principle of "separation of church and state" bars such activity. But even Thomas Jefferson's famous letter to the Danbury Baptists did not infer that churches could not express their views on public issues to political leaders.

In a recent case, the United States Supreme Court again

noted that churches have such a right: "Adherents of particular faiths and individual churches frequently take strong positions on public issues including . . . vigorous advocacy of legal and constitutional positions. Of course, churches as much as secular bodies and private citizens have that right" (*Walz* v. *Tax Commission*).

In 1977, in *McDaniel* v. *Paty,* Justice William Brennan in an opinion that struck down a Tennessee law barring clergymen from running for public office, stated:

> That public debate of relgious ideas, like any other, may arouse emotion, may incite, may foment religious divisiveness and strife, does not rob it of constitutional protection. . . . The mere fact that a purpose of the Establishment Clause is to reduce or eliminate religious divisiveness or strife, does not place religious discussion, association, or political participation in a status less preferred than rights of discussion, association, and political participation generally. . . .
>
> The state's goal of preventing sectarian bickering and strife may not be accomplished by regulating religious speech and political association. The Establishment Clause does not license government to treat religion and those who teach or practice it, simply by virtue of their status as such, as subversive of American ideals and therefore subject to unique disabilities. . . . Government may not inquire into the religious beliefs and motivations of office holders—it may not remove them from office merely for making public statements regarding religion, nor question whether their legislative actions stem from religious conviction. . . .

Justice Brennan also quoted Professor Laurence Tribe of Harvard Law School:

> In much the same spirit, American courts have not thought the separation of church and

state to require that religion be totally oblivious to government or politics; church and religious groups in the United States have long exerted powerful political pressures on state and national legislatures, on subjects as diverse as slavery, war, gambling, drinking, prostitution, marriage, and education. To view such religious activity as suspect, or to regard its political results as automatically tainted, might be inconsistent with First Amendment freedoms of religious and political expression—and might not even succeed in keeping religious controversy out of public life, given the political ruptures caused by the alienation of segments of the religious community.

If clergymen who are ordained to full-time service in the church cannot be deprived of their rights as citizens, those sitting in the pews cannot be deprived of their rights to assemble together and appeal to their government simply because they do so as a church. Those who contend that churches should not interfere in governmental affairs cite Supreme Court language in *Lemon* v. *Kurtzman* in 1971. In this case the Court struck down several forms of tax aid to parochial schools, holding that such aid was unconstitutional because it encouraged political divisiveness along religious lines:

Ordinarily, political debate and division, however vigorous, or even partisan, are normal and healthy manifestations of our democratic system of government. But political division along religious lines was one of the principal evils against which the First Amendment was intended to protect. The potential divisiveness of such conflict is a threat to the normal political process. . . . The history of many countries attests to the hazards of religion's intruding into the political arena or of political power intruding into the legitimate and free exercise of religious belief.

As the Court noted in *Walz,* "adherents of

particular faiths and individual churches frequently take strong positions on public issues."
We could not expect otherwise, for religious
values pervade the fabric of our national life.
But in *Walz,* we dealt with a status under state
tax laws for the benefit of all religious groups.
Here we are confronted with successive and
very likely permanent annual appropriations
that benefit relatively few religious groups.
Political fragmentation and divisiveness on
religious lines are thus likely to be intensified.

The issue in *Lemon,* however, was not that it was improper
for churches to press for financial aid for their church-related
schools. Rather, it was simply held improper for the legislature
to yield to those efforts.

Scripture, American history, the principle of separation of
church and state, and decisions by the United States Supreme
Court do not bar religious groups from pressing their views on
moral issues that have become political issues. However, churches must be circumspect in their political involvement—particularly in reference to supporting or opposing political candidates—so they do not run afoul of the tax laws and lose their
ability to attract tax-deductible contributions.

In 1934, Congress enacted a limitation on lobbying activities of public charities, including religious groups, under Section 501 (c) (3) of the Internal Revenue Code. The limitation was
stated in the form of a definition of a charitable entity: an
organization in which "no substantial part of the activities is
carrying on propaganda or otherwise attempting to influence
legislation." This limitation has created definitional problems.
What is "legislation"? What constitutes "attempting to influence legislation"?

Efforts that have been seen as such attempts include:
publications and broadcasts appealing to the public to act on
certain issues, writing legislators and urging members and others
to contact representatives, and unsolicited congressional
testimony and personal contacts with members of Congress and
staff. On the other hand, certain activities have been seen as OK:
presenting testimony in response to invitation by congressional
committee, nonpartisan research and dissemination to the

public, and communications with members of legislative bodies examining broad social or economic issues (which are not directly addressed to specific legislation).

There is likewise no definitive test to determine what is considered to be a "substantial part" of the organization's activities. The courts have held that this can only be resolved on a case-by-case basis. Although 5 percent of the organization's budget has not been seen as substantial, 16 percent was considered substantial by one court.

However, churches are definitely not allowed to intervene in political campaigns. Under the Internal Revenue Code, tax exemption is afforded only to organizations that do "not participate in or intervene in any political campaign on behalf of any candidate for public office (including the publishing or distributing of statements)."

Examples of activities that the IRS deems prohibitive include:
- publication or distribution of written or printed statements on behalf of or in opposition to a candidate;
- evaluation and support of candidates in a school board election;
- comparative rating of candidates as average, good, or excellent, and disseminating ratings to the public;
- directly approaching candidates to ask them to endorse or sign a code of ethics for political campaigns;
- publishing in a voter education guide the responses of candidates to a questionnaire, which contains questions evidencing a bias on certain issues;
- distribution of a voter education guide concentrating on a narrow range of issues during an election campaign;
- attacking incumbents and candidates in broadcasts and publications, urging the election or defeat of candidates, and endorsing a presidential candidate.

In view of this detailed list, what are the practical options for religious groups who desire to have a role in politics? Churches may speak out on public issues, and may participate in secular, temporal, and political affairs when religious principles are at issue. Lobbying with regard to a law that affects the organization's tax status, power, or existence is permissible. The cases are unanimous in allowing for such self-preservation. Also, giving a nonpartisan analysis is viewed as offering expert advice rather than lobbying.

But a religious organization should not become identified with a named political candidate.

Finally, religious organizations do have the option of organizing entirely separate entities for the purpose of political activity. The IRS regulations allow for action groups, which exist for the purpose of engaging in substantial political activity under Section 501 (c) (4) rather than 501 (c) (3). As a 501 (c) (4) organization, the entity's income is tax-exempt, although supporting contributions are not tax deductible to the individuals. Care should be taken, however, that the 501 (c) (4) organization is not too closely integrated with the religious organization; the IRS might view the (c) (4) activities as simply part of the "parent" organization.

The role of churches in American politics has been so important that they owe no apology to any other interest group or party. Churches have no choice but to be concerned about men's personal relations with one another. They are not "meddling" when they become involved in affecting public policy. Churches have been appointed to "preach good news . . . to set at liberty those who are oppressed, to proclaim the acceptable year of the Lord."

26

Zoning Powers and Religious Activities

$\mathbf{A}$s the United States shifted from an agricultural to an industrial economy, new cities sprang up and older cities grew rapidly. Before zoning or city planning, noisy factories might be found on the same block with single family homes. A mansion converted into a funeral home might be surrounded by hundreds of look-alike tenement dwellings. In response to the increasingly congested and hazardous conditions, New York City passed the first comprehensive zoning ordinance (public control over the private use of land) in 1916. This ordinance became a model for many others, and the United States Supreme Court has held land-use planning through zoning schemes to be constitutional.

The most frequently stated purpose for zoning ordinances is to protect public safety, health, morals, and welfare. Other purposes are to ensure an appropriate use of the land, to preserve the character of the neighborhood, to stabilize and protect property values and uses, to safeguard future development, and, in some cases, to promote aesthetic considerations.

When the framers of the New York zoning plan were discussing what buildings should be excluded from residential districts, it did not occur to them that churches, schools, and hospitals would ever be excluded. They considered these uses an integral part of American residential life. Yet, today, at least three states (Oregon, Florida, and California) have approved the exclusion of churches and synagogues from residential areas. Seven states, however, have held that religious facilities may not be so excluded, while the remaining forty have not dealt with the issue at this time.

In September 1980, the mayor of Los Angeles wrote: "A Bible study would not be a permissible use in a single family residential area" since "this would be considered a church activity." In Atlanta, a zoning official stated that individuals who held a regular home Bible study that included nonresidents would be issued a citation for using their home for worship services without a use and occupancy permit.

In New Jersey, an Episcopal congregation of twenty people could no longer afford the $300 per month rental for the school room at a local public school. They began meeting in the pastor's family room until the city closed them down for violating local zoning laws. A lower state court ruled in favor of the city, and the case is now on appeal. This decision could affect other home churches in other states.

Finally, a number of Romanian refugees fleeing their country to escape religious persecution started a new life in California. They formed a church, pooled their resources, and purchased an old house in the neighborhood where most of the congregation lived. It was the only affordable facility within their geographical reach, since many of them did not drive. The city went to court seeking a restraining order on the grounds that the religious use of the property violated the zoning ordinance of the city.

When communities raise objections to the building of a church sanctuary and other facilities, a number of governmental interests are used to justify the restriction. These interests must be measured against the standards set forth in *Sherbert* and *Yoder*, which demand that the state accommodate religious activities wherever possible. The most frequently raised interests fall generally into six categories.

First, public inconvenience and annoyance have been asserted as a governmental interest sufficient to allow restrictions on the religious use of land. A church facility in a residential district would undoubtedly inconvenience someone. However, to restrict churches to areas where no one will be inconvenienced would exclude churches entirely from those communities. The existence of places for worship is such a valuable right that their location should not be constitutionally denied simply because of the inconvenience to some in the community.

A second reason raised by communities is based on the argument that such land use will have a substantially negative impact on the tax base. There is a common misconception that churches are the only or principal beneficiaries of property tax exemptions. A 1967 study in New York City found that religious property was less than 5 percent of all the tax-exempt property in the city and less than 2 percent of the total property in New York City.

As a corollary to the property tax concerns, some communities have sought to restrict religious uses of land on the grounds that it would have a negative impact on property values. Again, the overwhelming majority of courts confronted with this argument have rejected it, contending that the positive benefits flowing from churches in the community far outweigh any alleged negative impact on property values.

A fourth governmental argument has been that such use will cause an increase in the level of noise. Clearly, a community has a legitimate interest in preventing noise. But there are certainly less drastic methods of dealing with this problem. In one state the court responded to neighbors' complaints about the noise and bright lights of a church recreation field by simply limiting the operation of the field to the hours of 7:00 A.M. to 10:00 P.M.

A fifth and more frequent objection deals with traffic. Churches and religious activities attract large numbers of people and vehicles that create hazardous traffic conditions. Here churches can take the initiative by developing means to control potential traffic problems, such as lowering the speed limit in the area and installing warning lights or traffic signals. In some areas churches encourage parishioners to organize car pools or use public transit; churches can also provide shuttles to and from areas away from the main church property.

The last and perhaps most frequent objection to church facilities involves parking requirements. As in the case of traffic safety, an off-street parking requirement alone is not a sufficient basis to justify the exclusion of church facilities. Creative alternatives can deal with these problems (public transportation, the use of shuttle buses, etc.).

The central issue in zoning is not the ability to accommodate religious activities and church facilities as much as it is the willingness of the church and the community to work together. As a people who are called to love their neighbors, rather than provoke them, Christians should go out of their way to lessen the burden of their activities on their communities.

ZONING AND CHURCH EDUCATIONAL FACILITIES

In our increasingly secularized society, the church steeple is the symbol of what religion and churches are about. A sermon, a song, a prayer, and an offering to many make up the "church." When churches start ministries beyond those parameters. and begin using facilities for functions viewed as "secular," problems often arise.

In the 1960s, the Christian school movement began to gain momentum. As many Christian parents questioned the effectiveness of the public education system as well as the values taught there, churches rediscovered their role in education. As a result, the facilities, which had previously been used for Sunday school classes a few hours per week, were now put into use Monday through Friday.

The reaction in many communities across the nation was to challenge this use of church facilities on zoning grounds. Often operating from the underlying assumption that education was secular, rather than religious, local communities pressed the issue. The question was no longer whether or not a church should be allowed to use land for religious purposes, but what was the definition of a "religious purpose."

The results in the courts have been mixed. In some cases the courts agreed with the church that zoning permits allowing for religious use of land can encompass education of children during the weekday. In others, the courts were not as friendly and found distinctions between the use of a facility for worship on Sunday and for day schools during the week (for example *Damascus Community Church* v. *Clackamas County,* Oregon Court of Appeals, 1980, and *Faith Baptist Church of Boca Raton* v. *City of Boca Raton,* Florida Court of Appeals, 1981).

This clash of interests is seen in a Washington State case. In 1978 the Faith Baptist Church of Sumner established a school, the Washington Academy, in the basement of the church. The city objected because the school's facilities, it said, violated the city building code and the zoning ordinance. A trial court agreed, and when the church failed to comply with the regulations, the court issued a contempt citation.

The church appealed to the Washington State Supreme Court, alleging that the building code and the zoning ordinance, when uncompromisingly applied to the church, violated its religious rights. The Washington Supreme Court was apparently troubled by the case, because it heard arguments twice, once in October of 1980 and again in November of 1981.

Finally the court reversed the trial court's decision, saying that the practical effect of this uncompromising enforcement was to deny church members their constitutional rights to guide the education of their children. The Supreme Court sent the case back to the trial court, instructing the lower court to seek to balance the interests of the parties (*City of Sumner* v. *Faith Baptist Church of Sumner*).

Government's efforts to exclude or restrict religious uses of church facilities must meet the constitutional tests discussed in this and other chapters. Unless the government can show that the zoning regulations serve a compelling state interest (which cannot be achieved by less drastic, alternative means), a zoning scheme to bar churches' educational activities during the week would probably not pass constitutional scrutiny.

THE HOME BIBLE STUDY

The most recent application of zoning regulations has focused on religious activities in private homes. The incidents involving home Bible studies that were previously mentioned are unsettling. After all, the rule of thumb in most communities in the United States today is that consenting adults should be left undisturbed to do anything in the privacy of their home. There is a blatant double standard when a community seeks to close down an activity because it happens to be a weekly Bible study.

When zoning officials require special permits from religious groups in advance of their meeting, the effect is to discourage the exercise of religion, thereby violating the First Amendment. The United States Supreme Court has held that any law or action by the government that imposes prior restraint on the exercise of a First Amendment right raises a heavy presumption against its constitutional validity.

It would seem that when a community seeks to impose restraints on religious speech (such as Bible studies) through its zoning regulations, the First Amendment is violated in both its free exercise protection as well as free speech. Bible studies and religious functions in private homes should not be treated differently from other activities such as socials, bridge parties, and political meetings; this is a violation of the Equal Protection Clause.

Although the Free Speech and Equal Protection Clauses are central to zoning and home Bible study issues, the most serious infringement occurs with regard to the Free Exercise Clause and the Establishment Clause of the First Amendment. Under the test adopted in *Sherbert* v. *Verner* and *Wisconsin* v. *Yoder,* the statute or government action must first be examined to determine whether a burden is created on the free exercise of religion. Then it must be shown that there exists a sufficiently compelling state interest to justify this burden on religious liberty. Finally, the court must determine whether the state is using the least drastic means possible.

Clearly, by choosing Bible study in the home for special treatment by zoning laws, a burden is placed on the free exercise of religion. There is no compelling state interest to justify this infringement, since the only reason for imposing the burden is that the subject matter is the Bible rather than bridge, poker, or politics. If the community is concerned about the parking, traffic, or noise created by religious activities, laws controlling parking, traffic, and noise already exist. They can be enforced against such violations, whether they stem from Bible studies, political meetings, or bridge parties.

The attempt to zone and regulate a religious activity in the home would also violate the Establishment Clause of the First Amendment. The tripartite test under *Lemon* v. *Kurtzman* requires that any statute, government act, or policy meet all three prongs of the following test: first, the purpose or intent must relate to a legitimate secular purpose and not aid or inhibit religion; second, the primary effect, notwithstanding the purpose, must not aid or inhibit religion; and third, the result must not excessively entangle the government in the affairs of religion.

Singling out Bible studies and other religious activities in the home for special treatment clearly violates all three prongs of the test. First, there is no legitimate secular end in regulating Bible studies or religious activities, especially when no such regulation is imposed on other subject matters. Second, the primary effect of the zoning regulation clearly inhibits religion. Finally, the scheme will inevitably require excessive entanglement as the authorities seek to determine the content of the meetings going on in private homes throughout the community.

For example, zoning officials must determine whether or not the subject matter for discussion is religious. If, perchance, a committee to elect Tom Smith meets each Friday in a private residence to discuss strategy and tactics for an upcoming election, and then shifts to an hour of discussing Christian faith and public policy as seen in the Epistles of the apostle Paul, one might ask at what point the meeting would require the city to intrude and exact special zoning permission.

In most of the incidents reported in this chapter, the communities' concerns focused on parking, traffic, and noise problems. Again, the most effective solution to these problems is for Christians to be sensitive to the concerns of their neighbors. Rotation of Bible study locations, organizing car pools, avoiding excessive noise, and dispersing parking can go a long way to maintain a positive witness, rather than confrontation with our neighbors.

In two recent 1982 cases, the rights of those conducting home religious studies were also upheld. In Florida the attempts to shut down the Orthodox Jewish group mentioned in the first chapter of this book were struck down by a court. And in Seattle, the city dropped charges against Maranatha Ministries for holding Bible study groups in its facility.

Your authors are not aware of any instance where a home Bible study was finally closed down.

Every time Christians have explained the constitutional protections that allow them to meet in their homes for Bible study, the authorities have responded favorably. In the Los Angeles instance, the mayor changed his position and indicated that religious activities would not be treated any differently than other meetings in a private home. This is an indication that authorities have been misinformed about the law and are not maliciously trying to limit religious liberties.

If your right to hold a Bible study in your home is questioned, you might want to present a statement of your constitutional rights to the zoning officials, who may change their minds. In order to preserve our religious liberties we must resist any infringement of them.

27

Government Licensing
of Religious Ministries

The government is seeking to confine the "church" to only those activities carried on in a building with a steeple on the roof.

William Ball, attorney

The mandate found in both the Old and New Testaments to be charitable toward the poor, to help the elderly, the orphaned, and the widowed has been a traditional endeavor of churches and synagogues. In the Book of Jeremiah, God asks, Is this not what it means to know me? To defend the cause of the poor and needy (Jer. 22:16). And Christ asked his disciples to care for others as they would care for him: "For I was hungry and you gave me something to eat, I was thirsty and you gave me something to drink, I was a stranger and you invited me in, I needed clothes and you clothed me, I was sick and you looked after me, I was in prison, and you came to visit me. . . . I tell you the truth, whatever you did for one of the least of these brothers of mine, you did for me" (Matt. 25:35, 36, 40, NIV).

Up until the twentieth century, American churches provided most of the assistance to the vulnerable in our society. But with the growth of the welfare state, many churches shifted the costs of such programs to the broader tax base so they could serve more "spiritual" needs. This trend has been reversed in the past decade. Many churches are once again providing for the poor, the needy, the elderly. But now the church is caught in a tension between God's mandate and a government perspective that seeks to confine the church to a "building with a steeple."

Christian ministries that are different from this limited concept are myriad, but the principal ones fall into the following categories:
- children's homes and orphanages;
- child-care, day-care, and preschool programs;
- foster home and adoption placement agencies;
- charities, storehouses of food and used household goods, and temporary meals and lodging;
- alcohol and drug treatment programs;
- counseling and chaplaincy services;
- youth recreational programs, camps, and retreat centers;
- maternity shelters for expectant unwed mothers;
- hospitals and medical clinics;
- halfway houses for criminal offenders and other prison ministries;
- nursing and invalid homes for the elderly; and,
- centers for the handicapped, retarded, or mentally ill.

The church and the government tend to become entangled because these ministries are subject to government regulations, such as state-required licenses.

For instance, officials of the Georgia Department of Human Resources removed nine girls from the Ruth Home of Compassion (organized by the Faith Baptist Church of Thomaston, Georgia) when it was found to be operating without a state-required license for group-care homes. But the officials were unable to cite any health or safety hazard on the premises or any evidence that the children were neglected or abused. The children were "deprived" merely because the home did not have a license.

Entanglement can also occur over employee relations, salary, and certification. The Eighth Circuit Court rejected the argument of the St. Louis Christian Home (an emergency residential treatment center for battered, abused, and neglected children, which is sponsored by the Christian Church Disciples of Christ) that it should be exempt from the National Labor Relations Board's jurisdiction and its attempt to organize the home's employees. The court ruled that the situation was not parallel to the United States Supreme Court's 1979 decision in *Catholic Bishop of Chicago* v. *NLRB*. In *Catholic Bishop,* the religious character of the school existed at three levels: the church, the church-operated institution, and the institution's employees. The Supreme Court had found that NLRB's involvement in mediating between two of these levels would "pose a significant danger of impermissible entanglement between church and state."

However, the court said that such a danger did not exist at the St. Louis Christian Home, which differed from a Catholic school and resembled a "nonreligious institution . . . because both the home and its employees perform essentially secular functions." The court noted that the home's activities "related only tangentially to the religious mission of the Christian Church."

But in 1981 the United States Court of Appeals for the Eighth Circuit ruled that the St. Louis Christian Home did "not devote itself to the propagation of religion" and operated "in the same way as a secular child care institution." Therefore, the home was not exempt from the National Labor Relations Board's jurisdiction.

These reports from Georgia and Missouri herald increasing church-state conflicts in the area of social and human services. Recent litigation and legislation has focused on state efforts to force certification or licensing requirements on religious organizations, programs, and personnel.

The organizational structures of social and human services ministries vary widely. Some are tightly integrated into a church or synagogue, with no existence apart from the body that conducts worship services. Others exist as lay religious groups or para-church organizations, often incorporated under Section 501 (c) (3) of the Internal Revenue Code, with operations worldwide and owing allegiance to no particular organized denomination. The differences in organization are the result of varying doctrinal interpretations, structures imposed by founding fathers, tax considerations, and state corporation law.

Once a certain activity is declared religious, the state must demonstrate a compelling interest to limit or prohibit this religiously motivated conduct. Further, the state must show that the method of regulation is the least intrusive.

Rather than carry this heavy burden, government has often sought to define the regulated activity as "secular." This position has perhaps caused the greatest outcry from religious organizations, because they are unable to accept their vocation as anything less than a religious calling.

THE CASE LAW

The first case in this area was *Roloff Evangelistic Enterprises Inc.* v. *Texas.* The Department of Public Welfare brought suit against Reverend Lester Roloff, asking that his three childrens' homes comply with the Child-Care Licensing Act.

The thrust of the testimony by Reverend Roloff and others was twofold: a license from the state implied, first, state headship over a Christian ministry, and second, a state role in the upbringing of children. Roloff admitted responsibility only to God and the parents placing the child in the home. Despite this testimony, the trial court ordered Roloff to secure licenses and allow welfare department employees to inspect the homes.

The Texas Court of Civil Appeals upheld the lower court. In so doing, the court noted that the act was addressed solely to the physical and mental well-being of the children and did not encroach into the area of their religious beliefs or training. Moreover, the mere requirement that a church obtain a piece of paper from the state before proceeding with its ministry did not, in the court's opinion, amount to a free exercise violation. The court was unmoved by Roloff's arguments for church autonomy.

In a turnabout decision in April of 1981, a Texas district court issued an opinion that Reverend Roloff's homes did not have to be licensed by the state. The decision in this case (*Texas* v. *Corpus Christi Peoples Baptist Church, Inc.*) effectively reversed the earlier court's decision. However, the state of Texas has appealed.

Other case law dealing with First Amendment challenges to state regulation of social and human services ministries is sparse. In *Tabernacle Baptist Church* v. *Conrad,* the Department of Social Services in South Carolina was sued by a church. The church sought relief from the Child Welfare Agencies Act and the Children's Foster Care Review Board, who were charged with reviewing and coordinating the activities of local foster care homes.

Integral to the church's program for neglected and disadvantaged children was their instruction in fundamentalist Christian training and discipline. But the Child Welfare Agencies Act issued rules that set minimum standards for the homes (including that a home's program be "well-rounded" with "appropriate community activities") and required a home to submit a report, which "clearly defined and explained" its purpose. The children's home did not object to compliance with the local fire and health regulations or to inspection by the department, but it did object to the analysis of its program and purpose.

In its decision, the federal district court struck down the act and the regulations as they applied to the religious children's home, noting that the act was too broad. In particular, the court felt guidelines that the program be "well-rounded" or that it make available "appropriate community activities" were so vague as to be void when dealing with sensitive constitutional rights.

In a decision, which was characterized as "strange, shocking, and unprecedented" by W. Stanley Mooneyham (president of World Vision International), Family Ministries, a California-based Christian foster and adoptive agency, lost the right to place children exclusively with families who were active members of an evangelical Protestant church.

The case of *Scott* v. *Family Ministries* involved the unusual instance of twenty orphans lifted from Cambodia on the eve of its fall to the Khmer Rouge in April 1975 and brought to the state-licensed Family Ministries organization for adoptive placement. When the children first arrived in the United States, an attending physician, Dr. Richard Scott, inquired about adopting one of the children. He was told that he and his wife were ineligible because they were not members of an evangelical Protestant church. Dr. and Mrs. Scott filed suit seeking to enjoin Family Ministries from enforcing this religious eligibility requirement. California law (like most states) permits matching religious preferences in adoptive placement.

The lower court found for the Scotts, and granted the requested injunction against Family Ministries.

The appellate court affirmed the decision against Family Ministries. The court declared that the involvement of the state in licensing private adoptive agencies was sufficient to make the agencies subject to Establishment Clause prohibitions. Thus, it reasoned, if the state must be neutral in matters of religion, so must private agencies such as Family Ministries.

The implications are far-reaching. Family Ministries exists for the very purpose of discriminating in favor of its particular religious persuasion, as do other adoptive agencies sponsored by other faiths. What about the free exercise and establishment rights of Family Ministries, its employees, and sponsoring churches? The court of appeals makes no mention of having considered this argument.

The holding of *Scott* v. *Family Ministries* hopelessly frustrates the religious activities and underlying motivations of social service ministries. Not only is a ministry not allowed to choose the community it seeks to serve, but its evangelization and spiritual counseling would be prohibited altogether. In light of this decision, one can understand the clergy's hesitancy to license their social service ministries.

Although it can be hoped that the *Scott* decision will be given a quick burial, the story of the twenty children had a bittersweet ending. In return for Family Ministry's promise not to appeal the decision to a higher court, the Los Angeles County Department of Adoptions approved the children's adoptions by the families chosen by Family Ministries. But because of the cost of litigation, Family Ministries was forced to close its doors.

No decisions have been reported that use licensure or certification requirements to unfairly burden the religious activities of charities, counseling and chaplaincy services, nursing and invalid homes, alcohol and drug treatment programs, hospitals and medical clinics, halfway houses and other prisoner ministries, or youth recreational programs, camps, and retreats.

LEGISLATIVE DEVELOPMENTS

Recent legislation in the area of child care has recognized the difficult First Amendment issues involved when the state seeks to regulate and accommodate religious ministries while still protecting the health, safety, and welfare of its citizens.

Statutes have taken two approaches. The states of Indiana, Virginia, and Louisiana have eliminated licensing requirements and regulations for certain religious organizations. They have substituted a registration and notice provision with authority to inspect the ministry's activities. The states of New Mexico and Texas have written into their statutes a general statement that the act and regulations are not to burden the exercise of religious beliefs or activities, except where the safety or health of the children are endangered.

The impetus for the state to regulate religious ministries is complicated by two key factors. First, counterparts to the religious ministries are operated by public or private secular organizations. Accordingly, the state sees itself as neutral when it regulates the activity the same way. This neutrality is often asserted by the state to sanction its regulatory interference.

Second, a religious organization is motivated to minister to a certain community because the people it serves are vulnerable and in need of help. The state, for the same reason, wishes to protect those who are not as able to help themselves. With both the religious organization and the state moving to assist or protect the same community of people, a collision of interests often results.

Challenging the power of the state to license or otherwise control the activities of social and human services ministries primarily raises free exercise and excessive entanglement issues. The argument addressing excessive entanglement of the state in church affairs is that state licensing creates a relationship between religion and the state, which too closely "entangles" them. The free exercise claim states that certain regulations unreasonably and unnecessarily interfere with certain religious convictions.

State regulations typically address the following: (1) purposes, policies, and procedures of the organization; (2) administration and its functions; (3) staff qualifications; (4) financial practices and records; (5) insurance; (6) fees or other charges; (7) criteria or qualifications for assistance or admission; (8) case records; (9) minimum space and personnel requirements; and (10) nutritional, health, building code, and fire concerns. No ministry should object to complying with reasonable nutritional, health, building code, and fire protection requirements. However, the regulatory activity of the state creates an ongoing relationship, with resulting surveillance of religious concerns by the state. Such continual supervision or organic relationship may be contrary to Establishment Clause values.

Concerning the free exercise contentions, the social ministries begin by readily conceding the power of the state to establish minimum standards regarding the health and safety aspects of their ministries. However, the state soon encounters stiff resistance as it begins to cross over into areas of program and personnel. A list of recurring areas of conflict between social ministries and the state follows:

Regulation: Requiring a license for operation of the ministry.

Objection: The ministry is not separate from the church or parachurch organization. To deny a license to the ministry is to close down part of the church. For the state to license the church implies that the state is superior, whereas the church doctrinal position is that church and state are coequals, with each assigned a separate sphere of authority. When children are involved, the ministry is principally responsible to the parents, not the state.

Regulation: Requiring a written statement of a ministry's purposes and policies, and a submission of character references on behalf of the operator, in order to obtain a license.

Objection: Because a ministry's purposes and policies are integrated with its religious beliefs and organizational structure, this requirement is tantamount to a religious test. An operational statement of purposes would repeatedly refer to Scripture and denominational documents, with which the state should have little involvement. The regulation either expresses or implies state authority to assess the quality and content of a ministry's program, all under the threat of licensure denial. A church or parachurch organization should set the scope and limits of its ministry, not the state. The requirement of character references or showings of "good moral character" are vague, and could result in the state sitting in judgment over a priest or pastor.

Regulation: Requiring professional certification of staff and minimum education and minimum job experience for supervisor. Staff cannot be employed on a discriminatory basis.

Objection: Staff members are considered

religious employees serving in a lay ministry position, even though some have no formal religious training. The employees are under the direct supervision of the church or religious authorities; it is they who determine who has the gifts to minister. Because of the religious nature of the program or training, state certification requirements may be at odds with the selection process. To discriminate on a religious basis in staff employment is at the very essence of propagation of the particular faith.

Regulation: Requiring case records to be kept on the individuals served and made available to the state.

Objection: The records of a church or religious organization are confidential and protected by the clergyman-parishioner or priest-penitent privilege. When children are involved, no records should be available to the state without permission of the parents.

Regulation: Prohibiting discrimination in providing the service; the organization is to be open to the public.

Objection: Certain organizations choose to make their ministry available only to members of their faith, church, or organization. The church is called of God to serve certain needs. When the ministry is privately funded, the state should not be able to interfere in this decision.

Regulation: Requiring periodic reports and inspections.

Objection: Health and safety regulations are not objectionable. However, where the regulations address broader concerns, reports and inspections are resisted because they enforce objectionable regulations.

Regulation: Prohibiting corporal and other

means of punishment (such as withholding of mail and isolation) when children are involved.

Objection: In certain instances of last resort, corporal punishment is required, but never so as to physically harm a child. Corporal punishment in extreme cases is required by Scripture. Certain forms of discipline are used to teach the child the consequences of improper conduct. Existing child abuse laws are sufficient to control any excesses.

Regulation: Requiring financial records to be kept, an annual audit to be conducted, and records to be inspected by the state.

Objection: Financial records of a church or religious organization are confidential, subject only to reasonable disclosure to tax authorities or upon investigation for fraud, based upon probable cause. The ministry takes no public funds, and, thus, is accountable only to its members.

Regulation: Requiring liability insurance.

Objection: Some religious faiths oppose insurance. In any event, this is a church financial decision in which the state has no compelling interest.

Regulation: Requiring adherence to health, safety, fire, and building codes that are more stringent than codes applicable to the same building when used as a church on Sunday.

Objection: A ministry using church facilities during the week is just as much a church activity as the Sunday worship. If the building is safe on Sunday, it is safe during the balance of the week.

Regulation: Requiring that, upon receipt of a complaint from a parent or member of the public, a state grievance investigation and resolution procedure shall be followed.

Objection: A church or religious organization has a right to establish and set its own procedures for the resolution of disputes, at least when the complainant is a member of the religious group.

Not all the regulations summarized above are objected to by any one given religious organization, neither would they be opposed for the same reasons. Sometimes legislation is opposed because of poor draftmanship in this sensitive constitutional area and because of the unnecessary financial burden entailed in order for the religious organization to comply.

Perhaps the most difficult question to resolve is how to define those "religious" organizations to which religious exemption applies. Since the establishment test requires that an entanglement be avoided if an organization is "pervasively religious," the best definition of an exempt organization may be one that was applied in Louisiana legislation, which exempts any organization that does not receive "state or federal funds."

Christians need to be sensitive to a well-known "golden" rule in the secular world: "He who controls the gold rules." Maybe church ministries need to reject all state and federal funding so they can maintain control of their outreach.

28

Regulation of Solicitation by Religious Organizations

Freedom of religion has a higher dignity under the Constitution than municipal or personal convenience.

Justice Frank Murphy

Solicitation of funds by religious groups has traditionally been recognized as a necessary and effective means of financing their ministries and activities. Nevertheless, solicitation by unscrupulous organizations can abuse the public. In recent years, state and local governments have increasingly sought to protect their citizens from crime, fraud, and undue annoyance by regulating religious solicitation. This increased regulation touches another sensitive area in American life, involving the separation of church and state as it affects our money, our privacy, and our faith.

A number of states have sought to impose strict regulations on the solicitation of funds by parachurch organizations (such as Campus Crusade, Youth for Christ, and the Billy Graham Association) and many of the new religions we think of as cults, whose membership is different from local churches. These groups obtain much of their support from direct solicitation of a broad spectrum of the public rather than Sunday morning offerings.

For example, the Minnesota Charitable Solicitations Act required that any organization that received less than half of its contributions from actual members had to register with the state and provide information about the amount and source of its donations and the organization's structure (so the state could determine if the organization was accountable to its donors). This type of statute treats one religious group differently from another, based simply on membership policy. Even churches that do not have official membership roles, such as some independent churches, would be judged differently from the church across the street with a traditional structure.

In April of 1982 the Supreme Court declared that the Minnesota Act was unconstitutional because it violated the Establishment Clause (*Larson* v. *Valente*). The Court said:

> The clearest command of the Establishment Clause is that one religious denomination cannot be officially preferred over another. . . .
>
> This kind of state inspection and evaluation of the religious content of a religious organization is fraught with the sort of entanglement that the Constitution forbids. It is a relationship pregnant with danger of excessive government direction . . . of churches.

As this case shows, the courts are increasingly asked to review the constitutionality of regulations aimed at religious solicitation. These regulations fall into two general categories: those designed to preserve public order and peace by controlling the time, place, and manner of solicitation and those designed to protect the public from fraudulent solicitation by unscrupulous persons or by careless fund raisers who use funds so inefficiently that little money ever finds its way to charitable or religious purposes.

The intensified interest in regulating religious groups stems in large part from two relatively recent phenomena. One is the increased growth of less traditional churches, some of them bizarre cults or sects who have actively taken their witness into the streets, airports, fairgrounds, and other public places.

The second phenomenon springs from the conduct of churches themselves. Over the last two or three decades, traditional religious groups have become increasingly active and vocal concerning social and political issues. This activity is viewed by many state and local officials as secular, and therefore subject to regulation. These officials feel they have the authority as well as the responsibility for differentiating activities that are religious from those that are secular. One way to control the activity is by regulating solicitation efforts.

The courts are well aware of the serious dangers, as well as nuisances, threatened by uncontrolled solicitation. Yet courts have upheld the right of solicitors, relying on the historical value of contact made by door-to-door visitation. As one court noted, "door-to-door distribution of circulars is essential to the poorly financed causes of little people."

In 1943, the United States Supreme Court found unconstitutional an ordinance that prohibited summoning occupants to the door for distribution of religious literature. While the Court (in *Martin* v. *City of Struthers*) set aside the ordinance in a steel mill town in Pennsylvania where many inhabitants worked on "swing shifts"—working nights and sleeping days—the court admitted:

> Ordinances of the sort now before us may be aimed at the protection of the householders from annoyance, including intrusion upon the hours of rest, and at the prevention of crime. Constant callers, whether selling pots or distributing leaflets, may lessen the peaceful enjoyment of a home as much as a neighborhood glue factory or a railroad yard which zoning ordinances may prohibit. . . .

Although some control of solicitation is permissible, the degree of control must be "reasonable," so as not to intrude upon First Amendment guarantees. The regulation must demonstrate a compelling state interest and use the least intrusive means available.

The city of Jeanette, Pennsylvania, passed an ordinance requiring a license fee in an effort to control solicitation by groups such as the Jehovah's Witnesses. The cost of the license varied according to the length of time the individual planned to solicit. However, the Supreme Court held that such fee schedules violate freedom of speech, press, and religion when used to control religious solicitation. The Court distinguished this ordinance from those merely requiring registration of strangers in the community or one imposing a nominal fee to defray "the expense of policing the activities in question." The Court stated that the "power to tax the exercise of a privilege is the power to control or suppress its enjoyment."

The fact that these traveling ministers sold their literature instead of giving it away did not transform their evangelism into a business enterprise. The Court noted that the donation was small compared to the cost of printing the pamphlets and the unpaid work of the witnesses. "Freedom of speech, freedom of press, freedom of religion are available to all, not merely those who can pay their own way."

One of the earliest and most important cases is *Cantwell* v. *Connecticut* in 1940. A Connecticut law required solicitors for religious causes to be certified by the secretary of the Public Welfare Council. The secretary was to determine whether the cause was religious and whether the organization conformed to reasonable standards of efficiency and integrity; he could revoke the certificate at any time. Three Jehovah's Witnesses were convicted under the statute for failing to obtain the certificate prior to soliciting. The Supreme Court overturned their convictions, and established four basic principles with regard to solicitation, which still control cases in this area:

- The state may regulate the time, manner, and place of solicitation to safeguard the peace.
- The state may, to prevent fraud, require a stranger in the community to establish his identity and authority to act for the cause.
- The state may regulate religious solicitation, but not in a manner that involves a religious test or unreasonably delays the collection of funds.
- There may not be prior restraint, even if there is a provision for judicial review.

In view of these general principles laid down by the United States Supreme Court, solicitation statutes and regulations can be evaluated under four general categories: (1) registration for identification; (2) registration as a prior restraint; (3) the extent of regulation; and (4) regulations preventing fraud.

REGISTRATION FOR IDENTIFICATION

The simplest and least burdensome regulation of solicitation is one that merely requires the solicitor to register—give notice of his activities. The solicitor identifies himself and clearly establishes his authority to solicit for a particular cause. In general, mere registration (without allowing officials discretion to deny a license) is not unduly burdensome.

Courts have been concerned that the power to license can easily be abused by denying licenses to disfavored groups. Therefore any statute is carefully reviewed to assure that no official has too much latitude in determining who may and may not receive a license. Government officials' authority must be narrowly drawn so that the important interest of protecting citizens from crime, fraud, and undue annoyance will be served without screening out what messages residents may hear. When First Amendment rights are at stake, the courts will not presume that a licensing official will perform his duty in a fair and impartial way.

Some courts have held such registration enforceable against groups who believe that any kind of state approval is an insult to God. These decisions have emphasized the reasonableness of the regulation and the lack of burden on the solicitor. Other courts have found registration unenforceable against such groups, emphasizing the regulation's denial of the right to worship according to one's own conscience.

In order to pass the constitutional test, the registration ordinances must have very definite standards for determining the identification necessary. Even a small fee for anything other than administrative costs has been considered an impermissible burden. Moreover, an unreasonably restrictive time period during which an applicant may register is also forbidden. In sum, registration that simply serves to identify those who solicit must operate for that purpose and not for the purpose of discouraging solicitation.

PRIOR RESTRAINT

A central requirement in legally regulating solicitation is that there must be no prior restraint. Religious organizations and others cannot be prohibited from soliciting on the grounds that their cause is unpopular or that the officials suspect that improprieties may occur. The regulation must provide definite standards which, if met, require the official to issue the license. The standards cannot include a religious test, which gives anyone other than the organization itself the power to determine what is or is not a religious cause.

Nor may the state decide what are "good" causes or "bad" causes. Generally, the courts have held that an official may not determine by his own unguided judgment whether a group has in fact a religious, charitable, political, or philanthropic aim. It is up to each individual resident to determine whether the group approaching his door should be allowed to take his time. Neither will an official be given the authority to decide if the applicant solicitor is the type of person who should distribute information from house-to-house nor whether the cause is proper or advisable.

EXTENT OF REGULATION

There are proper boundaries for regulating solicitation. If the state can show a compelling need, it may regulate solicitation to the extent necessary to meet that need. An airport authority may confine solicitation to specified public areas to insure the orderly flow of traffic. State fairgrounds may require the sale and distribution of literature to be only from booths available on a first-come, first-serve basis. Officials may also suspend solicitation entirely in an emergency situtation, so long as the definition of an emergency is explicit. This definition cannot be left up to the discretion of the official in charge.

The restrictions on religious solicitation can be no more intrusive than necessary to fulfill the compelling need. For example, a city cannot limit solicitation to one day per year and allow unrestrained solicitation on that one day. Such restriction is more than is required to protect the public from possible fraud. Regulations governing the time, place, and manner of solicitation can neither be so restrictive as to render the right to solicit meaningless nor limit solicitation to times when the fewest people are available and solicitation is least effective. Finally, regulation cannot limit soliciting to isolated places where solicitation would be the least successful.

An interesting case illustrating the tension between First Amendment rights and preserving public order is a 1981 decision by the Ninth Circuit Court of Appeals, *Rosen* v. *Port of Portland*.

Moshe Rosen, leader of the Jews for Jesus, was arrested at the Portland International Airport after he began distributing literature. He was cited for violating an ordinance that required twenty-four hour, advance registration of the name, address, and telephone number of the sponsoring person. The Ninth Circuit Court of Appeals held that the ordinance imposed a prior restraint and had a "chilling effect" on free speech.

> We acknowledge the legitimacy of the state's interest and recognize that many of those who communicate with the public, whether they represent Jews for Jesus, the Ku Klux Klan, the Socialist Workers Party, or the Moral Majority, may deeply offend or antagonize members of the public. We cannot agree that this interest of the Port justifies the infringement of fundamental First Amendment Rights.

The court said that a function of free speech is to invite dispute, and noted that such speech may be protected even if it stirs people to anger.

FRAUD

The state has the right to regulate solicitation to prevent fraud in the representation of religious beliefs by individuals or religious organizations. If the fund-raising activity is primarily commercial, it is subject to the same laws applicable to nonreligious groups. Thus, when an organization sells interest-bearing notes to the general public, the First Amendment does not shield the religious organization simply because the sales pitch was that the funds would be used "in God's work."

A religious fund raiser can be prosecuted successfully for diverting funds to a use other the one designated during the solicitation. But, again, no religious test may be invoked. If the funds were solicited merely for "God's work," it is not the role of the state or the courts or any official to determine what is "God's work." If, on the other hand, a person or organization solicits funds for a specified religious project (such as feeding the hungry in Cambodia) and diverts the money to other uses (such as building a retreat for the staff of the organization), the court or jury may determine that the group is guilty of fraud.

REGULATING FUND-RAISING EXPENSES

In 1980, in *Village of Schaumburg* v. *Citizens for a Better Environment,* the United States Supreme Court held unconstitutional a municipal ordinance prohibiting solicitation by any charity that does not use at least 75 percent of its receipts for charitable purposes. The Schaumburg ordinance made no provision for the charity to demonstrate that large fund-raising expenses were reasonable. The court held that an absolute percentage requirement was unconstitutional, since it does not relate sufficiently to the legitimate interest to prevent fraud and protect the public safety and residential privacy.

Schaumburg does not settle the question of what percentage of an organization's receipts could properly be used to cover fund-raising or other noncharitable costs. In an earlier decision in the Fifth Circuit Court of Appeals (National Foundation v. City of Fort Worth), the court upheld an ordinance in which an organization was supposedly held ineligible if the costs of solicitation exceeded 20 percent of the amount collected. However, Fort Worth's ordinance was different from Schaumburg's in that it allowed the organization to demonstrate that its fund-raising expenses were reasonable.

The Schaumburg decision casts serious doubt on the constitutionality of any law that prohibits solicitation if less than a specified percentage of receipts is applied to a charitable purpose. This may weaken the future effectiveness of any licensing laws, which often have the purpose of limiting fund-raising expenses.

AN ALTERNATIVE: FULL DISCLOSURE

In light of these court decisions, it is doubtful that licensing legislation can effectively regulate religious solicitation and still meet constitutional tests. Instead, some states and cities are turning to registration and disclosure statutes. In the Village of Schaumburg v. Citizens for a Better Environment, the Supreme Court referred to the Illinois disclosure statute as an acceptable alternative to prevent fraud. According to the Court, a disclosure statute "may assist in preventing fraud by informing the public of ways in which their contributions will be employed."

Some courts have expressed doubt that the government may constitutionally require an organization to disclose its membership lists and names of contributors, since disclosing membership lists would deter potential supporters from associating with groups or ideas that are not popular.

An alternative would be the disclosure of the names of officers and expenditures. Disclosure laws would neither prevent any religious organization from soliciting funds nor operate as governmental assurance that a cause is worthy. Such laws would simply enable a potential contributor to determine if an organization spends its funds in a way that is consistent with his own beliefs. The religious group can then solicit and spend its funds in any way it desires, so long as an informed public is willing to contribute.

29

Church Autonomy

The purpose of the First Amendment is to allow churches to control their own affairs; domination of the church by the state or the state by the church is to be avoided. However, some degree of involvement in the internal affairs of each by the other appears inevitable. In a number of cases, government has intervened in church controversies, and the state's inclination to do so appears to be growing.

PROPERTY DISPUTES

When two rival church factions contest the ownership of property, the state often intervenes at the request of one of the parties. But even the resolution of property disputes may draw the state into determining doctrinal issues, since they are often the cause of the schism. A frequent pattern has been a dispute between two factions, each claiming they are the "true" church.

In order to keep the state's involvement in religious issues to a minimum, the courts have followed the rule that places churches in one of two categories: "congregational" or "hierarchical." If a dispute arises among factions of a local congregational or Baptist church, the majority decision of the congregation will ordinarily be accepted by the courts as binding. On the other hand, if the dispute is between factions of the Roman Catholic, Methodist, or other hierarchical churches (where members of a local church are under the control of a larger body in ecclesiastical matters), the courts will generally follow the decision of the proper institutional authority.

The first case to reach the United States Supreme Court was *Watson* v. *Jones* in 1872. A faction of the Walnut Street

Presbyterian Church of Louisville, Kentucky, split from the General Assembly of the Presbyterian Church in 1866, after the Assembly decreed that persons who had voluntarily aided the Confederates, or who believed in slavery as a divine institution, could not become church members unless they first agreed to "repent and forsake these sins." The Kentucky Supreme Court found in favor of the "splinter" group, even though the General Assembly had decided that the faction that followed the decree was the "true" Walnut Street Church.

When the case reached the Supreme Court, the Court rejected the "departure-from-doctrine" standard. Some state courts had applied this standard when it was felt that the momentary majority had departed from the fundamental doctrines on which the church was founded. The Supreme Court noted that the Presbyterian Church had a hierarchical form of church government, and therefore the decision of the General Assembly was final. Justice Miller, speaking for the Court, stated:

> The law knows no heresy, and is committed to the support of no dogma, the establishment of no sect. . . . All who unite themselves to such a body . . . [the denomination] do so with the implied consent to its government, and are bound to submit to it. But it would be a vain consent and would lead to the total subversion of such religious bodies, if anyone aggrieved by one of their decisions could appeal to the secular courts and have those decisions reversed. It is of the essence of these religious unions, and of their right to establish tribunals for the decision of questions arising among themselves, that those decisions should be binding in all cases of ecclesiastical cognizance, subject only to such appeals as the organization itself provides for.

This meant that the courts were not to become involved in reviewing decisions of authorized church bodies.

In 1929, the *Watson* decision was reiterated in *Gonzalez* v. *Archbishop* where the Court accepted without question the

Roman Catholic archbishop's appointment of a chaplain to the Philippines. However, Justice Louis Brandeis in the majority opinion created an exception to the "departure-from-doctrine" prohibition by suggesting that secular courts may give marginal review to decisions by church authorities in order to ascertain whether or not there has been "fraud, collusion, or arbitrariness."

In 1952, in *Kedroff* v. *St. Nicholas Cathedral*, the Supreme Court struck down a New York law aimed at freeing the Russian Orthodox Church in America from Moscow's control. This law would have given the American church title to St. Nicholas Cathedral and other assets of the church in the United States. The Supreme Court held that the First Amendment prevented New York from determining which group was to control the cathedral.

Finally, in 1969, in *Presbyterian Church in the U.S.* v. *Mary Elizabeth Blue Hull Memorial Presbyterian Church*, the Supreme Court categorically ruled out further use of the departure-from-doctrine standard in state courts. Two local Presbyterian churches in Georgia had voted to withdraw from the Presbyterian Church in the United States on the grounds that the denomination had departed from its original doctrines and tenets. They cited ordination of women, the use of neo-orthodox literature, membership in the National Council of Churches, and public stands against the Vietnam conflict.

The denomination sought to conciliate this intrachurch dispute by use of a special church commission set up by the Regional Presbytery of Savannah. When the local churches refused to change their position, the commission took over their properties. The local churches filed suit in the secular courts to stop the General Assembly from trespassing on the properties.

At the trial, the jury decided that the General Assembly had departed from its original doctrines and could not therefore deprive the local churches of the property. The Supreme Court of Georgia upheld this verdict, but the United States Supreme Court reversed. In strong language, the Supreme Court ruled out further use of the departure-from-doctrine guideline. The Court agreed that a secular court is a proper forum for the settlement of property disputes, but held that the *Watson* v. *Jones* rule meant that courts may not interpret and weigh church doctrine in resolving the disputes. Interpretation of religious doctrines is reserved exclusively to the appropriate church authority.

However, the court suggested that the states might develop "neutral principles of law" to apply in all kinds of property disputes—religious as well as secular—in line with the comment by Justice Brandeis in *Gonzalez,* noting that church decisions can be reviewed for "fraud, collusion or arbitrariness."

In the most recent decision about church property (*Jones* v. *Wolf*), the Supreme Court ruled that the states are free to follow "neutral principles of law" in deciding church property disputes unless the dispute involves an "issue of doctrinal controversy."

The Court said that civil courts must "defer to the resolution of issues of religious doctrine or polity by the highest court of a hierarchical church organization." As long as civil courts stay out of "doctrinal matters, . . . the ritual and liturgy of worship or the tenets of faith," they may adopt any approach for settling church property disputes. The Court suggested that courts might examine the deed of the local church's property, its corporate charter, the state statutes dealing with implied trusts, and the constitution of the parent church. If none of these documents clearly shows that the property of the local congregation is held in trust for the denomination, the state courts may award the property to the local congregation, even if it has seceded from the parent church.

NONPROPERTY DISPUTES

In a nonproperty dispute that reached the Supreme Court in 1976, *Serbian Eastern Orthodox Diocese for the United States and Canada* v. *Milivojevich*, the Court addressed the "neutral principles of law" concept. Milivojevich had been suspended and defrocked in 1963 by the mother church of the Serbian Orthodox Church in Belgrade, Yugoslavia. The Illinois Supreme Court ordered the bishop's reinstatement upon reviewing the action by the mother church, contending that the prescribed church procedure had not been followed. The Supreme Court held, however, that this type of detailed review "under the umbrella of arbitrariness" far exceeded the minimal review allowed by the courts. Thus, the most recent holding by the Supreme Court underscores their reluctance to intervene in matters of ecclesiastical custom or law.

Another major area of state interference in matters of church administration concerns employee rights. In *McClure* v.

Salvation Army, a female minister charged (under Title VII of the Civil Rights Act of 1964) that the Salvation Army had unlawfully practiced sex discrimination by offering male ministers higher salaries and additional benefits. The Fifth Circuit Court of Appeals dismissed the plaintiff's complaint on the grounds that a secular court should not attempt to resolve intrachurch disputes that involve the court in the process of interpreting and weighing church doctrines. The court noted that:

> An application of the provisions of Title VII to the employment relationship between . . . a church and its minister would . . . cause the state to intrude upon matters of church administration and government which have so many times before been proclaimed to be matters of a singular ecclesiastical concern. . . . The church would then be without the power to decide for itself, free from state interference, matters of church administration and government.
>
> Moreover, in addition to injecting the state into substantive ecclesiastical matters, an investigation and review of such matters . . . as a minister's salary, his place of assignment and his duty, which involve a person at the heart of any religious organization, could only produce by its coercive effect the very opposite of that separation of church and state contemplated by the First Amendment.

There are perhaps no more important ecclesiastical decisions by any church than the freedom to choose and train the staff that is to carry out its ministries. The qualifications, skills, training, and other standards followed by churches in hiring may, on occasion, clash with generally accepted employee rights. The only issue for secular courts to determine is whether or not the asserted religious belief is sincerely held.

The issue of a church's right to follow its beliefs in determining the qualifications of its employees was raised in *Walker* v. *First Orthodox Presbyterian Church of San Francisco* in 1979. Walker was hired as the congregation's organist after an audition and interview with the pastor. Soon afterward, the pastor learned that Walker was a practicing homosexual who declined the pastor's exhortations to repent. Walker was subsequently discharged from his position because of his homosexuuality.

The church organist claimed that the church's firing of him violated a San Francisco, gay right's ordinance, which made it unlawful for any person to discriminate in employment on the basis of an employee's sexual orientation. But the trial court held that the organist was constitutionally prohibited from relying on the ordinance, which unconstitutionally infringed upon the rights of the local church and its members to freely exercise their religious beliefs. The city and county of San Francisco had no compelling interest to overcome the significant burden placed on the defendants' rights.

Although some involvement of the church and state in each other's affairs is unavoidable, as these cases show, the First Amendment does provide for church autonomy. Such autonomy is essential to our religious freedom and should be protected by Christians everywhere.

THERE IS A BETTER WAY

We have touched on the legal approach to resolving disputes within the church. Yet there seems to be a better way—in fact, a biblical way—to handle such disputes. The alternative is identified by Christ in Matthew 18 (verses 15-18) and by Paul in 1 Corinthians 6: tell it to the church. Let the matter be resolved within the church rather than through the secular courts.

Paul is very blunt about Christians suing one another. He asks in 1 Corinthians 6, "How dare you sue one another?" Paul is dealing with the reproach Christians bring to Christ's name when they sue one another in secular courts. Christ said that the world would know us as his disciples by the love we have one for another. Yet, what is the world to believe when they see these "loving" Christians fighting it out hammer and tong in the courts?

Up until recently there were few alternatives available to Christians other than "throwing in the towel." Now the Christian Conciliation Service of the Christian Legal Society has developed an effective, biblical method for Christians and churches to deal with conflict within the Christian community.*

Your authors have used this biblical approach in dealing with many disputes.

One controversy involved over 1.2 million dollars of property owned by the Wallace Presbyterian Church in Maryland. In 1981 the church voted to leave its national denomination after it had lost a series of appeals contesting the ordination of a pastor who did not unequivocally affirm the diety of Christ. The local congregation had paid for the property, although the denomination had granted the original loan.

As was the custom in the Presbyterian faith, the deeds were in the name of the national denomination. Naturally a dispute arose over who "owned" the property; both sides were seriously considering the most common option: litigation.

Yet the local congregation, led by its pastor and board of elders, chose not to violate Paul's injunctions and to proceed along biblical lines. The national denomination agreed. After much prayer and discussion, the local church was allowed to keep the property as long as it continued to meet its short-term financial obligations to a number of missionaries. The bitterness, anger, and hurt that often flows from litigation was avoided; the individuals were reconciled with one another although the local congregation never rejoined the national denomination. Christ's name was not compromised in the secular courts.

When it comes to disputes within the Christian community, there is a better way than the courts. It is within the church. Let's use it.

---

*For more information about the Christian Conciliation Service's biblical approach read *Tell It to the Church,* another book within the Issues and Insights Series.

30

The IRS:
Render unto Caesar

Much of this book focuses on one central issue: sovereignty. Who has legitimate jurisdiction? Who makes the final decision?

In the church-state arena, persons become most vocal when the issue of sovereignty involves one of the least popular words in any language: taxes. Apart from death, there are few subjects that cause more controversy and tension. Everyone has an opinion.

A universal attitude is that if taxes must be paid, let someone else pay them. And, of course, those perceived as evading taxes—whether by loophole, windfall, or exemption—are viewed with suspicion, even contempt.

Let the state try to close down a religious school for failing to comply with state educational standards and a few religious groups may get involved and assist. Most will remain in the stands—many even applauding the state. But let the state attack the school's tax exemption, and everyone gets into the fray with the best legal talent money can buy.

We need to remember that few societies have been as benevolent to religious institutions in respect to taxes as America. This comes as no surprise when we consider that our nation was founded by those seeking religious freedom.

The Supreme Court has said often that the power to tax has within it the power to destroy. In the case of *Murdock* v. *Pennsylvania,* the Court struck down a local tax levied upon a door-to-door salesman of religious tracts saying: "The power to tax the exercise of a privilege is the power to control or suppress its enjoyment. . . . Those who can tax the exercise of this religious practice can make its exercise so costly as to deprive it of the resources necessary for its maintenance.''

Yet, obviously, someone must serve as the gatekeeper; someone must finally decide who pays and who is exempt. And someone must design, implement, and supervise the process. Four options are available.

First, some contend that no man can properly judge another man's religion or ministry. So, each man should make the decision as to whether or not his ministry qualifies for a tax exemption. Their anthem should be Judges 21:25: "In those days there was no king in Israel; everyone did what was right in his own eyes." The ultimate result of this free-for-all would be anarchy.

Another suggestion is that the religious community should judge who is worthy of exemptions. This proposal overlooks the basic self-serving nature of man and institutions. History has shown that every time the church becomes the gatekeeper, religious tyranny soon follows. Don't forget the Spanish Inquisition or the persecution in Europe that led to the settling of our country.

The third option is to place all gatekeeping authority in the state. Here again, history shows that such unqualified power will always be abused at the expense of religious freedom. We need only to look at the Communist countries to see what would happen. The fruit is tryanny.

Finally we can entrust the gatekeeping function to our representatives and their agents. This is the American pattern. Under our Constitution, the people grant Congress the right "to lay and collect taxes, duties, imposts and excises." Since pre-Revolutionary War days, churches have been exempt from taxes. They were not required to participate in underwriting the cost of the state. In fact, the reverse was true: state-financed churches were the norm at the time of the Revolution. Few Americans realize that Massachusetts had a state church until 1833.

In 1916, the people, through the Sixteenth Amendment, broadened Congress's power to tax by giving it authority "to lay and collect taxes on income, from whatever sources derived." The purpose of the amendment was to give Congress the authority to tax the *income* of individuals and profit-making (or *for*-profit) organizations. Nonprofit organizations, such as churches, were never considered the objects of possible taxes. Yet, since 1916, a substantial bureaucracy, armed with rules, regulations, and forms has been established within the Internal Revenue Service (IRS), which has begun to place ever-increasing burdens and requirements on nonprofit organizations to prove their status. Some perceive this gatekeeper as brewing its own rules without accountability to anyone.

The challenge is to find the balance that will prevent abuse and allow legitimate ministries. No doubt the framers of the Bill of Rights were fully aware of the potential for groups to abuse their religious liberties. Yet, they chose to err on the side of religious freedom, rather than to pull out every tare from among the wheat.

The debate over how much religious organizations should "tip their hat" to the state will never end. We can only be thankful that God provided a legal system so we can challenge the required obeisance if it goes too far. And if we lose, we can apply the "Golden Rule for Losers" set forth by Paul in 1 Thessalonians 5:18: "give thanks in all circumstances; for this is the will of God in Christ Jesus for you."

MISCONCEPTIONS

The government's fiscal crisis looms larger each year. At all levels of government, the gatekeeper is looking closely at many institutions that have enjoyed tax-exempt status as "fair game" in its search for funds.

It is not our purpose to repeat the material already in print on churches, taxes, and exemptions. A most readable book on this topic is *Why Churches Should Not Pay Taxes* by Dean M. Kelley, executive director for religious liberty for the National Council of Churches. As Kelley points out, we need to clear away some popular and widespread misconceptions on this subject.

The first misconception is that a church must file for tax-exempt status in order to be a legitimate church. Neither the state nor the IRS are in the church-making business. A church can be a church without filling out a single form or qualifying for anything. But if an entity wants to enjoy certain legal benefits and tax advantages, formalized organization and certification of tax exemptions are needed from the gatekeeper. For example, a small fellowship may choose not to formalize its legal entity. But if it chooses to purchase or hold real property in its name or to have its members' donations be tax deductible, then the fellowship needs to file for exempt status.

Many of those who seek to end income tax exemptions for churches misuse the word *income*. At first glance, people conclude that churches have lots of income. After all, look at all that property they own! Or look at the $24 billion dollars claimed as donations to religious groups on 1981 tax returns!

Yet, with relatively small exception, the funds received by churches are gifts, not income. The money placed in the Sunday morning offering plate is not like the steel worker's payroll check or the fee charged by the lawyer or the profit made by the utility company. The offering is not a compensation for services rendered, it is a gift to God.

Another common misconception is that tax exemptions are an abnormal condition, requiring special justification. The underlying and blatantly false assumption is that the state has the right, if not the duty, to take some tax from everything that exists. Under our Constitution of *delegated* powers, the state has no autonomous sovereignty apart from that which the citizenry vests in it. Thus, the state is accountable to the people and cannot take anything, property or otherwise, without the people's permission.

The fact that churches and religious organizations are tax-exempt is not a unique or abnormal state of affairs. Historically many western societies have chosen to tax only those individuals and institutions that actually generate revenue to produce material wealth. Nonprofit organizations, which simply survive on gifts, are not revenue producers. Although many believe that just about everything is taxed these days, the list of exempt activities, which escape the tax collectors' grasp, is substantial.

The fourth common misconception is that tax exemptions are the equivalent of tax subsidies. A subsidy is a *direct* grant of a specific amount of tax monies to a program, entity, or individual. A tax exemption, however, involves no exchange of money between the government and the church. In and of itself, a tax exemption is not a tax expenditure. It does not give one cent to the church. The church must still rely almost entirely on the voluntary contributions of its supporters and occasionally on earnings from savings or endowments.

Subsidies on the other hand are specific amounts determined by legislatures or administrators. Thus, the pitched battles in Congress or other legislatures is over whether to retain, renew, or increase subsidies. Finally, a subsidy is an involuntary type of expenditure of tax monies. As a practical matter, the individual citizen has nothing to say about the amount of the subsidy or the selection of the recipient. However, the citizen does have the power to determine precisely who benefits from a gift and by how much.

Churches are neither the only nor the primary beneficiaries of tax exemptions. For example, in New York City, the real estate owned by religious groups is less than 5 percent of the total tax *exempt* property in the nation's largest city. The remaining 95 percent of tax exempt property is owned by nonprofit groups such as hospitals, airports, parks, public housing, public education, and public works. Church-owned property represents a very minor fraction of the total amount of exempt property in the United States.

Another misconception is that churches use their tax-exempt status to engage in commercial ventures in unfair competition with tax-paying businesses. One notorious example was the purchase by a well-known church ministry of a girdle factory in Brooklyn, New York, which was then operated with tax-exempt benefits. There has never been more than a few such instances. In any event, churches took the initiative to close this loophole by proposing the Tax Reform Act of 1969, which eliminated the benefit. Few institutions can claim credit for taking the lead in closing the door on a tax benefit for themselves!

Some people believe that churches receive exemptions in exchange for surrendering their right to influence the legislative and political process. It is true that restraints contained in federal and most state tax-exemption statutes place some restrictions on the nature and scope of influence that the *corporate* organization may exert on legislation. However, serious constitutional issues, which have yet to be addressed by the Supreme Court, surround the concept that a church must give up *any* of its birthright of influence for its tax-exempt status.

A final misconception is that tax exemptions to churches are granted in return for public services, which the government would otherwise have to provide. Although this argument may have some merit with respect to many nonprofit groups such as hospitals, libraries, parks, and schools, it is not applicable to churches. The state is not to be involved in providing spiritual and religious services. This would violate the Establishment Clause.

In the only Supreme Court decision dealing specifically with the tax exemption of churches, *Walz* v. *Tax Commission*, the Court clearly recognized the problems created when a church's tax exemption is determined by an evaluation of its social welfare services or other good works. In other words, the IRS cannot ask if a church is "good" enough to qualify. In upholding the propriety of property tax exemptions for churches in New York, the Court said:

> We find it unnecessary to justify the tax exemp-
> tion on the social welfare services or "good
> works" that some churches perform for
> parishioners and others—family counseling,
> aid to the elderly and the infirm, and to
> children. Churches vary substantially in the
> scope of such services; programs expand or
> contract according to resources and need. . . .
> The extent of social services may vary, depend-
> ing on whether the church serves an urban or
> rural, a rich or poor constituency. To give em-
> phasis to so variable an aspect of the work of
> religious bodies would introduce an element of
> governmental evaluation and standards as to
> the worth of particular social welfare pro-
> grams, thus producing a kind of continuing
> day-to-day relationship which the policy of
> neutrality seeks to minimize. Hence, the use of
> a social welfare yardstick as a significant ele-
> ment to qualify for tax exemption could con-
> ceivably give rise to confrontations that could
> escalate to constitutional dimensions.

The same logic must be applied in restraining the growing intrusion by the IRS and other governmental bodies into selectively determining what are "acceptable" and "appropriate" ministries of the church.

WHAT IS AN
"ACCEPTABLE" RELIGION?

Even under the most ideal circumstances, mixing religion, race, politics, and constitutional law results in confusion. Thus, tax exemptions for religious schools became hot news on January 8, 1982, when the White House announced a change in the government's position in two cases on appeal to the Supreme Court. The first case involved Bob Jones University, which forbids interracial marriage and dating among its students. The second case involved Goldsboro Christian School in North Carolina, which excludes all blacks. Both schools insist that Scripture mandates these policies, and their sincerity in this religious belief is not challenged.

The IRS decided that neither of these schools was entitled to tax-exempt status on the ground that the policies violated "federal public policy" with respect to race. The two schools challenged the IRS in federal court. One lost and one won in the district court; both lost in the court of appeals, and both appealed to the Supreme Court.

In preparing their briefs, the attorneys for the Reagan administration rightly concluded that Congress had not given the IRS authority to deny tax exemptions to private religious schools who may be out of step with some "federal public policy." The annnouncement caused such an uproar that within four days the White House decided to send a bill to Congress to remedy this fact and give the IRS such authority. This simply added fuel to the fire, since many viewed this as an about-face.

Congress held brief "hearings," but failed to invite a single representative from the religious community to testify. Finding the issue too hot to handle, the White House and Congress finally urged that the case be left up to the Supreme Court to decide.

What are the underlying issues? Religious schools and most of the religious community contend that religious freedom is the issue. On the other hand, some religious groups and virtually all civil rights groups contend that the central issue is racial discrimination. The challenge, of course, is to find a way to reconcile these two concerns.

The First Amendment states that there shall be no law prohibiting the free exercise of religion. But, the state is not permitted to choose between religions. At its core, the issue is whether or not a sincerely held religious belief that results in segregative practices can bar a school from tax-exempt status.

There is a great danger when the law seeks to carve out what is an "acceptable" practice of religion. On a few occasions the Supreme Court has held that religious practices are impermissible. For example, in 1879, the Supreme Court decided that polygamy was so offensive to the fabric of society that a criminal law against its practice was held constitutional (*U.S.* v. *Reynolds*). The question now is whether or not exclusion from a private school, or prohibition of interracial marriage and dating, should be viewed in the same way—and whether Congress may constitutionally enact a statute to authorize the IRS to deny tax-exempt status on these grounds.

Once we start down the path of listing "unacceptable" religious practices, there are grave dangers. For example, can a hospital with a strong prolife position lose its tax exemption if "federal public policy" favors abortion? Likewise, will religious schools, seminaries, and churches that follow their understanding of Scripture on the roles of men and women lose their tax exemption for failing to treat both sexes "equally" in line with "federal public policy"?

Perhaps no issue causes more soul-searching for Christians than taxation. Yet, Scripture may offer some helpful guidelines.

AN ISSUE OF SOVEREIGNITY

First, we must remember that the issue is both a legal and a spiritual problem. Christ was not opposed to paying taxes—even to the pagan Roman authorities of his day. Instead, he stressed the issue of sovereignty.

By far the best known incident in Scripture concerning Christ and taxes is the report of the Pharisees' unsuccessful attempt to trick Jesus. The legal-eagle Pharisees asked Jesus whether or not it was lawful for Jews to give a poll tax to Caesar. The Pharisees thought they had Christ cornered: if he said no, he would have to answer to the Roman authorities. If he said yes, he would have to answer to the Jewish religious leaders. Jesus simply asked for a coin. Since the legal currency of the day was Roman, Caesar's likeness and inscription was on the coin. "Render therefore to Caesar the things that are Caesar's, and to God the things that are God's," he answered.

Checked in their tracks, the Pharisees remained silent. They had overlooked the fact that only one Sovereign exists in the universe. Yet, he ordains government as his ministers for our good. Government, even the despised Caesar, reigns as his servant. So, when you render taxes to Caesar, you are concurrently rendering to the Sovereign.

CHRIST'S PERCEPTION

Second, we must also keep our priorities in order. We need to examine our hearts so that we never sacrifice righteousness on the altar of a tax exemption. According to Christ, nothing blurs the vision more than mammon—the power of money.

Christ addressed the issue of mammon in the Sermon on the Mount. "For where your treasure is, there will your heart be also" (Matt. 6:21). A moment later he made it clear that man cannot serve two masters concurrently: "You cannot serve God and mammon" (v. 24). You must choose one or the other.

Often overlooked is the fact that Christ had an infinite number of choices to place in juxtaposition to God. Why didn't he say one cannot serve political power and God? Or fame and God? Or education and God?

Perhaps it is because money, more than any of the other options, gives man a false sense of independence. We speak of the independently wealthy: someone who is seemingly removed from the whims of fate—or, more accurately, "free" from dependence on God. Money can so easily become the ultimate idol if we perceive that it gives us independence. Sandwiched in-between the two oft-quoted statements about treasure and mammon, we find the real meat of Christ's message:

> The eye is the lamp of the body. So, if your eye
> is sound, your whole body will be full of light;
> but if your eye is not sound, your whole body
> will be full of darkness (Matt. 6:22, 23).

The key issue, Christ said, is our perspective. How we perceive anything will determine how we act with regard to it. How we perceive our treasure—or mammon—will control our lives. In the final analysis, our perspective will determine who is truly sovereign in our life.

CALL FOR AN ACCOUNTING

Finally, when the law is violated, even by agents of the

state, the Christian involved should call the agents to account. For example, when the apostle Paul appeared before Festus, he appealed to Caesar because those under Caesar's authority had acted contrary to the law in their treatment of Paul. In the present tax exemption cases, contrary to the misinformation reported by most of the media, the IRS clearly acted without statutory authority in its actions against the religious schools. Thus, it is appropriate to call the IRS to account for its actions.

There are those who perceive the government in general, and the IRS in particular, as persecuting religious people. Let us even pray for those gatekeepers, since they have authority over us. On occasion, Christians may have to render to Caesar unrighteous mammon. But when we do so, we are ultimately respecting the sovereignty of our God who has allowed them to have dominion over us.

PART FOUR
THE CHRISTIAN RESPONSIBILITY

31

Never Be Fooled!

Don't let this book fool you! Its focus is on problems, many of them urgent and serious. Problems can cause us to lose a clear perspective and distort reality. Problems also generate reactions. There are many possible reactions to this book. We will discuss five, which may clarify some objectives for those who have read this book.

THE OBSERVER

Is there really anything urgent about the issues of religious freedom today? The answer of this volume is yes. Issues of rights of conscience and religious liberty are compelling problems in America as well as many other countries of the world. We err, and fatefully so, if we think that these issues are simply individual struggles—a series of fascinating and sometimes tragic war stories. To be sure, there are stories worth telling and some unforgettable characters. But the real plot and theme is larger than the troubles of Adell Sherbert or Levi Whisner. The struggle involves the character of our society and the way it nourishes or penalizes vibrant religious faith; the battle revolves around whether or not our culture will acknowledge the legitimacy of religious values and expression in our public life.

If your reaction to this book is merely that of a legal voyeur, you have missed the central message for the Christian community—namely that these issues involve you and your neighborhood and your society. These are issues that demand more than observers. If you haven't sensed that these issues touch your life, you've been fooled.

THE LOSER

No doubt there are those who will conclude after reading this book that religious freedom is dying in America, and some may even say it is dead. Like Chicken Little, they conclude that the sky is falling. The end is near. Only the eulogy needs be said, and the funeral dirge sung. Like those on the Titanic, let us close with "Nearer My God to Thee." If that is your reaction, we suggest the book has fooled you.

There are indeed cases that disturb and frustrate the believer. There are times when one senses "principalities and powers." And there are certainly instances in communities where government officials seem incredibly insensitive and inflexible. When these things happen, we ought to be alarmed, even outraged and take decisive stands.

However, we would not have written this book if we thought the response of Christians should be to wring our hands. Rather we believe that we still possess great opportunities to contribute to the preservation of liberty. We shall tragically abdicate our rights if we simply complain.

Don't forget: the Lord has yet to lose a case. He remains sovereign, even though temporal circumstances and events may look bleak to us. There may be times when we suffer an occasional loss in the church-state arena, but the final outcome is determined. "For the wicked shall be cut off; but those who wait for the Lord shall possess the land" (Ps. 37:9).

THE FIGHTER

Then there are those who may be angered by what they have read. They believe that it is time to hit the streets. Christians have been nice guys too long. It's time to get militant. Let's build the barricades and bring in the big guns. Forget the funeral song. Let's hear the trumpets and drums and march out singing "Onward Christian Soldiers." If that is your reaction, we suggest the book has fooled you.

We are concerned that too many persons lose a sense of perspective and balance when they approach these problems. They fail to see positive developments, clear court decisions for liberty. These persons only see—and relish—the negative. They perceive every act of government as if it were a deliberate and cancerous conspiracy designed to take away their freedoms.

David warns us in Psalm 37 not to fret, because it "leads

only to evil." Christ taught that when salt loses its preserving quality it becomes worthless—except to be trampled on. So, let us not fret.

David also counsels us not to envy the position and successes of wrongdoers. There are many Christians who wish they were in control, so they could give those bureaucrats and secular humanists some of their own medicine. Again, David says this is the wrong attitude. Why? Because the wrong of evildoers is only temporary. "They will soon fade like the grass, and wither like the green herb" (v. 2).

THE CYNIC

A third type of reaction is that of the cynic. He remains indifferent. This book has shown him nothing new, and is viewed simply as an effort by two authors to play on people's fears. In his opinion, the problems mentioned are overplayed. The real problem is that a few religious zealots demand too much and refuse to be reasonable. These cynics speak too easily about the "public good" and "society," but have an inadequate appreciation for the rights of conscience and personal religious freedom. They fail to recognize that the Yoders and Whisners of this world not only have the right to swim against the stream, they enrich us all by their faithfulness. Our nation's life is enhanced by our assurance of their rights.

We suggest that this person has also been fooled, perhaps more by his own refusal to listen and consider the issues than by the content of the book.

THE CONCERNED

A final reaction comes from the reader who now feels better informed on these church-state issues. But since he is not a constitutional lawyer, he concludes that he can't really do anything meaningful. The issues are all so complex, intimidating, and awesome. He decides to leave it to the experts, hum "Oh, for a Thousand Tongues," and leave the singing to the soloists. Again, if this is your reaction, we suggest that you may have been fooled.

There are certainly many challenges in the church-state arena. And many are complex. Yet, that has always been the case. There are also many things that someone who is not an attorney can do.

We need to set aside our fear and anger and recognize the Lord's sovereignty in even the most trying situations. As constitutional lawyer William Ball noted, "We are not yet slaves of a People's Republic." Nor are the Courts by any means insensitive to religious freedoms. In recent years, the majority of Supreme Court decisions on issues of religious liberty have supported our liberties: *Wisconsin* v. *Yoder, Sherbert* v. *Verner, Widmar* v. *Vincent, Thomas* v. *Review Board,* and *NLRB* v. *Catholic Bishops.*

Admittedly there are some persons in public service whose hostility to Christian values is transparent and dangerous; they must be challenged and called to account. But these deliberate evildoers are rare. Even where serious problems have emerged, they are often the result of misguided rather than ill-intentioned policies. We need to trust the future to our Lord.

But trusting the Lord is only one side of the coin. We must also "do good and dwell in the land." Unfortunately, many people are sitting on their hands, trusting in the Lord, but doing nothing.

What can we do in the area of religious freedom? Your authors would like to suggest an agenda for those who wish to make a positive contribution to religious liberty in our country.

DEVELOPING AN INFORMED PERSPECTIVE

Christians should remain informed about issues that affect our religious freedom. Groups such as the Christian Legal Society have publications that will notify you of current decisions. Listening to newscasts and reading the newspaper with a new concern for legal issues will also help.

We must always attempt to "read between the lines" to develop a rational perspective. Some issues of religious liberty seem relatively obvious. When students are virtually compelled by public school authorities to read literature with offensive language, and then subjected to ridicule when they refuse to do so, we all rise up and insist that government has overstepped its powers. When there are attempts to disqualify judges from hearing cases because they belong to a religious group, we all sense something is wrong. But not all the cases are that simple.

Those of us who spend time arguing religious issues before policymakers and courts are sometimes disheartened by the popular religious media's failure to examine issues carefully. For example, one national religious newspaper reported a decision of the South Dakota Supreme Court that upheld the firing of a teacher who was teaching creation as an attack on religion and a victory for humanism. An examination of the facts reveals that this teacher was allowed to teach creation, but he was repeatedly asked to limit the time he devoted to this subject, since the general course had a broader scope. The teacher refused, and was finally dismissed. The case is quite different when you read the facts carefully.

We must also avoid the temptation to cry wolf every time a government action seems to reduce our "freedom." Not long ago one of your authors received a set of documents from a person urgently claiming a violation of her religious rights. It seems that a county zoning ordinance limited the number and kind of animals she could keep in her yard. This woman insisted that God had told her to have two goats, and city officials had declared that she could only keep one. Was her religious liberty threatened? Of course not.

INFLUENCING SOCIETY

Our next step toward insuring religious freedom and justice is to participate in the shaping of our society. Many complain about the "rascals in office," but they are not even registered to vote. We have a great opportunity in our country to choose our decision makers. We need to use this privilege.

We also need to be faithful in communicating our concerns to both elected and appointed officials. However, politicians and bureaucrats should be seen as more than power brokers. They get enough of angry, self-serving politics. Our contact with them needs to reflect the gifts of the spirit: love, patience, goodness, and self-control. As William Ball notes, "The voice must not be strident, but kindly and intelligent, and reflecting homework diligently done."

So far our concern for freedom and justice has been little more than a self-serving desire to be free from interference. Many groups who are now vocal on the rights of Christians were noticeably silent about First Amendment and civil rights until their own interests were threatened. They neglected the Christian mandate to be salt and light to the world.

Christians with a perspective on the gospel that encompasses all of life are going to insist on participating in public life. They are going to serve on public school boards and parent-teacher organizations, on local government and political committees, and on other community boards. Many of us see the free exercise of religion as essential to assuring that values and the moral life are a vigorous part of the pluralism of our day.

An experiment of monumental danger is taking place in much of western civilization—a test of whether or not a society may survive when it cuts off its moral roots and rejects any informing ethic. The issue is not whether one sectarian religious system will control a society—but whether society may in its search for freedom reject a central value system. Your authors are not at all convinced it can, and writers such as Solzhenitsyn warn the West about this loss of moral commitment.

UTILIZING OUR LIBERTIES

In Psalm 37, David exhorts us to cultivate faithfulness. Christ repeatedly taught that if we are not faithful in using what we have, we will not be entrusted with greater things. In fact, the Lord made it clear that we may lose it all! We must be faithful stewards of the many fragments of freedom all around us, for these fragments are wide open doors that few bother to use. It is often much more fun to fight the closed doors, than to walk through the open ones. However, we are more accountable for the privileges we neglect. As examples, let us mention some open doors that seem to be ignored.

Courts have consistently protected rights of evangelism. Yet few of us speak to others about our faith with eagerness and earnestness. Courts generally protect rights of conscience, but we meld pretty easily into prevailing values. Opportunities to worship, to teach our children our faith, to fellowship together, to give of our resources have hardly ever been threatened. Yet we often remain narcissistic, hardly ever challenging the values of our society and teaching our children almost nothing except consumerism.

Release-time for religious education is another open door. Local churches may work together with school boards to release students for religious instruction a few hours each week. Thirty years ago, Justice William O. Douglas of the United States Supreme Court made this comment about release-time programs:

When the state encourages religious instruction
or cooperates with religious authorities by ad-
justing the schedule of public events to sectarian needs, it follows the best of our traditions. For it then respects the religious nature of
our people and accommodates the public service to their spiritual needs. To hold that it may
not, would be to find in the Constitution a requirement that the government show a callous
indifference to religious groups. That would be
preferring those who believe in no religion over
those who do believe.

Few churches bother going through this open door. An effective release-time program requires work, planning, prepara-
tion, administration, and most of all, time. Tragically, many
Christians have written off the 75 percent of American children
still attending the public schools, because they no longer feel
that they can influence the educational system. This door is still
open. Let's use it before we do lose it!

A third door was identified twenty years ago when the Supreme Court said that it was appropriate to teach Bible as
literature in public schools. Many Christians view this as de-
meaning God's Word by seeing it as merely literature or an intellectual experience. Yet, the Bible is the mind of God, and, as
many intellectuals such as C. S. Lewis and Malcolm Muggeridge
have found out, academic scrutiny often leads to belief.

Another open door was also mentioned twenty years ago.
The Supreme Court said that it was permissible to teach comparative religion in public schools. Before you close the door on
comparative religions, remember that Christ taught in this way.
He said, "You've heard that it was said . . . but I say to
you. . . ." Are we afraid to compare the Christian religion to a
religion invented by man? If we do our job, the Holy Spirit will
do his. Yet, how many comparative religion courses are taught
in the public schools? Probably not very many.

A BIBLICAL PROCESS

Finally we feel that Christians need to commit themselves to
a method of pursuing religious liberty that reflects biblical principles and insights. One of the most difficult tasks facing the

Christian community is to contribute to the character of our society without adopting a worldly style or process. In our quest for spiritual goals and values we must avoid the temptation to adopt a Watergate philosophy: the end justifies the means.

We must remember that the goal is not essentially a political one. The goal of the believing community is more than winning elections by outnumbering the opposition. We need to realize that our political power is severely limited, as is the law, in its capacity to achieve a just society. The struggle we are engaged in is essentially a spiritual one. Secularism, materialism, and egotism are not rooted out by statute or judicial fiat. The combatants in the struggle for society are spiritual, and the essential weapons are spiritual as well. How tragic it will be if Christians try to force religion and moral life on persons when we have failed to win these people with the attractiveness of redemption and the gospel.

In any spiritually ordered agenda we shall have to account for the biblical call to servanthood and the cross. Biblical prophets, however honored today, were a ridiculed and notably unsuccessful bunch who proclaimed with faithfulness the Word of God. It was not by power nor by might but by the Word of God that salvation would come, they declared. Israel was in danger precisely when this nation confused its role and thought it was powerful because of its own character or clever planning. Israel ministered when it suffered and wandered.

The Christian community does not need to be politically successful in order to be faithful. We do not need to win. Perhaps we must learn how to thrive in captivity, in conditions that are not seen as powerful, dynamic, or successful.

A spiritual perspective will also assist us in distinguishing mere political agendas from the basic moral and religious issues facing our society. While Christian views may indeed impact political questions such as the Panama Canal Treaty and school busing, these issues are radically different from such problems as the role of the family, abortion, and personal rights of conscience. To confuse core moral issues with political issues tragically waives our commitment to a real moral witness.

God through Christ has reversed this world's notions of power and success. We must never succumb to simply trying to outmaneuver, outspend, outthreaten, or outvote our opponents. We wrestle not against flesh and blood. Robert Toms, an attorney active in religious liberty cases, declared to an assembly of Christian lawyers, "We must guard all frontiers of liberty from enslavers in any guise. But, most of all, we must do all of this as redemptive servants of Christ, stilling the chaotic, stormy waters of contemporary life and law. . . . [We must] be agents for the discovery of . . . hope."

APPENDIXES

FOOTNOTES

Chapter 11

[1]Paul Blanshard, "Three Cheers for Our Secular State," *The Humanist,* March/April 1976, p. 17.

[2]G. Richard Bozarth, "On Keeping God Alive," *The America Atheist,* November 1977, p. 7.

[3]Charles E. Rice, "Conscientious Objection to Private Education: The Grievance and the Remedies," *Brigham Young University Law Review* 4 (1978):847-888.

Chapter 13

[1]James Panoch and David Barr, *Religion Goes to School* (New York: Harper and Row, 1968), p. 5.

Chapter 14

[1]"Can We Still Sing Christmas Carols in Public Schools?" *Music Education Journal,* November 1976, p. 71.

Chapter 16

[1]William J. Miller, "A Little School Against the Big Bureaucracy," *Reader's Digest* 117 (1980):159.

[2]William Sanders, "Regulation of Nonpublic Schools as Seen by the State Commissioner," *Public Controls for Nonpublic Schools* (Chicago: University of Chicago Press, 1969), p. 180.

[3]Kevin Phillips, "The Balkanization of America" *Harpers,* 256, No. 1536 (1978):47.

[4]Carl H. Esbeck, "State Regulation of Social Services Ministries of Religious Organizations," *Valparaiso University Law Review* 16 (1981):1.

[5]William Ball, "Law and the Educational Mission of Christianity," *Theology, News and Notes* (Pasadena, Calif.: Fuller Theological Seminary, 1980), p. 9.

[6]Peter L. Berger and Richard J. Neuhaus, *To Empower People: The Roles of Mediating Structures in Public Policy* (Washington, D.C.: American Enterprise Institute, 1977).

Chapter 17

[1]Gordon Sypkman, et al., *Society, State, and Schools: A Case for Structural and Confessional Pluralism* (Grand Rapids, Mich.: Eerdmans, 1981), p. 134.

Chapter 18

[1]Gray Hughes, "What Do the Supreme Court Prayer-and-Bible-Reading Decisions Really Mean?" *Liberty,* September/October 1979, p. 19.

[2]*Trustees of Schools* v. *People.*

[3]Alice Beshoner, "Home Education in America: Parental Rights Reasserted," *University of Missouri-Kansas City Law Review* 49 (Winter 1981).

Chapter 19

[1]Thomas Strahan, "The Rights of Conscience," unpublished monograph, 1980.

Chapter 23

[1]H. M. Weinstein and L. Russell, "Competency Based Psychiatric Education," *American Journal of Psychiatry* 133 (1976):935.

IMPORTANT CASE SUMMARIES

THE ESTABLISHMENT CLAUSE

Application of First Amendment to the States through the Fourteenth Amendment:

Everson v. Board of Education
330 U.S. 1

1947

Expressed absolute separation of church and state formula. Upheld a township school board that reimbursed parents for money spent in sending their children to parochial schools on local buses.

Financial Aid to Religious Endeavors:

Bradfield v. Roberts
175 U.S. 291

1899

Found no establishment violation in a government payment to a secular corporation operated by the Catholic church for the construction of a hospital and for supplying hospital care for indigent patients of all religions.

Quick Bear v. *Leupp*
210 U.S. 50

1905   Court saw no First Amendment objection to the use of Indian tribal trust funds to pay for parochial school training desired by members of the tribe.

Cochran v. *Louisiana*
281 U.S. 370

1930   Upheld public provision for textbooks in secular subjects for pupils attending church-related schools (unanimous).

Everson v. *Board of Education*
330 U.S. 1

1947   Upheld tax subsidy for bus transportation for children attending Catholic schools, NJ (5-4).

Board of Education v. *Allen*
392 U.S. 236

1968   Upheld N.Y. statute requiring tax-subsidized textbooks for parochial and private school students (6-3).

Tilton v. *Richardson*
401 U.S. 672

1971   Upheld Connecticut aid to colleges and universities with religious affiliations as long as a legitimate secular goal is present, and there is no pervasive religious atmosphere. It disallowed a twenty-year limitation, since the buildings could be used for religious purposes after twenty years.

Lemon v. *Kurtzman*
403 U.S. 602

1971   Held invalid Rhode Island's 1969 Salary Supplement Act, providing for a 15 percent salary supplement for teachers in non-public schools, because it involved the state and church in excessive entanglement.

Committee for Public Education and Religious Liberty v. Nyquist
413 U.S. 756

1973

Held invalid a N.Y. law providing for three distinct programs of financial aid to nonpublic schools. One program provided maintenance and repair expense of facilities and equipment for schools serving low-income families. Second program provided tuition reimbursement to low income families. Third program provided tax-benefit plan for the parents of children attending nonpublic schools.

Meek v. Pittenger
421 U.S. 349

1975

Struck down Pennsylvania statute (except for portions relating to loaned textbooks), which authorized furnishing "auxiliary services" to children enrolled in nonpublic elementary and secondary schools. The services included such items as counseling, testing, psychological services, speech and hearing therapy, and other related services. Instructional materials included periodicals, photographs, maps, charts, recordings, and films. Instructional equipment included projectors, recorders, and laboratory apparatus.

Roemer v. Board of Public Works of Maryland
49 L.Ed. 2d 179

1976

Upheld Maryland program of annual general grants to church-related colleges for use in secular programs in schools that meet certain minimum criteria and do not award seminary or theological degrees exclusively. Decision followed *Lemon* holding that (1) state aid shall have a secular purpose; (2) aid would have a primary effect other than the advancement of religion; and (3) there was no tendency to entanglement.

Religion and Public Schools:

Pierce v. Society of Sisters 268 U.S. 510	1925	Invalidated an Oregon statute requiring attendance of all children of school age at public schools.
McCollum v. Board of Education 333 U.S. 203	1948	Found unconstitutional the use of public school facilities for religious instruction of pupils (Champaign, Illinois; absolute separation formula).
Zorach v. Clauson 343 U.S. 306	1952	Permitted program of release time for religious instruction off the public school premises (N.Y.C.; absolute separation formula).
Engel v. Vitale 370 U.S. 421	1962	Found unconstitutional a prayer composed by the N.Y. regents to be recited voluntarily by students attending public school (absolute separation formula).
Abington School District v. Schempp 374 U.S. 203	1963	Found unconstitutional officially sponsored reading of Bible and recitation of Lord's Prayer in public schools. (Neutrality text suggested: There must be a secular purpose and a primary effect that neither inhibits nor advances religion. Important Brennan concurrence).
Widmar v. Vincent 102 S. Ct. 269	1981	Upheld equal access to public university and college facilities by students for religious functions. University must remain neutral in regulating use of public forum facilities.

Government Regulation of Conduct:

McGowan v. *Maryland*
366 U.S. 420

1961   Refused to characterize the Sunday closing laws of Maryland, Massachusetts, and Pennsylvania as establishment of Christian religion. Held economic and recreational goals to be the primary purpose of the legislation.

Braunfeld v. *Brown*
366 U.S. 599

1961   Upheld the constitutionality of Sunday closing laws as long as they were primarily designed to achieve legitimate secular goals.

THE FREE EXERCISE CLAUSE

Application of First Amendment to the States through the Fourteenth Amendment:

Meyer v. *Nebraska*
262 U.S. 390

1923   By inference, the Court applied Free Exercise Clause to states through the Fourteenth Amendment.

Hamilton v. *Regents of University of California*
293 U.S. 245

1934   Upheld state statute requiring all male students of the university to take military training even though some objected on religious grounds. Applied the free exercise to the states.

Cantwell v. *Connecticut*
310 U.S. 296

1940   Overturned the conviction of three Jehovah's Witnesses who violated a Connecticut statute requiring solicitors for religious causes to be certified on the basis that the Free Exercise Clause applied to the states via the Fourteenth Amendment.

Government Regulation of Religious Practices and Beliefs:

Reynolds v. United States
98 U.S. 145

1878   Court upheld the conviction of a Mormon in a polygamous marriage, reasoning that freedom of religion does not condone overt acts that may be disruptive of the social order.

Arver v. U.S.
245 U.S. 366

1918   Upheld draft law providing draft exemptions for conscientious objectors.

Cantwell v. Connecticut
310 U.S. 296

1940   Overturned the conviction of three Jehovah's Witnesses who violated a Connecticut statute requiring solicitors for religious cases to be certified, on the basis that it violated the Free Exercise Clause.

Minersville School District v. Gobitis
310 U.S. 586

1940   Upheld constitutionality of a Pennsylvania law that required all public school pupils to salute the flag. Reversed in *Barnette* (1943).

Cox v. New Hampshire
312 U.S. 569

1941   Held that local authorities may regulate parades by religious groups and charge license fees proportionate to the public expense incurred.

Choplinsky v. New Hampshire
315 U.S. 568

1941   Held that rights of free speech and free religious exercise do not extend to "fighting words."

Jamison v. Texas 318 U.S. 413	1943	Found constitutional protection for the distribution of hand-bills of a religious nature that incidentally solicit funds and invite purchase of books.
Martin v. Struthers 319 U.S. 141	1943	Found unconstitutional an ordinance prohibiting summoning of occupants to the door for distribution of religious literature.
West Virginia State Board of Education v. Barnette 319 U.S. 624	1943	Reversed *Gobitis*, and stated that statute requiring flag salute invaded the free exercise of religion guaranteed by the First Amendment (6-3).
Prince v. Massachusetts 321 U.S. 158	1944	Upheld the application to religious literature of a statute forbidding the sale by minors of religious papers or periodicals on public streets.
Marsh v. Alabama 326 U.S. 501	1946	Upheld right of itinerant evangelists to distribute religious literature in company towns.
Tucker v. Texas 326 U.S. 517	1946	Upheld right of itinerant evangelists to distribute religious literature in federal housing projects.
Watchtower Bible and Tract Society v. Metropolitan Life Insurance Co., 79 N.W. 2nd 433 335 U.S. 886	1949	Certiorari denied. Lower court denied right of itinerant evangelists to distribute religious literature in private apartment houses.

Case	Year	Summary
Niemotko v. Maryland 340 U.S. 268	1951	Declared it constitutional for public parks to be made available for the orderly use of religious groups.
Fowler v. Rhode Island 345 U.S. 67	1953	Upheld *Niemotko*.
Torcaso v. Watkins 367 U.S. 488	1961	Held unconstitutional a Maryland requirement that belief in God was necessary for holding office. Important because it broadened the definition of religion.
Sherbert v. Verner 374 U.S. 398	1963	State may not constitutionally exclude from unemployment compensation a claimant who, for reasons of conscience, turned down a suitable job involving work on Saturday.
Wisconsin v. Yoder 406 U.S. 205	1972	Wisconsin forbidden from imposing compulsory school attendance law on Amish whose deep religious convictions would be violated. The state lacked a compelling state interest to force the Amish to comply.
Thomas v. Review Board of Indiana Employment Security Division 49 U.S.L.W. 4341	1981	Ruled that Indiana's denial of unemployment compensation benefits violated free exercise protection when a Jehovah's Witness terminated employment after transfer to department producing weapons. Fact that other Jehovah's Witnesses did not object to manufacturing weapons did not reduce an individual's rights based on his religious beliefs.

Heffron v. ISKCON 101 S. Ct. 255	1981	Court upheld a state regulation restricting the distribution of literature and solicitation of funds by any group, including religious groups, to a fixed location within the fairgrounds.
U.S. v. Lee 50 U.S.L.W. 4201	1982	Court held that a compelling state interest exists, which justifies a limitation on free exercise when such restriction is needed to maintain a sound social security tax system.

THE FREE EXERCISE CLAUSE

Taxation of Religious Organizations and Activities:

Jones v. Opelika	1942	Upheld right of a community to levy a tax on itinerant evangelists who peddle religious tracts door to door.
Murdock v. Pennsylvania 319 U.S. 105	1943	Reversed *Jones v. Opelika.* State cannot tax religious activities *in se.*
Follet v. Town of McCormick 321 U.S. 573	1944	Extended *Murdock* to evangelists who make their living selling religious literature.
Walz v. Tax Commission of City 397 U.S. 664	1970	Upheld tax exemption for religious bodies, stating that legislative purpose for exemption is not aimed at establishing religion but creates less involvement in religion than taxation would. Neutrality formula used.

Valley Forge Christian College v. Americans United for Separation of Church and State 50 U.S.L.W. 4103

1982   AUSCS did not have standing to challenge under Establishment Clause a conveyance of real property from U.S. government to Christian college.

Larson v. Valente 50 U.S.L.W. 4411

1982   Court declared unconstitutional Minnesota Charitable Solicitations Act, which provided that only those religious organizations receiving more than 50% of their total contributions from members were exempt from registration and reporting requirements. One religious denomination cannot be preferred over another.

THE FREE EXERCISE CLAUSE

The Judiciary and Internal Ecclesiastical Dissension:

Kedroff v. St. Nicholas Cathedral 344 U.S. 94

1952   Ruled that legislation regulating the appointment of Russian Orthodox clergy in New York invaded the freedom of religious exercise.

Kreshik v. St. Nicholas Cathedral 363 U.S. 190

1960   Ruled that free Exercise Clause gives hierarchical religious organizations exclusive power to decide matters of church government.

Presbyterian Church v. *Blue Hull Church*
393 U.S. 440

1969

Ruled that free exercise values are jeopardized when church property litigation is made to turn on the resolution by civil courts of controversies over religious doctrine and practice. Courts must decide church property disputes without resolving underlying controversies over religious doctrine.

Jones v. *Wolf*
443 U.S. 595

1979

Ruled that in hierarchical church organizations, the First Amendment does not dictate that state must follow particular method of resolving church property disputes. Court can apply "neutral principles of law" for resolving such disputes by examining "certain religious documents, such as church constitution, for language of trust in favor of the general church."

INDEX

NOTE TO THE READER:
If the subject of this book interests you, here are other books
you might wish to read:

[

    Crossroads by Leon Jaworski
    SCHOOLS: They Haven't Got a Prayer! by Lynn R. Buz-
      zard
    Tell It to the Church by Lynn R. Buzzard and Laurence Eck
    The Second American Revolution by John Whitehead

If you would like to receive supplements or updates concerning
the issues discussed in this book, please fill out this form and
send it to: David C. Cook Publishing Company, Book Division
—Department CD, Elgin, IL 60120.

Name: _____

Address: _____

              _____
              City   State   Zip

How did you obtain this book?

☐ Bookstore ☐ Mail Order ☐ Church or Conference
                      ☐ Gift

76874